Politics, Position, and Power

HAROLD SEIDMAN

Politics, Position, and Power

The Dynamics of Federal Organization

THIRD EDITION

OXFORD UNIVERSITY PRESS
New York 1980 Oxford

Library of Congress Cataloging in Publication Data

Seidman, Harold.
Politics, position, and power.

Bibliography: p.
Includes index.
1. United States—Politics and government.
I. Title.
JK421.S44 1980 353 79-15319
ISBN 0-19-502658-6
ISBN 0-19-502659-4 pbk.

This reprint, 1981

Printed in the United States of America

*For Peg
and the Memory
of Howard Schnoor*

Preface to the Third Edition

My task in writing the third edition was greatly simplified by the perceptive analyses of the Carter reorganization proposals prepared by Ronald C. Moe, Specialist in American National Government, Congressional Research Service. While we did not always agree about approaches, I am grateful to W. Harrison Wellford, Executive Associate Director for Reorganization and Management, Office of Management and Budget, for our stimulating dialogues about the politics of reorganization and the frustrations of reorganizers. The suggestions of David B. Walker, Assistant Director, Advisory Commission on Intergovernmental Relations, and my colleague Professor Robert Gilmour were very helpful. I again wish to thank Mrs. Jean Gosselin for her assistance and for typing the manuscript.

H.S.

Storrs, Connecticut

Preface to the Second Edition

Events since the publication of *Politics, Position, and Power* in 1970 have tended to confirm the principal themes developed in the book. President Nixon's far-reaching proposals for restructuring the executive branch clearly were designed to accomplish political purposes, and, if they had gone into effect, might well have altered the balance of power in our constitutional system. Except for the updating of statistics and the deletion of obsolete references, the revisions in the main consist of additions to the original text, notably a detailed analysis of President Nixon's organization strategy and the highly significant materials produced in hearings before the House Select Committee on Committees, the House Committee on Government Operations, and the Senate Select Committee on Presidential Campaign Activities. Wherever possible, I have attempted to cite and take into account the relevant scholarly literature published subsequent to the first edition.

In preparing the second edition, I again found myself in the position of discussing certain events in which I had been either a direct or indirect participant, this time as a consultant to the President's Council on Executive Organization and the Reorganization Subcommittee of the Senate Committee on Government Operations. In the very few instances where no sources are cited to support the statements made in the book, the material is drawn from my own files and records.

I wish to express my appreciation to Mrs. Jean Gosselin who typed the manuscript and to Mrs. A. F. Willbond who prepared the bibliography. Mr. Charles F. Parker was exceedingly helpful in meeting my many requests for White House press releases and official publications. That outstanding institution, the Office of Management and Budget Library, once more demonstrated its ability to track down the documents and information I required. I am grateful also to the University of Connecticut Research Foundation for a grant to study the backgrounds and the professional experience of members of the Council of Economic Advisers.

Finally, I am in debt to my colleagues and students at the University of Connecticut for many lively discussions which helped to sharpen my thinking about the dynamics of Federal organization.

H.S.

Storrs, Connecticut

Preface to the First Edition

In some respects this is a very personal book. It depicts the Federal scene as observed for almost a quarter of a century through a particular window in the Bureau of the Budget. The same scene might well be described somewhat differently if viewed from the White House, the Congress, or an operating department. I was involved either directly or indirectly in a number of the events discussed in the book. Wherever possible I have endeavored to find citable sources for the material used in this study. In the relatively few instances where no source is cited, the material is derived from my own notes and records.

My basic purpose in writing the book was to capture and record in a reasonably systematic and scholarly way my observations of the various phenomena which determine and influence Federal organization structure and administrative arrangements. As one brought up to believe that politics and administration must be kept separate and that efficiency was the single overriding goal of organization and administration, I became aware increasingly, along with many others, that the orthodox doctrines had little relevance to the organization issues with which I was dealing and were of marginal help in finding solutions. There were few issues that were not "political" and concerned with the balance of power among several contending forces: the President of the United States, congressional committees, the bureaucracy, State and local governments, and organized groups in the private community which are affected in one way or another by Federal policies and programs.

It seemed to me that I would be making a constructive contribution if I could identify and describe the strategic and tactical uses of organization type and structure; the interrelationships among the executive branch, the Congress and State and local governments in the administrative process; the linkages between executive branch and congressional organization; institutional culture and personality as a determinant of organizational behavior; and the political and administrative significance of various coordinating devices and the rich variety of institutional types. If we are to discover meaningful solutions to the organization problems that now confront us, we must start with a realistic understanding of how the system operates and the political consequences of organizational decisions.

I have not attempted to develop "models" or to explore in depth the implications of my observations for organization theory. I recognize that I have posed many fundamental questions to which I furnish no complete and comprehensive answers. My own convictions, some might call them "biases," will be apparent to the reader and in the last chapter I do present several rather specific suggestions for possible courses of action. In emphasizing the need for a President to have an organization strategy, I do not imply that every President should have the same strategy, or try to prescribe in detail what the strategy should be. Every President should know how to use organization and reorganization to support his long-range goals, but his strategic plan necessarily must be tailored to his objectives.

I am deeply indebted to George A. Graham, Executive Director of the National Academy of Public Administration, for giving me the opportunity to write the book as the Academy's first scholar-in-residence and for arranging for the grant from the Ford Foundation, which made the study possible.

Several of my former colleagues in the Executive Officers' Group, consisting of the Assistant Secretaries for Administration and their equivalents in the non-Cabinet agencies, were most generous with their time and encouragement. They assisted me greatly in verifying the facts and clarifying my thinking, although, needless to say, they do not necessarily share all of my conclusions.

While this book was in draft form, a number of friends and colleagues read the entire manuscript and gave me the benefit of their comments: Marver Bernstein, Roy Crawley, Herbert Emmerich, Neil Hollander, Dwight Ink, Roger W. Jones, Herbert Kaufman, Harvey C. Mansfield, Frederick C. Mosher, Charles F. Parker, Don K. Price, Howard Schnoor, James L. Sundquist, Dwight Waldo, and Robert C. Wood. James E. Webb and Ernest C. Friesen, Jr., read and commented upon substantial parts of the draft manuscript. I have profited significantly from their suggestions, but responsibility for any errors of omission or commission in the book is strictly my own.

Ruth Fine and her very able staff in the Bureau of the Budget Library provided invaluable assistance in tracking down documents and in identifying relevant bibliographical material. My task in collecting and analyzing data was made more manageable by Peter J. Jones, who served as my research assistant during the summer of 1968, and C. Spencer Platt, who prepared a special study of the backgrounds and characteristics of Federal "Supergrade" employees. I am grateful for the cooperation of the U.S. Civil Service Commission and Seymour Berlin and Sally Greenberg in making available to me computer printouts from the Federal Executive Inventory. My secretary, Mrs. Pauline Daigle, not only typed the manuscript, but also cheerfully did some of the tabulations and other miscellaneous chores connected with the production of the book.

Finally, I would be remiss if I did not acknowledge my debt

to the Bureau of the Budget and my associates in the Office of Management and Organization and to the professional staffs of the House and Senate Committees on Government Operations, particularly James Lanigan, Elmer Henderson, Herbert Roback, James Calloway, Eli Nobleman, Paul Danaceau, and Win Turner, who gave me a liberal education in the theory and practice of Government organization.

H.S.

January 1970
Washington, D.C.

Contents

I

The Politics of Government Organization

1

Introduction

ORTHODOX THEORY: CULT OF EFFICIENCY

Reorganization has become almost a religion in Washington. It has its symbol in the organization chart, Old Testament in the Hoover Commission reports, high priesthood in the Office of Management and Budget, and society for the propagation of the faith in sundry groups such as the Citizens Committee for Government Reorganization.[1]

Reorganization is deemed synonymous with reform and reform with progress. Periodic reorganizations are prescribed if for no other purpose than to purify the bureaucratic blood and to prevent stagnation. Opposition to reorganization is evil and attributable, according to Mr. Hoover, to the "gang up, log-rolling tactics of the bureaus and their organized pressure groups."[2]

For the true believer, reorganization can produce miracles:

1. The name of the Bureau of the Budget was changed by Reorganization Plan No. 2 of 1970 to Office of Management and Budget. The Citizens Committee for Government Reorganization headed by James Roche, board chairman of General Motors, was organized to promote President Nixon's reorganization proposals. It was modeled on the Citizens Committee for the Hoover Report.

2. Herbert C. Hoover, *The Memoirs of Herbert Hoover: The Cabinet and the Presidency, 1920–1933*, The Macmillan Co., 1952, pp. 282–83.

eliminate waste and save billions of dollars; restore to health and economic vigor a chronically ill maritime industry; abate noise at airports; control crime in the streets, to name but a few. The myth persists that we can resolve deep-seated and intractable issues of substance by reorganization. The report of the Senate Subcommittee on National Policy Machinery to the contrary, the conviction that the weaknesses of one organization can be cured by creating another remains a widely held article of faith.[3] Rare indeed is the commission or presidential task force with the self-restraint to forgo proposing an organizational answer to the problems which it cannot solve.

The organizational commandments laid down by the first Hoover Commission constitute the hard core of the fundamentalist dogma.[4] The devils to be exorcised are overlapping and duplication, and confused or broken lines of authority and responsibility. Entry into the "nirvana of economy and efficiency" can be obtained only by strict adherence to sound principles of executive branch organization. Of these the most essential are the grouping of executive branch agencies as nearly as possible by major purposes so that "by placing related functions cheek-by-jowl the overlaps can be eliminated, and of even greater importance coordinated policies can be developed"; and the establishment of a clear line of command and supervision from the president down through his department heads to every employee with no subordinate possessing authority independent from that of a superior.

The commission's report on "General Management of the Executive Branch" represents the most categorical formulation of the orthodox or classical organization doctrine derived

3. Senate Committee on Government Operations, Subcommittee on National Policy Machinery, "Organizing for National Security," Vol. 3, 1961, p. 4. The staff report criticized most of the proposals for additions to national policy machinery as based "on the mistaken assumption that the weakness of one organization can be cured by creating another."

4. The Commission on Organization of the Executive Branch of the Government, "General Management of the Executive Branch," A Report to the Congress, February 1949.

largely from business administration and identified with the scientific management movement during the early decades of this century and the writings of Gulick, Urwick, Fayol, and Mooney. Government organization is seen primarily as a technological problem calling for "scientific" analysis and the application of fundamental organizational principles: a single rather than a collegiate executive; limited span of control; unity of command (a person cannot serve two masters); a clear distinction between line and staff; and authority commensurate with responsibility.

For Luther Gulick, "work division is the foundation of organization; indeed, the reason for organization."[5] In his view, "the theory of organization, therefore, has to do with the structure of coordination imposed upon the work division units of an enterprise."[6] "Organization as a way of coordination requires the establishment of a system of authority whereby the central purpose or objective of an enterprise is translated into reality through the combined efforts of many specialists, each working in his own field at a particular time and place."[7] Organization structure should be designed to create homogeneous combinations of work units on the basis of major purpose, process, clientele or materiel, or place.

Orthodox theory is preoccupied with the anatomy of government organization and concerned primarily with arrangements to assure that (1) each function is assigned to its appropriate niche within the government structure; (2) component parts of the executive branch are properly related and articulated; and (3) authorities and responsibilities are clearly assigned.

The important caveats and qualifications emphasized by Luther Gulick in his "Notes on the Theory of Organization,"

5. Luther Gulick, "Notes on the Theory of Organization" in *Papers on the Science of Administration* edited by Luther Gulick and L. Urwick, Institute of Public Administration, 1937, p. 3.
6. *Ibid.*
7. *Ibid.*, pp. 6–7.

particularly coordination "by the dominance of an idea," the futility of seeking a single most effective system of departmentalism, the need to recognize that "organization is a living dynamic entity," the limitations of command and the role of leadership, have been largely ignored by both his critics and disciples.[8] Such reservations were not entertained by the Hoover Commission whose report echoes, often in identical language, the organization "truths" first expounded by Herbert Hoover in the 1920's and early 1930's.[9]

Central to the understanding of orthodox theory are certain basic assumptions about the nature and purpose of organization and administration. The starting point is a rigid interpretation of the constitutional doctrine of separation of powers. Public administration is viewed as concerned almost exclusively with the executive branch, "where the work of government is done,"[10] with only grudging recognition given to the legislative and judicial branches' role in the administrative process. Preoccupation with the executive branch is coupled with an ill-concealed distrust of politics and politicians as the natural enemies of efficiency. Politics and administration are regarded as two heterogeneous functions, "the combination of which cannot be undertaken within the structure of administration without producing inefficiency."[11] Execution of policy is a matter for professional, technically trained, nonpartisan career managers, not amateurs. "Efficiency" is held to be the single overriding goal of organization and administration. On this point, Luther Gulick is unequivocal. In his words: "Efficiency is thus axiom number one in the value scale of adminis-

8. *Ibid.*, see pp. 6, 31, 37.

9. Library of Congress, *A Compilation of Basic Information on the Reorganization of the Executive Branch of the Government of the United States, 1912–1947*, Washington, 1947, pp. 1214–23.

10. Luther Gulick, "Science, Values and Public Administration" in *Papers on the Science of Administration* edited by Luther Gulick and L. Urwick, Institute of Public Administration, 1937, p. 191.

11. Gulick, *op. cit.*, p. 10.

tration. This brings administration into apparent conflict with the value scale of politics, whether we use that term in its scientific or popular sense."[12]

Since World War II, public administration theologians have become increasingly disenchanted with the orthodox dogmas. Skeptics and agnostics have dismissed the "principles of organization" as mere "proverbs" and exercises in "architectonics." Heretics have challenged the politics-administration dichotomy, notably Paul Appleby who classified administration as "the eighth political process,"[13] and a few even have gone so far as to question whether efficiency and economy are "the ultimate good."[14] Behavioral scientists have attacked the assumptions about human behavior which they believe are implicit in the orthodox theology, namely that authority flows from the top and employees are inert instruments performing the tasks assigned to them by their superiors. They condemn orthodox organization theory for almost completely ignoring the interplay of individual personality and interpersonal relations, informal groups, interorganization conflict, and the decision process in their conception of formal structure.[15] New cults worship the same gods of "economy and efficiency" but hope to achieve salvation by nonorganization means through the mysteries of systems analysis and Zero Based Budgeting. The literature of dissent is vast and growing.[16]

12. Gulick, *op. cit.*, p. 192.

13. Paul H. Appleby, *Policy and Administration,* University of Alabama Press, 1949.

14. Dwight Waldo, *The Administrative State,* The Ronald Press Co., 1948, Chapter 10.

15. William G. Scott, *Organization Theory: A Behavioral Analysis for Management,* Richard D. Irwin, Inc., 1967, p. 109.

16. For critiques of orthodox organization theory see: Warren G. Bennis, *Changing Organizations: Essays on the Development and Evolution of Human Organization,* McGraw-Hill Book Co., 1966; Bertram M. Gross, *The Managing or Organizations: The Administrative Struggle,* Vol. I, The Free Press of Glencoe, 1964; Daniel Katz and Robert L. Kahn, *The Social Psychology of Organization,* John Wiley & Sons, Inc., 1966; Douglas McGregor, *The Human Side of Enterprise,* McGraw-Hill Book Co., 1960; John D. Millett, *Organization*

Some of the criticism represents a form of intellectual exhibitionism which in its own way is as incomplete and parochial as the orthodox dogmas it condemns. While the observations on the discrepancies between the orthodox dogmas and the facts of organizational life and behavior are often pertinent and valid, these do not add up to a rational well-articulated set of working hypotheses for dealing with the present and emerging problems of federal organization. It is easy to pick the flaws in the concepts of unity of command, straight lines of authority and accountability, and organization by major purpose; it is far more difficult to develop acceptable alternatives.

Warren Bennis is one of the few who has had the courage to make the attempt with his proposal that organizations of the future be "adaptive, rapidly changing temporary systems." These will be organized around problems to be solved. The function of the executive will be to coordinate various project groups. Bennis emphasized that "people will be differentiated not vertically according to rank and role but flexibly according to skill and professional training."[17] But whatever its potential for private institutions or intradepartmental organization, the Bennis approach does not and was not intended to provide a grand design for executive branch structure.

Flawed and imperfect as they may be, the orthodox "principles" remain the only simple, readily understood, and comprehensive set of guidelines available to the president and the

---

for the Public Service, D. Van Nostrand Co., Inc., 1966; William G. Scott, *Organization Theory: A Behavioral Analysis for Management,* Richard D. Irwin, Inc., 1967; Herbert A. Simon, *Administrative Behavior,* 2nd Ed., The Macmillan Co., 1957; Herbert A. Simon, Donald W. Smithburg, and Victor A. Thompson, *Public Administration,* Alfred A. Knopf, 1950; Dwight Waldo, *The Administrative State,* The Ronald Press Co., 1948; Stephen J. Wayne, *The Legislative Presidency,* Harper and Row, 1978; Herbert Kaufman, "Reflections on Administrative Reorganization," in *Setting National Priorities: The 1978 Budget,* The Brookings Institution, 1977.

17. Bennis, *op. cit.,* p. 12.

Congress for resolving problems of executive branch structure. Individual members of Congress can relate them to their own experience within the Congress or in outside organizations. They have the virtue of clarity, a virtue often scorned by the newer orthodoxies, especially the behavioralists and social psychologists, who tend to write for each other in an arcane language which is unintelligible to the lay public. Dwight Waldo was correct when he concluded:

> . . . not only is the classical theory still today the formal working theory of large numbers of persons technically concerned with administrative-organizational matters, both in the public and private spheres, but I expect it will be around a long, long time. This is not necessarily because it is "true," though I should say it has much truth in it, both descriptively and prescriptively; that is to say, both as a description of organizations as we find them in our society and as a prescription for achieving the goals of these organizations "efficiently." *But in any event a social theory widely held by the actors has a self-confirming tendency and the classical theory is now deeply ingrained in our culture.*[18]

Publication of the *Papers on the Science of Administration* in 1937 may have marked the "high noon of orthodoxy in public administration theory in the United States,"[19] but someone apparently stopped the clock.

Herbert Hoover's fundamentalist dogmas have been enshrined by the Reorganization Act of 1949 (Chapter 9, Title 5 of the U.S. Code) as the lawful objectives of government reorganization. The president is directed from time to time to "examine the organization of all agencies" and to "determine what changes in such organization are necessary" to carry out

18. Italics supplied, Dwight Waldo, "Organization Theory: An Elephantine Problem," *Public Administration Review,* Vol. 21, No. 4, 1961.

19. Wallace S. Sayre, "Premises of Public Administration: Past and Emerging," *Public Administration Review,* Vol. 18, No. 2, 1958.

the following purposes which are declared by the Congress to be "the policy of the United States."

> (1) to promote the better execution of the laws, the more effective management of the executive branch of the government and of its agencies and functions, and the expeditious administration of the public business;
> (2) to reduce expenditures and promote economy to the fullest extent consistent with the effiicient operation of the government;
> (3) to increase the efficiency of the operations of the government to the fullest extent practicable;
> (4) to group, coordinate, and consolidate agencies and functions of the government, as nearly as may be, according to major purposes;
> (5) to reduce the number of agencies by consolidating those having similar functions under a single head, and to abolish such agencies or functions thereof as may not be necessary for the efficient conduct of the government; and
> (6) to eliminate overlapping and duplication of effort.

Necessary though it may have been to establish a legal foundation for an extraordinary grant of powers to the president, the long-run effects of freezing the purposes and principles of organization into law have been most unfortunate. They have inhibited creative thinking about federal structure and the development of fresh approaches adapted to the needs of our times. They have sometimes provided the right answers, but often for the wrong reasons. Organizers in the Office of Management and Budget and elsewhere have been compelled to develop and justify reorganization proposals within a narrow set of legal constraints. The talents required are more those of a Talmudic scholar than those of a sophisticated political scientist. Witness the tag paragraph found in most reorganization plans to conform with the provision that the president "specify the reduction of expenditure which it is probable will be brought about by the taking effect of the plan" (itemized so far as practicable). A typical example is to be found in the message transmitting Reorganization Plan No. 1 of 1962 to create a Department of Urban Affairs and Housing:

> Although the taking effect of the reorganizations provided for in the reorganization plan will not in itself result in immediate savings, the improvements achieved in administration will in the future allow the performance of necessary services at greater savings than present operations would permit. An itemization of these savings in advance of experience is not practicable.

By its overemphasis on observance of prescribed rituals, the statute has contributed materially to congressional failure, both in hearings and floor debates, to expose to public view the basic political questions posed by reorganization proposals. The more knowledgeable members of the Congress and the executive branch are generally quite well aware what these issues are—and they seldom have anything to do with economy and efficiency. But the real issues are openly discussed, if at all, by indirection and in a language which only insiders can understand. Occasionally these issues do surface, as in the case of Reorganization Plan No. 3 of 1967 to reorganize the government of the District of Columbia, where the major points of difference were more concerned with the power and prerogatives of the House District Committee than the strengths and weaknesses of a commission form of government.

Congress has insisted on more, not less, orthodoxy. Congressman John Erlenborn was highly critical of the lack of specificity in presidential reorganization messages concerning which of the purposes of the reorganization statute would be fulfilled by a plan. On Erlenborn's initiative the House in 1968 adopted an amendment to the statute requiring the president to specify, one-by-one, which of the enumerated purposes would be accomplished by each plan and to estimate the "aggregate" reduction of expenditures which would result. When the budget director promised in 1969 that in the future the requested data would be supplied, the House agreed to extend the reorganization authority without including the Erlenborn amendment.[20]

President Carter proposed that the Reorganization Act of 1949 be amended to eliminate the requirement for detailed savings estimates. Instead the president would provide information on the improvements in management efficiency and delivery of services which would be realized as the result of reorganization. Carter's suggested language was included in the 1977 statute extending presidential reorganization authority, but the Congress retained the requirement that the president "estimate any reduction or increase in expenditures (itemized so far as practicable)."

The theoretical assumptions underlying the orthodox dogmas have been transformed into unassailable eternal verities. Executive branch spokesmen are loath to challenge established "truths" on fear of excommunication. Custom, culture, and role all require OMB officials openly to profess their faith in "economy and efficiency" as the prime goals of organization and reorganization, with emphasis on economy. When Congressman Erlenborn commented that "it would be refreshing sometimes if your messages would say there are no economies," Deputy Budget Director Phillip S. Hughes replied: "It might be refreshing but it might also be disastrous."[21]

Almost every president from Theodore Roosevelt to Richard M. Nixon, with the notable exception of Franklin D. Roosevelt, has at one time or another found it necessary to defend reorganization as a means of reducing expenditures. The Nixon administration sought to downplay economy as a major purpose of the president's proposed restructuring of the executive departments, but Roy L. Ash, chairman of Mr. Nixon's Advisory Council on Executive Organization, testified that the reorganization to create Departments of Community Develop-

20. *Congressional Record,* April 22, 1968, pp. H3057–61, House Report No. 91–80, 91st Congress, 1st Session.

21. Committee on Government Operations, House of Representatives, Hearing on H. R. 15688 to extend the reorganization statute, March 13, 1968, p. 13.

ment, Economic Affairs, Human Resources, and Natural Resources would produce savings of $5 billion.[22]

"We have to get over the notion that the purpose of reorganization is economy," FDR told Louis Brownlow and Luther Gulick in 1936. "I had that out with Al Smith in New York. . . . The reason for reorganization is good management."[23] The overwhelming weight of empirical evidence supports the Roosevelt view that reorganizations do not save money.

Of the reorganization plans transmitted to the Congress from 1949 through 1978, only six—Reorganization Plan No. 3 of 1952, which would have ended Senate confirmation of postmasters; Reorganization Plan No. 1 of 1965 reorganizing the Bureau of Customs; Reorganization Plan No. 5 of 1966 abolishing the National Capital Regional Planning Council; Reorganization Plan No. 1 of 1973 abolishing the Office of Science and Technology, the Office of Emergency Preparedness, the National Aeronautics and Space Council, and other components of the Executive Office of the President; Reorganization Plan No. 1 of 1977 reorganizing the Executive Office of the President; and Reorganization Plan No. 3 of 1978 consolidating emergency preparedness functions—were supported by precise dollar estimates of savings. Plan No. 3 of 1952 was disapproved by the Congress. Granted executive branch reluctance to offer savings estimates which can be later used in evidence by the appropriations committees, it is clear that the failure to itemize expenditure reductions reflects the reality that economies are produced by curtailing services and abolishing bureaus, not by reorganization.

Emphasis is placed more on form than on substance. Frequently, studies of executive branch structure degenerate into

22. Committee on Government Operations, Legislation and Military Operations Subcommittee, Hearings on Reorganization of Executive Departments (Part 1—Overview), June and July 1971, p. 231.

23. Richard Polenberg, *Reorganizing Roosevelt's Government,* Harvard University Press, 1966, p. 8.

sterile box-shuffling and another version of the numbers game. This approach is typified by President Nixon's citing as indisputable evidence of the need for "comprehensive reform" of the federal government, the fact that "nine different Federal Departments and 20 independent agencies are now involved in education matters. Seven departments and eight independent agencies are involved in health. . . . Three departments help develop our water resources and four agencies in two departments are involved in the management of public lands. Federal recreation areas are administered by six different agencies in three departments of the government. Seven agencies provide assistance for water and sewer systems. Six departments of the government collect similar economic information—often from the same source—and at least seven departments are concerned with international trade."[24] One White House task force on government organization found that if you pushed this approach to its logical conclusion you would end up with a Department of Foreign Affairs, a Department of Domestic Affairs, and a Department of Defense, and even then all overlaps would not be eliminated.

Established organization doctrine, with its emphasis on structural mechanics, manifests incomplete understanding of our constitutional system, institutional behavior, and the tactical and strategic uses of organization structure as an instrument of politics, position, and power. Orthodox theories are not so much wrong when applied to the central issues of executive branch organization as they are largely irrelevant.

Executive branch structure is in fact a microcosm of our society. Inevitably it reflects the values, conflicts, and competing forces to be found in a pluralistic society. The ideal of a neatly symmetrical, frictionless organization structure is a dangerous illusion. We would do well to heed Dean Acheson's sage advice that "organization—or reorganization in govern-

24. *Papers Relating to the President's Department Reorganization Program*, revised February 1972, U. S. Government Printing Office, p. 6.

ment, can often be a trap for the unwary. The relationships involved in the division of labor and responsibility are far more subtle and complex than the little boxes which the graph drawers put on paper with their perpendicular and horizontal connecting lines."[25]

EXECUTIVE BRANCH ORGANIZATION: THEORY VS. PRACTICE

Organizational arrangements are not neutral. We do not organize in a vacuum. Organization is one way of expressing national commitment, influencing program direction, and ordering priorities. Organizational arrangements tend to give some interests and perspectives more effective access to those with decision-making authority, whether they be in the Congress or in the executive branch. As Richard Neustadt has pointed out: "In political government, the means can matter quite as much as the ends; they often matter more."[26]

Institutional location and environment, administrative arrangements and type of organization, can raise significant political questions concerning the distribution and balance of power between the executive branch and the Congress; the federal government and state and local governments; states and cities; the federal government and organized interest groups, particularly the principal beneficiaries of federal programs; and finally, among the components of the executive establishment itself, including the president's relationship to the departments and the bureaucracy.

If our democratic system is to be responsive to the needs of *all* our people, organization structure and administrative arrangements need to so balance the competing interests within given program areas that none is immune to public control

25. Dean Acheson, "Thoughts about Thoughts in High Places," *The New York Times Magazine,* October 11, 1959.
26. Richard E. Neustadt, *Presidential Power—The Politics of Leadership,* John Wiley & Sons, Inc., 1960, p. 47.

and capable of excluding less powerful segments of our society from effective participation in the system and an equitable share of its benefits. Failure to maintain this balance has contributed to the present malaise.

President Eisenhower in his farewell address to the nation warned against "the acquisition of unwarranted influence, whether sought or unsought, by the military-industrial complex." Other complexes, notably the science-education and agricultural establishments, wield power equal to or exceeding that of the perhaps overly dramatized military-industrial combine. Scientific research is said to be the only pork barrel for which the pigs determine who gets the pork.

The political implications of organization structure were recognized as early as 1789 when the states endeavored to control the extension of federal power by limiting the creation of executive departments. In 1849 the bill to establish the Department of the Interior was opposed because "it meant the further extension of federal authority to the detriment of the states."[27] Opposition to the establishment of the Department of Education in the 1970's stemmed from much the same concern.

Application of "economy and efficiency" as the criteria for government organization can produce serious distortions, if political and environmental factors are ignored. It led the first Hoover Commission to proceed from the indisputable finding that the Farmers Home Administration's functions duplicated and overlapped those of the Farm Credit Administration and Agricultural Extension Service to the seemingly logical conclusion that the Administration ought to be liquidated and its functions divided between its two competitors. The conclusion was obviously faulty to anyone in the least familiar with the histories of the Farm Credit Administration and the Extension Service as creatures of the American Farm Bureau Federation

27. Lloyd M. Short, *The Development of National Administrative Organization in the United States*, The Johns Hopkins Press, 1923, p. 89.

and the most conservative elements in the agricultural community. The Farm Bureau was proud of its role in scuttling the Rural Resettlement Administration and Farm Security Administration, the immediate predecessors of the FHA.[28] If there were ever a case of letting the goats loose in the cabbage patch, this was it. The FHA was created to furnish special assistance to farmers who constitute marginal risks and possess little political clout. Commissioners Acheson, Pollock, and Rowe observed in their dissent that "the purpose of the Farmers Home Administration is to make 'good' tenant farmers out of 'poor' tenant farmers, and not to restrict credit to 'good' tenant farmers who can probably obtain credit from other sources."[29]

Some now question whether the Farmers Home Administration or any other agency within a department so conceived and so organized as the Department of Agriculture can respond adequately to the needs of the rural poor in the South, most of whom are black. It was no coincidence that the 1968 Poor People's Campaign in Washington singled out the Department of Agriculture for special attention. The Citizens Board of Inquiry into Hunger and Malnutrition in the United States asserted that the Department of Agriculture and the congressional Agriculture committees are "dominated by a concern for maximizing agricultural income, especially within the big production categories. Other objectives always yield to this one . . . almost never does our agricultural policy take a direct concern with the interests of consumers."[30] The board

28. For excellent analyses of the role played by the American Farm Bureau Federation in organizational politics see Sidney Baldwin, *Poverty and Politics,* University of North Carolina Press, 1968; Philip Selznick, *TVA and the Grass Roots,* University of California Press, 1949.

29. The Commission on Organization of the Executive Branch of the Government, "Federal Business Enterprises," A Report to the Congress, March 1949, p. 102.

30. Reprinted in hearings before the Subcommittee on Executive Reorganization of the Senate Committee on Government Operations on "Modernizing the Federal Government," January–May 1968, p. 355.

proposed reorganization and removal of food programs from Agriculture's jurisdiction as the answer.

Powerful groups in the commercial banking, research, and educational communities regard overlapping and duplication not as vices, but as positive virtues. The American Bankers Association through the years has successfully blocked efforts to consolidate bank supervisory and examining functions in a single federal agency. The division of responsibility among the Comptroller of the Currency, the Federal Deposit Insurance Corporation, and the Federal Reserve Board is viewed by the ABA as "wholly in keeping with the broad principle that the success and strength of democracy in America is largely due to the sound safeguards afforded by the wisely conceived checks and balances which pervade our composite governmental system."[31] The system is defended because banks retain the option of changing their federal supervisors and thus gaining "some possible relief from unduly stringent examinations."[32]

Whatever advantages may have been gained by these "checks and balances" now appear to be more than offset by the loss of power within the councils of government. Without a single spokesman, the common interests of the commercial banks may be obscured in a chorus of discordant voices. This was a matter of little importance when most commercial banks enjoyed *de facto* monopolies and did not face competition from newly chartered commercial banks and an aggressive, politically wise savings and loan industry. The commercial banks are now in a position where they might be better served by organizational arrangements designed to stimulate and influence, not prevent, federal action. Unwillingness to abandon long cherished positions is not the exclusive disease of government bureaucracies.

Overlapping and duplication among federal agencies mak-

31. American Bankers Association, "Reply to Questionnaire of U.S. Senate Committee on Banking and Currency," April 1941, p. 65.
32. *Ibid.*, p. 67.

ing research grants do not alarm scientists and educators. On the contrary, diversity in support is held essential to maximize the opportunities for obtaining federal funds and to minimize the dangers of federal control. The Committee on Science and Public Policy of the National Academy of Sciences strongly endorsed a "plural system" which has many roots for its authority "and many alternative administrative means of solving a given problem."[33]

Assignment of administrative jurisdiction can be a key factor in determining program direction and ultimate success or failure. Each agency has its own culture and internal set of loyalties and values which are likely to guide its actions and influence its policies. A number of satellites grow up and around and outside the institution and develop a mutual dependence. Private bureaucracies in Washington now almost completely parallel the public bureaucracies in those program areas where the federal government contracts for services, regulates private enterprise, or provides some form of financial assistance.

Shared loyalties and outlook knit together the institutional fabric. They are the foundation of those intangibles which make for institutional morale and pride. Without them, functions could not be decentralized and delegated with the confidence that policies will be administered consistently and uniformly. But because people believe what they are doing is important and the way they have been taught to do it is right, they are slow to accept change. Institutional responses are highly predictable, particularly to new ideas which conflict with institutional values and may pose a potential threat to organizational power and survival. Knowledgeable Budget Bureau officials once estimated that agency positions on any major policy issue can be forecast with nearly 100 percent accuracy, regardless of the administration in power.

There is an ever-present danger that innovative programs

33. National Academy of Science, "Federal Support of Basic Research in Institutions of Higher Learning," Washington, D.C., 1964.

which challenge accepted norms, demand new skills and approaches, and create conflicts with agency constituencies will be assimilated into the "system" and their purposes muffled or distorted. One way to kill a program is to house it in a hostile or unsympathetic environment.

The Congress tacked a rider to the 1953 RFC Liquidation Act authorizing the president to designate an agency to make loans to public bodies for the construction or acquisition of public facilities.[34] Budget Bureau staff recommended that the Housing and Home Finance Agency be designated because its mission was most closely related to urban and community development, but the then budget director preferred Treasury "because it wouldn't make the loans." Treasury obviously would be less susceptible to pressure from state capitols and city halls and could be expected to apply strict banking criteria in reviewing loan applications. The final solution was not to make any designation. The Congress solved the problem by enacting legislation vesting program responsibility in the Housing and Home Finance Agency.

In their zeal to construct neat and uncluttered organization charts, professional reorganizers and reorganization commissions tend to downgrade, when they do not wholly ignore, environmental influences. Certainly, the poverty program would have been different, whether better or worse depends on one's point of view, if, as many advocated, responsibility at the outset had been given either to the Department of Health, Education, and Welfare or to the choice of the big-city mayors, the Department of Housing and Urban Development. Creation of a new agency is likely to present fewer problems than reform of an old one and enables the president and the Congress to finesse competing jurisdictional claims. Compromise arrangements are possible, and program seedlings under some circumstances can take root and grow within established departments if protected during the developmental period by a self-contained, relatively autonomous status.

34. Reconstruction Finance Corporation Liquidation Act, 1953 (40 U.S.C. 459).

Adherence to the principle of organization according to major purposes provides no automatic answers. Herbert Hoover would have resolved the problem by having the Congress define "major purpose" and then leaving it to the president to reorganize executive agencies in accordance with their purposes as set forth in law.[35] Granted that Mr. Hoover made this proposal in 1924, when federal programs were simple by today's standards, it is incredibly naïve.

Federal programs are likely to have multiple purposes. Disagreements as to priorities among diverse and sometimes conflicting objectives are a major source of current controversies. Is the major purpose of the food stamp program to dispose of surplus agricultural commodities or to feed the poor? Is mass transportation a transportation or an urban development program? Are school lunches a nutrition or an education function? Should the federal water pollution control program have as its principal objective health protection, or should it be concerned more broadly with the development of water resources?

Major purposes cannot be ascertained by scientific or economic analysis. Determination of major purpose represents a value judgment, and a transitory one at that. Thus President Nixon could argue in 1971 that the Department of Transportation "is now organized around methods and not around purposes," although transportation was assumed to be a major purpose when the department was established in 1966.[36] What is the secondary purpose for one, is a major purpose for another. To quote Miles's law: "Where one stands depends on where one sits."[37] Major purposes are not constants but variables shifting with the ebb and tide of our national needs and aspirations.

Debates about organizational type also may mask basic dif-

35. Library of Congress, *op. cit.*, p. 1216.

36. *Papers Relating to the President's Departmental Reorganization Program, op. cit.*, pp. 14–15.

37. Attributed to Rufus Miles, formerly assistant secretary for administration, Department of Health, Education and Welfare.

ferences over strategy and objectives. Orthodox theory postulates that all federal agencies, with the possible exception of the independent regulatory commissions, be grouped under a limited number of single-headed executive departments and consequently ignores the other possible forms of organization. Except for the regulatory commissions and government corporations, the Hoover Commissions and President's Committee on Administrative Management took little interest in the typology of organization—a disinterest shared by most students of public administration.

The significance of institutional type has been underrated. In Part II we will endeavor to identify and analyze the rich variety of organizational types which have been developed within our constitutional system: executive departments, independent agencies, assorted commissions, boards, councils, authorities, wholly-owned corporations, mixed-ownership corporations, "captive" corporations, institutes, government-sponsored enterprises, foundations, establishments, conferences, intergovernmental bodies, compact agencies, and a wide variety of interagency and advisory committees. The differences among these institutional types are more a matter of convention and tradition than legal prescriptions. Yet some have acquired a "mystique" which can profoundly influence public attitudes and executive and congressional behavior for good or ill. Institutional type can be crucial in determining who controls—the president, the Congress, or the so-called "special interests."

Institutional type, for example, was a major issue when Congress authorized the Marshall Plan. Republicans wanted the plan administered by a government corporation because by definition it would be more "businesslike."[38] A corporation would also make it more difficult for the State Department to meddle in the European recovery program. The compromise

38. House Select Committee on Foreign Aid, "Preliminary Report Eleven—Comparative Analysis of Suggested Plans of Foreign Aid," November 22, 1947.

was to establish an independent agency outside the State Department and to authorize creation of a corporation, if and when needed.

Scientists devised a new government institution named a "foundation" when existing institutions would not support their postwar grand design of "science governed by scientists and paid for by the public."[39] The ostensible aim was to duplicate within the executive branch a typical university structure. Effective control over the proposed National Science Foundation was to be vested in a twenty-four-member National Science Board to be appointed by the president after giving due consideration to nominations submitted to him by the National Academy of Sciences, the Association of Land Grant Colleges and Universities, the National Association of State Universities, the Association of American Colleges, or by other scientific or educational institutions. The board would be required to meet only once a year. It would, in turn, select biennially from among its members a nine-member executive committee which would meet six times a year and exercise the board's powers. The foundation's full-time executive officer, a director, would be appointed by the executive committee unless the board chose to make the appointment itself.

A bill incorporating the scientists' proposal was enacted by the Congress but drew a strongly worded veto from President Truman.[40] Truman recognized that "the proposed National Science Foundation would be divorced from control by the people to an extent that implies a distinct lack of faith in the democratic process" and would deprive the president "of effective means for discharging his constitutional responsibility." He took particular exception to the provisions insulating the director from the president by two layers of part-time boards

39. Daniel S. Greenberg, *The Politics of Pure Science,* The New American Library, Inc., 1967, p. 107.

40. Harry S Truman, Memorandum of Disapproval of the National Foundation Bill (S.526), August 6, 1947.

and warned that "if the principles of this bill were extended throughout the government, the result would be utter chaos." Truman's views only partially prevailed. The Congress deleted the most objectionable feature by making the foundation director a presidential appointee, but retained the basic structure desired by the science establishment.

Institutional advisory bodies often are as much of a potential threat to executive power as the National Science Foundation proposal, but they are far more difficult to combat. Creation of the National Security Council properly could be construed as a ploy by a Republican Congress to circumscribe a Democratic president's powers in areas where he was constitutionally supreme. Not only did the Congress designate those officials who were to "advise" the president in the exercise of his constitutional powers, but it also included the curious provision that other secretaries and undersecretaries of executive departments could be appointed council members only with the advice and consent of the Senate. Advice is potentially one of the most powerful weapons in the administrative arsenal.

Up to now we have been discussing mainly the strategic implications of executive branch organization. But power relationships are not always involved in organization decisions. The president, the Congress, and even outside groups may use organizational means to obtain some immediate tactical advantage.

Herbert Hoover himself was not above using organization for tactical purposes. He claimed that he was "a much misunderstood man on this question of committees and commissions." According to Mr. Hoover,

> There is no more dangerous citizen than the person with a gift of gab, a crusading complex and a determination "to pass a law" as the antidote for all human ills. The most effective diversion of such an individual to constructive

> action and the greatest silencer on earth for foolishness is to associate him on research committee with a few persons who have a passion for truth, especially if they pay their own expenses. I can now disclose the secret that I created a dozen committees for that precise purpose.[41]

Presidents have continued to employ committees and commissions to capture and contain the opposition. Committees and commissions can also offer an immediate, visible response in times of national catastrophe, such as the assassinations of President Kennedy and Senator Kennedy or the Watts riot. Study commissions are employed as a kind of tranquilizer to quiet public and congressional agitation about such matters as pesticides, crime, and public scandals. Attention, it is hoped, will be diverted to other issues by the time the commissions report. A poem appearing in *Punch* some years ago put it very well:

> If you're pestered by critics and hounded by faction
> To take some precipitate, positive action,
> The proper procedure, to take my advice, is
> Appoint a commission and stave off the crisis.[42]

Prestigious commissions can also build public support for controversial courses of action. What is wanted is endorsement, not advice, although "run-away" commissions are not unknown. On sensitive issues such as congressional pay, where members of Congress are politically vulnerable, a commission report helps to take them off the hook. Both Presidents Kennedy and Johnson used commissions to support legislation to increase executive, congressional, and judicial salaries.[43]

41. Hoover, *op. cit.*, p. 281.

42. Geoffrey Parsons, "Royal Commission," *Punch,* August 24, 1955. © *Punch,* London.

43. For a perceptive analysis see Elizabeth D. Drew, "How to Govern (or Avoid It) by Commission," *Atlantic Monthly,* May 1968.

Interagency committees sometimes create an impression of neatness and order within the executive establishment, even when a president cannot or will not resolve the basic differences and jurisdictional conflicts. If differences surface publicly and become embarrassing to the administration, the president's reflex reaction is to appoint another committee or to reorganize existing committees. The pressure is almost overwhelming "to do something" which might do some good and certainly will do no harm. No president can confess that he is stumped by a problem.

Pressure for immediate, tangible answers to highly complex problems may result in reorganizations. President Eisenhower's first response to the national trauma caused by the Soviet Union's successful launching of Sputnik in 1957 was to appoint a special assistant to the president for Science and Technology and to transfer the Science Advisory Committee from the Office of Defense Mobilization to the White House office. Creation of the Department of Energy in 1977 was a response to the energy crisis caused by the 1973 oil embargo.

Reorganization may provide a convenient way to dump an unwanted official, particularly one with strong congressional or constituency ties. The maneuver is not always successful, as was seen with Secretary of State Dean Rusk's abortive plan to abolish the Department's Bureau of Security and Consular Affairs. Mr. Abba Schwartz's version of this incident is highly colored, but there is no question that Secretary Rusk's timing was influenced by his desire to shift Mr. Schwartz from the bureau directorship to another post. The Bureau of Security and Consular Affairs was the brainchild of Senator Joseph McCarthy, and the Bureau of the Budget had targeted it for reorganization long before Mr. Schwartz arrived on the scene.

Use of reorganization to bypass a troublesome committee or subcommittee chairman in the Congress can also be hazardous when it does not succeed. Transfer of civil defense activities from the Office of Civil and Defense Mobilization to the secretary of defense in 1961 was expected as an incidental benefit to remove the shelter program from the jurisdiction of an unfriendly appropriations subcommittee chairman.[44] Albert Thomas, however, had the power to retain jurisdiction to the great discomfiture of the civil defense officials.

Organization choices may be motivated almost entirely by a desire to exclude billions in expenditures from budget tabulations. The 1969 budget was the first to include trust funds and mixed-ownership government corporations in the administrative budget. President Eisenhower's 1955 proposal to create a Federal Highway Corporation for financing the construction of the National System of Interstate Highways was deliberately designed to keep the authorized payments of $25 billion out of the budget totals. The proposal was later abandoned when it was found that establishment of a highway trust fund could serve the same purpose. Conversion of the Federal National Mortgage Association from a wholly-owned to a mixed-ownership government corporation in 1954 also had as its principal appeal the appearance of a multi-billion-dollar budget reduction. When the ground rules were changed with the 1969 budget, legislation was enacted to turn the Federal National Mortgage Association into a "government sponsored private corporation" so as to keep its expenditures out of the budget.

To escape arbitrary and unrealistic ceilings on civilian personnel, federal agencies have been compelled to utilize so-called "nonprofit intermediaries" to carry out programs mandated by congressional enactments. The Labor Department's organizational choices were limited when it was allowed forty-nine full-time positions in order to design and implement a complex multi-million dollar youth employment and training program.[45]

44. Executive Order No. 10952, July 20, 1961.

45. National Academy of Public Administration, *Government Sponsored Non-Profits,* November 1978.

A new name and a new look may be necessary to save a program with little political appeal, particularly one which congressional supporters find difficult to sell to their constituents. At times reorganization supplies the rationale needed by members of Congress to explain their vote. The frequent reorganization and renaming of the foreign aid agency reflect efforts to bolster congressional support and to demonstrate presidential interest, rather than to introduce new policies and improve management. There have been no less than eight successive foreign aid agencies—from the Economic Cooperation Administration in 1948 to the Agency for International Development in 1961—until 1961 an average of a new agency less than every two years.[46]

For many, organization is a symbol. Federal councils on aging, mental retardation, physical fitness, consumers, and the arts, for example, are more important as evidence of national concern than as molders of federal policies.

Some seek the creation of new federal agencies or reorganizations to enhance their status in the outside community. The demand for an independent National Archives disassociated from the government's "housekeeper," the General Services Administration, in part stems from the archivists' desire to improve their standing as a scholarly profession. Several years ago the firemen's association sought Bureau of the Budget support for a Federal Fire Academy. While the academy was not perceived at the time as fulfilling any identifiable federal need, it would place firemen on a par with policemen, who had a federal "sponsor" in the Federal Bureau of Investigation, and thus strengthen their bargaining position in dealing with mayors and city councils.[47]

The Congress is highly skilled in the tactical uses of organization and reorganization. If you come from a district with a

46. Michael K. O'Leary, *The Politics of American Foreign Aid,* Atherton Press, 1967, p. 117.

47. A National Academy for Fire Prevention and Control was authorized by the Federal Fire Prevention and Control Act of 1974.

jet airport, establishment of an Office of Noise Abatement in the Department of Transportation has tremendous voter appeal. Even though there is doubt that a separate office could do much to reduce noise levels, at least it offers a place where members of Congress can send constituent complaints. While the administration was able to defeat an amendment to the Department of Transportation bill to create such an office on the valid grounds that aircraft noise was a research and development and traffic control problem, Secretary Alan Boyd later found it expedient to create an Office of Noise Abatement by administrative action. Members of Congress are more susceptible to pressures from sectional, economic, and professional interests than is the president, and these often become translated into organizational responses.

Economy and efficiency are demonstrably not the prime purposes of public administration. Even such a single-minded and zealous advocate of "efficiency" and "competency" in government as President Jimmy Carter has acknowledged:

> Nowhere in the Constitution of the United States, or the Declaration of Independence, or the Bill of Rights, or the Emancipation Proclamation, or the Old Testament or the New Testament, do you find the words "economy" or "efficiency." Not that these words are unimportant. But you discover other words like honesty, integrity, fairness, liberty, justice, patriotism, compassion, love—and many others which describe what human beings ought to be. These are the same words which describe what a government of human beings ought to be.[48]

Supreme Court Justice Louis D. Brandeis emphasized that the "doctrine of separation of powers was adopted, not to promote efficiency but to preclude the exercise of arbitrary power."[49] The basic issues of federal organization and administration relate to power: who shall control it and to what ends?

48. Jimmy Carter, *Why Not the Best?* Bantam Books, 1976, p. 132.

49. Cited in Lewis Meriam and Lawrence F. Schmeckebier, *Reorganization of the National Government,* The Brookings Institution, 1939, p. 132.

The questions that now urgently confront us are as old as the Republic itself. How can we maintain a government structure and administrative system which reconcile liberty with justice and institutional and personal freedom with the general welfare?

What we are observing today are the strains and tensions inevitably produced by revolutionary changes in the federal government's role and its relationships to other levels of government, institutions of higher learning and other nonprofit institutions, and the private sector. Dividing lines have become increasingly blurred. It is no longer easy to determine where federal responsibilities end and those of state and local governments and private institutions begin. These changes began with the "New Deal" in the 1930's, but the most dramatic developments have occurred since 1961.

Organizational ills are not easily diagnosed. Organization problems are often merely symptoms of growing pains or more deep-seated organic disease. Institutions do not perform well when called upon to accomplish significant transformations in the economic and social structure of our society within a one- or two-year time frame. Yet this is exactly what we have done in the poverty and model cities programs. In piling one new program on top of another, we have tended to ignore the need to find or develop the necessary managerial capability at all levels of government and have overloaded the system.

Yardsticks for measuring organizational health are admittedly inadequate and may be misleading. Strong public and congressional criticism may reflect effective performance, not the reverse. Servile obedience to congressional and constituency pressures, or inaction, may win more influential "friends" and supporters than would vigorous pursuit of the public interest.

Growth has been a factor. Expenditures for major social programs, such as health and education, now exceed $67 billion a year. Federal aid to state and local governments jumped from about $7 billion in 1961 to an estimated $82.9 billion in 1980. In the same period annual expenditures for research and development have increased from approximately $9 billion to between $31 and 32 billion.

As a percentage of Gross National Product, federal outlays for civilian programs rose from 1 percent or less in the 1920's to about 5 percent in immediate postwar years to 16 percent in fiscal 1980.[50]

These increases would not be significant if they represented in the main stepped-up spending for traditional programs (welfare payments, price supports, veterans benefits, public works, highway construction) which could be smoothly channeled through the comfortable time-worn, single-purpose, single-agency groove. But the new programs to combat poverty, air and water pollution, crime and urban blight rewrote the ground rules. Under these programs, the federal government directly participates in specific projects in states and communities and acts as a co-equal partner with state and local governments, either individually or as a member of joint federal-state organizations such as the Appalachia Regional Commission. These programs call for participation by many federal agencies and cut across established jurisdictional lines at all levels of government.

The Hoover Commission solution of "placing related functions cheek-by-jowl" so that "the overlaps can be eliminated, and of even greater importance coordinated policies can be developed" is not workable when you must combine the major purpose programs—health, education, manpower, housing—in alleviating the social and economic ills of a specific region, city, or neighborhood. We could regionalize the executive branch, as some have proposed, but members of Congress, governors, and mayors would be unwilling to accept such a concentration of power in any one federal agency. Such modest proposals as those to establish HUD "urban expediters" in

50. The Budget of the United States for Fiscal Year 1980, p. 82.

key cities are viewed with suspicion. If one official could control the flow of federal funds into a region, that person would be in a position to dictate state and local policies.

Senator Robert Kennedy posed the fundamental question when he asked: "Do the agencies of Government have the will and determination and ability to form and carry out programs which cut across departmental lines, which are tailored to no administrative convenience but the overriding need to get things done?"[51]

Straight lines of authority and accountability cannot be established in a nonhierarchical system. The federal government is compelled to rely increasingly for accomplishment of its goals on cooperation by nonfederal institutions which are not legally responsible to the president and subject to his direction. Federal powers are limited to those agreed upon and enumerated in negotiated contracts. Success of the foreign aid, energy, space and defense research and development programs depends almost as much on performance by contractors as by the government's own employees. About 80 percent of federal expenditures for research and development are made through nonfederal institutions, under either grants or contracts.[52] The government since 1948 has caused to be organized and wholly financed a host of university- and industry-sponsored research centers and so-called nonprofit corporations for the sole purpose of providing services to the government. Legally these are private organizations, but many, such as the Institute for Defense Analyses, Aerospace Corporation, Urban Institute, Lincoln Laboratory, Public/Private ventures, and Oak Ridge National Laboratory, have more in common with traditional government agencies than with private institutions.

51. Senate Committee on Government Operations, hearings on "Federal Role in Urban Affairs," 1967, p. 40.

52. U.S. Bureau of the Budget, "Report to the President on Contracting for Research and Development," April 30, 1962.

Fundamentalist dogmas were developed for a different universe—for the federal government as it existed in the 1920's and early 1930's. It was a time when Herbert Hoover could be told by one of his predecessors as secretary of commerce that the "job would not require more than two hours of work a day. Indeed that was all the time that former secretaries devoted to it. Putting the fish to bed at night and turning on the lights around the coast were possibly the major concepts of the office."[53] In the 1920's the Department of Commerce was engaged in what were then typical government services: collection and dissemination of statistics, preparation of charts and maps, operation of lighthouses, issuance of patents, and licensing, inspection, and regulation. Except for public works projects, timber, grazing and mineral rights, agricultural loans, and land permits, the federal government had little power to confer or withhold economic benefits. Federal intervention in the economy was indirect through economic regulation, the tariff, fiscal, monetary, and credit policies.

Government and business regarded each other as adversaries, not as potential partners. Theodore Roosevelt argued that establishment of a Department of Commerce would represent "an advance toward dealing with and exercising supervision over the whole subject of the great corporations doing an interstate business."[54] Roosevelt considered that the secretary's first duty would be to regulate commerce and industry, rather than to act as a spokesman for their interests.

The regulatory approach reached its high-water mark with the New Deal. To the Interstate Commerce Commission, Federal Trade Commission, and Federal Power Commission, there were added the Securities and Exchange Commission, Federal Communications Commission, Civil Aeronautics Board, U.S. Maritime Commission, and the National Labor Relations Board. As far as the regulated industries were concerned, ex-

53. Hoover, *op. cit.*, p. 42.
54. Library of Congress, *op. cit.*, pp. 1205–6.

cept for maritime and aviation subsidies, the less the federal government did the better. Tactics were defensive and designed to weaken, capture, and control the regulators.

It is highly significant that in *Public Administration and the Public Interest,* which was published in 1936, and is a groundbreaking analysis of the role played by special interest groups in the administrative process, Pendleton Herring devotes 150 pages to the regulatory agencies and internal revenue and only 74 to the executive departments—State, Agriculture, Commerce, and Labor. The War, Navy, and Interior departments receive only passing mention.[55] If the book were written today, the emphasis would be reversed.

In the years since World War II, the federal table has become crowded with dependents, each clamoring to be fed and demanding the biggest slice of pie. Where before the federal government was tolerated as a nuisance or at best a marginal customer, major industries, universities, and other institutions have now come to depend on federal funds for survival.

In contrast to the situation in World War II, and even that during the Korean War, a large share of defense production is performed by highly specialized defense contractors, many of whose products bear little resemblance to civilian items, and who have had little experience outside defense production. For many companies their only important customer is the United States government. Fifteen companies in 1968 derived more than half of their business from United States government contracts. For Lockheed Aircraft, McDonnell Douglas, AVCO, Newport News Shipbuilding, and Thiokol, government purchases accounted for more than 70 percent of sales.[56]

The federal government currently finances almost two thirds of university research and development programs. This money goes for basic research in such fields as chemistry,

55. E. Pendleton Herring, *Public Administration and the Public Interest,* McGraw-Hill Book Co., 1936.

56. *Congressional Quarterly,* Special Report on "The Military-Industrial Complex," May 24, 1968.

physics, biology, astronomy, materials, oceanography, and earth sciences.

States and cities see no solution to their critical financial problems other than more federal money. Federal aid has risen as a proportion of state and local expenditures from 12 percent in 1958 to 26.7 percent in 1978.

The federal government may not be loved, but its capacity to raise revenues is greatly envied. Industry interests, however, may go beyond money. Otto Klima, Jr., and Gibson Wolfe, for example, advocate one federal agency with overview and program responsibility for all of this nation's interests in the oceans primarily as a means of helping U.S. industry by providing it with better decisional criteria.[57]

Unlike the regulated industries, it is not enough for these federal dependents to maintain a strong defensive posture. Under our system of checks and balances, it is relatively easy to block action. It is far more difficult to persuade the executive branch and the Congress to do something, particularly when there are strong competing demands for limited resources. Offense demands a new team and a different strategy. Some industries, such as the railroads, have been penalized because they were too slow in getting their defensive team off the field.

Each of the dependents endeavors to manipulate the organization structure and assignment of program responsibilities so as to maximize its ability to obtain federal funds and to minimize federal interference in the allocation and use of funds. Scientists had these objectives in mind when they developed their original design for the National Science Foundation. Farm organizations were inspired by identical motives when they convinced President Eisenhower to support legislation which provided independent financing for the farm credit system and immunized it to effective federal control. Not all de-

57. Otto Klima, Jr., and Gibson M. Wolfe, "The Oceans: Organizing for Action," *Harvard Business Review,* May–June 1968.

pendents have been as successful as the farm credit organizations in gaining the four freedoms: freedom from financial control by the Congress, freedom from independent audit by the comptroller general, freedom from budget review by the president, and freedom to use federal funds. But for many these freedoms remain the goals.

The struggle for power and position has contributed to fragmentation of the executive branch structure and the proliferation of categorical programs. By narrowing the constituency, agencies are made more susceptible to domination by their clientele groups and congressional committees.[58] Efforts to narrow the constituencies have been accompanied by demands for independent status or autonomy within the departmental structure.

Programs are packaged in such a way as to elicit congressional and clientele support. General programs have far less political appeal than specific programs. Support can be mobilized more readily for federal programs to combat heart disease, blindness, cancer, and mental illness than for such fields as microbiology or for general health programs. For this reason in 1955 the National Microbiological Institute was renamed the National Institute of Allergy and Infectious Diseases. As was explained at the time, the Institute had been handicapped in making its case to the Appropriations Committees because "no one ever died of microbiology."[59]

It would be a mistake to assume, however, that dependents always have the wisdom to know what is in their own best interests. The maritime unions have become so obsessed with the idea that an independent maritime agency would solve all of their problems that they have ignored the plain fact that any transportation agency outside the Department of Transportation would be in a very weak competitive position.

58. For a brilliant analysis of the significance of constituencies see Grant McConnell, *Private Power and American Democracy,* Alfred A. Knopf, 1967.
59. *The New York Times,* December 14, 1969.

We are faced with the strange paradox that the privilege of access to public funds is believed to carry with it the right to exercise public power, where the payment of large amounts in taxes does not. This thesis is expressed in such euphemisms as "decentralization," "grass-roots administration," and "freedom from politics." Thus Yale alumni were reassured that the university's independence has not been compromised by accepting federal money because "the men who fix the Government's policy in this respect are themselves university and college men. . . ."[60]

The issue of dependence vs. subservience is at the heart of our present dilemma. How can we reconcile a growing federal involvement in all aspects of our national life with the maintenance of deeply cherished pluralistic values? The typical answer is that offered by Alan Pifer, president of the Carnegie Corporation.[61] He proposed the creation of a federal center for higher education which would "depend heavily in all its activities on men and women co-opted from the colleges and universities *so that it is as much of higher education itself as it is of government*" (italics supplied).

Few would dispute that federal domination of science and education would be undesirable. Yet grave risks are run when public power is exercised by agricultural, scientific, and educational elites who are more concerned with advancing their own interests and the interests of the institutions they represent than the public interest. Serious distortions and inequities may occur in the allocation of funds among those eligible for assistance. Vested interests are created which are resistant to change and the reordering of priorities to meet new national needs.

As our one elected official, other than the vice president, with a national constituency, the president of the United States

60. *Report of the Treasurer of Yale University for the Fiscal Year Ended June 30, 1967*, p. 18.

61. Alan Pifer, Speech to the Association of American Colleges, January 16, 1968, reprinted in *Congressional Record,* May 1, 1968, p. E.3631.

stands almost alone as a counterweight to these powerful centrifugal forces. Sometimes the executive branch takes on the appearance of an arena in which the chiefs of major and petty bureaucratic fiefdoms, supported by their auxiliaries in the Congress and their mercenaries in the outside community, are arrayed against the president in deadly combat.

Herbert Emmerich, a highly perceptive student of federal organization, has said: "The Presidency is the focal point of any study of reorganization. . . . The Presidency focuses the general interest as contrasted with the centrifugal forces in the Congress and the departments for the specialized interests of subject matter and of region."[62]

It is significant that the lasting contributions of the first Hoover Commission, the President's Committee on Administrative Management, and the earlier Taft Commission on Economy and Efficiency are to be found in their recommendations to strengthen the office of the presidency, not in the long-forgotten proposals for reshuffling agencies and providing more efficient and economical administration. Institutional type and organization structure are important because they can help or hinder the president in performing his pivotal role within our constitutional system.

Reorganization also can be exploited by the president to alter the delicate balance within our constitutional system by eliminating or eroding the checks and balances resulting from the distribution of power within the executive branch as well as among the three branches of government. Watergate and its attendant "horrors" raise fundamental and disturbing questions about the centralization of power in the White House, the fractionalization of presidential power among assistants to the president, and the division of responsibilities between the White House Office and the statutory agencies within the Executive Office of the President, the executive departments, and

62. Herbert Emmerich, *Essays on Federal Reorganization*, University of Alabama Press, 1950, p. 7.

independent agencies. It is one thing to support and strengthen the president's capability to perform his pivotal role within the constitutional system. It is quite another to restructure the government so the president, in the words of Assistant to the President Bryce N. Harlow, "is running the whole government from the White House."[63]

63. Emmet J. Hughes, *The Living Presidency,* Coward, McCann & Geoghegan, Inc., 1973, p. 344.

2

Executive Branch Organization: View from the Congress

One could as well ignore the laws of aerodynamics in designing an aircraft as ignore the laws of congressional dynamics in designing executive branch structure. What may appear to be structural eccentricities and anomalies within the executive branch are often nothing but mirror images of jurisdictional conflicts within the Congress. Congressional organization and executive branch organization are interrelated and constitute two halves of a single system.

Executive branch structure and administrative arrangements are not matters of mere academic interest to members of Congress. Organization or reorganization of executive agencies may influence committee jurisdictions, increase or decrease the "accessibility" of executive branch officials to members of the Congress, and otherwise determine who shall exercise ultimate power in the decision-making processes.

To understand the organization of the executive branch, one must first understand the organization and culture of the Congress and the high degree of congressional involvement in administrative decisions.

It is highly misleading to speak of *the Congress,* as if it were a collective entity. According to James Rowe, Jr., "the Constitution and American political development make it apparent that there is really no such thing as 'the Congress.' It is not even an entity. There are instead 531 individuals, 96 Senators and 435 Representatives, who form among themselves temporary and shifting coalitions."[1] Conditions have not been altered materially since 1885 when Woodrow Wilson found "power is nowhere concentrated; it is rather deliberately and of set policy scattered amongst many small chiefs."[2] The structure, procedure, and culture of the Congress tend to obscure the general interest, encourage particularism, and create an environment in which organized interest groups and special pleaders can be assured a sympathetic response. There are highly articulate and effective spokesmen for the general interest within the Congress, but they are likely to be the exceptions.

Congressional power is divided among 18 major fiefdoms (standing committees) and some 120 petty fiefdoms (standing subcommittees) in the Senate; 22 major fiefdoms and over 140 petty fiefdoms in the House. The Legislative Reorganization Act of 1946 more than cut in half the number of standing committees, but this reduction has been offset by the proliferation of subcommittees. The number of Senate subcommittees has more than doubled in the past thirty years and comparable growth has occurred in the House. The shift from "committee" to "subcommittee" government is one of the most significant developments in the Congress.[3]

Subcommittees have become independent power centers and function with considerable autonomy. Under the subcommittee "bill of rights" adopted by the House Democratic

1. James Rowe, Jr., "Cooperation or Conflict? The President's Relationships with an Opposition Congress," *The Georgetown Law Journal,* Vol. 36, 1947.

2. Woodrow Wilson, *Congressional Government,* Meridian Books, 1956, p. 76.

3. See *Congressional Quarterly,* November 8, 1975, p. 2407. Walter Oleszek, *Congressional Procedures and Policy Process,* Congressional Quarterly Press, 1978, pp. 42, 60, 64.

caucus in 1973, committee chairmen were compelled to yield exclusive power to select subcommittee chairmen and to define subcommittee jurisdictions. This power is now exercised by all Democrats on a committee. Each subcommittee is guaranteed staff and an adequate budget. A chairman is required to refer most measures to subcommittees within two weeks.

Subcommittee reform has enabled more junior members of the Congress to assume posts of leadership and power. The impetus for reform came from what Congressman Thomas S. Foley called a "generational conflict."[4] But reform has been gained at the cost of further fractionalization of power and jurisdictions within the Congress.

Generalizations about congressional committees should be approached with caution. Each committee and subcommittee has its own culture, mode of operations, and set of relationships to executive agencies subject to its oversight, depending upon its constituency, its own peculiar tradition, the nature of its legislative jurisdiction, its administrative and legislative processes, and the role and attitude of its chairman. Richard F. Fenno, Jr.'s, analysis reveals significant differences among House committees with respect to member goals, environmental constraints, strategic premises, decision-making processes, and conclusions.[5] There are only two things committees have in common. First, power within a committee is earned by specialization. A new member is advised that "to make a great name for himself in the Congress a man must be a specialist."[6] Second, jurisdictional prerogatives are zealously guarded and raids by other fiefdoms are resisted with a jealous frenzy.

Growth of a congressional bureaucracy and institutionalization of committees and subcommittees have deepened the

4. *Congressional Quarterly, Ibid.,* p. 2409.
5. Richard F. Fenno, Jr., *Congressmen in Committees,* Little, Brown and Company, 1973.
6. Neil MacNeil, *Forge of Democracy—The House of Representatives,* David McKay Co., Inc., 1963, p. 130.

moats dividing the fiefdoms and accentuated the innate disposition of the Congress to concentrate on administrative details rather than basic issues of public policy. Professional staffing for all congressional committees became established only in 1946 with the passage of the Legislative Reorganization Act. Committee staff now exceed 3,000. Approximately 10,000 persons are employed on the personal staffs of senators and representatives.[7]

According to Samuel C. Patterson, "committee staff members tend to adopt the goal orientations dominant among the members of the committee for whom they work." He has found that there is minimal communication among the professional staffs of the different congressional committees, even when they have overlapping jurisdictions, and that staff appear "to be very much isolated from one another."[8]

Staff develop alliances with the executive branch bureaucracy and the bureaucracies representing interest groups. Most are highly capable, but some develop narrow interests in particular programs, are highly parochial in outlooks, and provide a rallying point for those fighting reorganizations that upset committee jurisdictions. Roger H. Davidson and Walter J. Oleszek acknowledge that the House Select Committee on Committees seriously underestimated the ability of staff to mobilize outside allies in protecting their domains.[9] Those who hope further expansion of the congressional bureaucracy will make it possible for the Congress to look at the big picture and regain legislative leadership are pursuing a will-o'-the-wisp.

Standing committees, like the major executive departments, tend to be composed of individuals who share much the same

7. Harrison W. Fox, Jr., and Susan Webb Hammond, *Congressional Staffs: The Invisible Force in American Lawmaking,* The Free Press, 1977, p. 3.

8. Samuel G. Patterson, "Staffing House Committees," in working papers, House Select Committee on Committees, June 1973.

9. Roger H. Davidson and Walter J. Oleszek, *Congress Against Itself,* Indiana University Press, 1977, p. 263.

background, interests, and values. Members seek assignments which will best advance their own interests and help win re-election. Organized groups outside the Congress may take a hand from time to time in the assignment process to see that the "right people" are designated.[10] Majority representation on the Agriculture committees goes to those from the wheat, cotton, tobacco, and peanut producing areas. In the 90th Congress only 8 of the 49 members of the Senate and House Agriculture committees came from cities of over 25,000. Many came from villages of less than 1,000 people. Eighteen of the members still resided in the town where they were born. At least half of the members were actively engaged in agriculture or related occupations, and the late Congressman Joseph Resnick asserted that a majority of the House committee members belonged to the American Farm Bureau Federation.[11] In contrast, 28 of the 33 members of the House Merchant Marine and Fisheries Committee came from port districts which have a major interest in ship construction and maritime subsidies. Membership on the House and Senate Interior committees was predominantly from the Western states where reclamation projects, grazing, timber, and mineral rights are issues of primary voter interest. Parochialism in the executive agencies reflects and is supported by parochialism in their oversight committees.

Reform proposals have focused mainly on distribution of power within the Congress, staffing, procedures, and processes. Efforts to reorganize the committee structure in the House failed. The Temporary Select Committee to study the Senate Committee System, chaired by Senator Adlai E. Stevenson III, was more successful than its House counterpart, since senators serve on several committees and have less to lose through committee restructuring than House members. Although the num-

10. Nicholas A. Masters, "House Committee Assignments," *American Political Science Review,* June 1961.

11. *Congressional Record,* July 12, 1967, p. H8531.

ber of Senate committees has been reduced, according to one informed observer, the realignment has left "jurisdictional lines pretty much untouched, concentrating instead on consolidating several obsolete committees." He concludes that "neither the House nor the Senate has succeeded in recasting its work groups in conformity with the altered shape of public problems."[12]

The Commission on Operation of the Senate found that "the legislative process as it presently operates appears to be organized primarily for incremental decision making rather than addressing major problems in a comprehensive manner."[13] In vital areas, such as energy, programs which have been reorganized or are effectively coordinated at the executive level remain fragmented in the Congress. Hoped for benefits are lost when comprehensive and well-integrated plans developed by the executive must be broken up and considered in separate pieces by the Congress. The Jackson Subcommittee was highly critical of the Congress for treating "as separable matters which are not really separable." It noted:

> Foreign affairs, defense matters, space policies, and atomic energy are handled in different committees. It is the same with money matters. Income and outgo, and the relation of each to the economy, come under different jurisdictions. There is no place in the Congress short of the floors of the Senate and House, where the requirements of national security and resources needed on their behalf, are considered in their totality."[14]

The Budget and Impoundment Control Act of 1974 did provide an institutional structure for coordinating congres-

12. Roger H. Davidson, "Our Changing Congress: The Inside (and Outside) Story," paper delivered at the Conference on Congress and the Presidency, Lyndon Baines Johnson Library, Austin, Texas, November 14–17, 1977.

13. Senate Document No. 94–278, December 1976, p. 42.

14. Senate Committee on Government Operations, Subcommittee on National Policy Machinery, "Organizing for National Security," Vol. 3, Staff Report and Recommendations, 1961, p. 7.

sional actions on budget and fiscal policy. But except for budget and fiscal policy, there remains no place short of the floor of the Congress where important programs which cut across established agency and committee jurisdictions can be considered in their totality. Diffusion of responsibility provides opportunities to divide and conquer by playing off one committee against another.

Committee jurisdictions are overlapping and cannot be neatly delineated. On March 22, 1973, Congressman Kenneth J. Gray introduced H.R. 6038, the National Energy Research and Development Policy Act, which was referred to the Interstate and Foreign Policy Committee. An identical bill introduced by Congressman Foley on April 4, 1973, was referred to the Interior Committee. The House Committee on Judiciary has jurisdiction over corrections. Yet jurisdiction as to employment of offenders in prison is lodged with the Education and Labor Committee; social security coverage of inmates with the Ways and Means Committee, and distribution of excess food commodities to prisons with the Agriculture Committee. Enactment of legislation to permit the Highway Trust Fund to be utilized for mass transit was impeded by fragmentation of committee jurisdiction for transportation.[15]

Inability to resolve competing jurisdictional claims among the House committees on Government Operations, Armed Services, Ways and Means, Education and Labor, Banking and Currency, and Judiciary led to the creation of a Commission on Government Procurement to evaluate the effectiveness of present statutes affecting government procurement. It was acknowledged that "a Commission on Government Procurement would be able to do what the congressional committees cannot readily do—examine in a concerted and comprehensive way many important procurement problems in their multiple

15. Statement of Congressman John C. Culver, *Congressional Record,* January 31, 1973, p. H591.

interrelationships and in terms of their impact on public policy and the national economy."[16]

Folklore has it that the camel is an animal conceived by an interagency committee. The camel is a perfectly fashioned animal compared with some spawned out of the maelstrom of conflicting committee jurisdictions. When jurisdictional problems could not be resolved, the Congress in 1966 created two agencies—the National Highway Safety Agency and the National Traffic Agency—to administer the highway safety program. The president was authorized to designate a single individual to head both agencies. All that was gained by creating two agencies—where only one was needed—was to give two Senate committees a voice in the confirmation of the agency head.

Organizational arrangements may be skewed to establish or maintain committee jurisdictions. A Senate bill authorizing the National Science Foundation to provide financial assistance to academic institutions for training, research, and advisory services to exploit marine resources was in normal course referred to the House Education and Labor Committee. To gain jurisdiction over the sea grant college program, the House Merchant Marine and Fisheries Committee introduced its own bill, which was subsequently enacted, to bring the program under the general policy guidance of the National Council on Marine Resources and Engineering Development. Thus, in one of its grant and contract programs assisting educational institutions, NSF policy-making responsibility was not centered in the National Science Board but was shared with an outside agency. The program was transferred from the National Science Foundation to the National Oceanic and Atmospheric Administration, Department of Commerce, in 1970.

In 1978 seabed mining legislation was held up by a dispute between the House Merchant Marine Committee and the Interior Committee. Each committee insisted that the program be administered by the executive agency subject to its over-

16. House of Representatives, 90th Congress, 1st Session, Report No. 890.

sight. The Merchant Marine Committee proposed that jurisdiction be vested in the Department of Commerce; the Interior Committee favored the Department of the Interior.[17]

Reorganization proposals repeatedly have foundered on the shoals of competing committee jurisdictions. Chairman Chet Holifield of the House Committee on Government Operations warned proponents of President Nixon's 1971 proposals to create Departments of Community Development, Natural Resources, Human Resources and Economic Affairs:

> If by this reorganization you affect in a major way the powers of the various committees in the Congress, you may as well forget it. The only way I know to get one or more of these departments through is to allow the committees that now have the programs within their jurisdiction to follow their programs, just as they are followed now, and authorize these programs wherever they are distributed.[18]

A bill to establish a Department of Community Development reported favorably by Holifield's committee in 1972, was blocked in the Rules Committee by the opposition of the chairmen of the Interior, Public Works, Banking and Currency, Education and Labor, Agriculture, and Appropriations committees.

Congresswoman Shirley Chisholm argued against President Carter's legislation to establish a Department of Education because creation of such a department might encourage renewed efforts to split the House Education and Labor Committee. "As members of Congress," Rep. Chisholm testified before the House Government Operations Committee, "we must also take note of the impact the reorganization of HEW and Federal education programs would probably have on the commit-

17. *Congressional Quarterly,* February 25, 1978, p. 525.
18. House Committee on Government Operations, Legislation and Military Operation Subcommittee, hearing on "Reorganization of Executive Departments," Part I, June–July 1971, p. 324.

tee structure in the House of Representatives. Although my distinguished colleague, Chairman Perkins from the Education and Labor Committee, has denied the likelihood of committee division, others may decide to spearhead a drive to divide this committee."[19]

Objections by appropriations subcommittees sometimes can be safely ignored, but presidents run grave risks when they threaten the jurisdiction of the major legislative committees. Legislative committee chairmen have what amounts to a veto. Interior Committee objections killed a plan to consolidate weather modification functions in the Environmental Science Services Administration, even though in this instance the three agencies administering weather modification programs—Interior, National Science Foundation, and Commerce—agreed that reorganization was desirable. Interior Committee disapproval also brought to a halt plans for consolidating general purpose cartographic activities in the Department of Commerce. The committee feared that transfer of the Topographic Mapping Division from Geological Survey to Commerce might result in the eventual transfer of the Geological Survey itself. The Agriculture Committees forestalled efforts to transfer responsibility from the Department of Agriculture to the Agency for International Development for foreign assistance programs involving surplus agricultural commodities. On the other hand, the Agriculture committees persuaded the Congress to enact legislation requiring that the president's budget classify expenditures for such programs "as expenditures for international affairs and finance rather than for agriculture and agricultural resources."[20]

Organizational arrangements for the conduct of federal water resource programs violate each of the organizational commandments handed down by Herbert Hoover. Almost

19. Hearings before a subcommittee of the House Committee on Governmental Operations, on H.R. 13343, to establish a Department of Education, July–August 1978, p. 380.
20. 7 U.S.C. 1703.

every objective observer has confirmed the Hoover Commission's findings that the existing sharing of water resource responsibilities among Interior, Agriculture, and the U.S. Army Corps of Engineers has resulted in poor planning, overlapping and duplication, working at cross purposes, and wasteful competition. Entrenched interests within the bureaucracy and outside community constitute major obstacles to needed reorganization. But these obstacles would not be insuperable, if the schism in the executive branch did not have its counterpart in the Congress.

Congressional organization and executive branch organization with respect to water resources are so closely interlinked that they cannot be considered separately. Control over project authorizations and funding are the essence of congressional power. Jurisdictional rivalries within the executive branch pale by comparison with those among congressional committees. The Senate Energy and Natural Resources Committee and the House Interior Committee exercise jurisdiction over the Bureau of Reclamation and the Senate Environment and Public Works Committee, the House Public Works and Transportation Committee over the Corps of Engineers, and the Agriculture Committees over the Soil Conservation Service.

The current organization of federal water resources functions results from a series of laws each of which was directed toward a single objective, such as improvement of rivers and harbors, flood control, irrigation, and watershed protection. Given the original limited missions, the logic of assigning rivers and harbors and flood control functions to the Corps of Engineers, reclamation to Interior, and watershed protection to Agriculture could not be reasonably disputed. West Point was our first engineering school and the Corps alone among federal agencies at the time possessed adequate engineering competence. The lands to be reclaimed were mostly arid Western lands under Interior's jurisdiction. Agriculture pioneered a watershed improvement program which extended to the major watersheds of the Mississippi and its tributary, the Missouri.

In contrast to the early laws directed toward a single objective, the Federal Power Act of 1920 expressed a multiple-purpose concept of river basin planning and development. Clientele groups and congressional committees who had come to identify their interests with those of the Corps, Interior, and Agriculture did not object to the new concept—provided that it was carried out on their terms and by "their" agency. Instead of awarding custody to a single agency or dividing the baby in three parts, the decision was to produce triplets. Initially the three factions, the secretaries of agriculture, interior, and war, constituted the Federal Power Commission.

Since 1920 the Corps, Interior, and Agriculture have obtained parallel and in some respects identical authorities for multiple-purpose development of water resources, although Interior's jurisdiction is limited to the Western states and Alaska and Agriculture's authority under the 1954 Act is limited in terms of the size of the structure for watershed improvement.

Except when all parties are agreed on the dominant project objective, the decision as to which agency will undertake a particular multiple-purpose project requires a time consuming, complex, and often bitter bargaining process. At some point the president must make a determination, but it is seldom final and can be upset by appeal to the Congress. Even the "peace treaties" negotiated by the Corps and Reclamation under which one assumed responsibility for construction and the other responsibility for operation and maintenance of certain projects have been negated by subsequent congressional actions.

The Kings River project in California is often cited as a classic illustration of the inherent weakness of federal resource management.[21] More significantly, this case history shows the

21. See Arthur Maass, *Muddy Waters—The Army Engineers and the Nation's Rivers,* Harvard University Press, 1951.

linkages between organization and legislative policy. The Bureau of Reclamation and the Corps of Engineers were in agreement on the design of the project. The differences resulted from the conflicting water use philosophies developed by the two agencies in keeping with their individual legislative mandates. Reclamation emphasized water conservation and maximum water use, and the Corps local flood protection. This was not solely a bureaucratic contest for power. Economy and efficiency were not the issues. The significant disagreements centered on the policy issues raised by the choice among administrative agencies. These included differences over repayments and distribution of benefits, restrictions on acreage and speculation, operation of irrigation facilities, power development, and method of congressional authorization. Such issues cannot be resolved by reorganization, and regardless of where the initial decision is made, the final arbiters will have to be the president and the Congress.

Former congressman and TVA director Frank Smith concluded:

> Ideally, the old concept of one single department of conservation and resource development, responsible for all Federal planning and action in the field, might still work if it could be achieved by waving a magic wand. It simply cannot be achieved, however, without a bloody, bone shattering fight, which would leave the landscape so scarred that the conservation cause would be lost in the critical years immediately ahead.[22]

The boldest congressional advocates of a Department of Natural Resources have been exceedingly timid in facing up to the problems of congressional organization. Senator Edward Kennedy reassured the Congress that the sponsors of a bill to establish a Department of Natural Resources had no intention of upsetting the status quo, and that because of the special ex-

22. Frank E. Smith, *The Politics of Conservation,* Pantheon Books, 1966, p. 306.

pertise acquired by the committees and their staffs, "legislative authority should remain where it is, relying upon effective administration of the programs to provide essential coordination."[23] With at least six congressional "bosses," the secretary of Natural Resources would be in an untenable position. The key to rationalizing executive branch structure lies in a reorganization of the Congress, not the reverse.

For many agencies, their natural allies are the legislative committees. As noted by one witness before the House Select Committee on Committees: "If you leave the same jurisdiction year after year, with the same bureaucrats appearing for 20 years, the same committee members for 20 years, and the same staff members, soon there isn't much to disagree about because everyone understands how they think their little piece of the world ought to be run."[24] Support is quickly forthcoming when they need help in blunting or negating presidential directives which they oppose or in chasing poachers from their domains. Within two hours after President Eisenhower privately advised the secretary of the Army of his intention of transferring supervision of the St. Lawrence Seaway to the secretary of commerce, Senator Charles E. Potter was denouncing the proposed action. A close affinity often exists between a committee chairman and the senior career staff of the departments and agencies under his jurisdiction. The chairmen and ranking committee members probably know more about the details of an agency's program and are better acquainted with the senior career staff than most agency heads who serve for relatively brief periods. New secretaries quickly find that some officials whom they want to reassign are "untouchables." Others whom they may want to keep must be replaced because they have been declared *persona non grata* by

23. Senate Committee on Government Operations, Subcommittee on Executive Reorganization, hearing on S. 886 to establish a Department of Natural Resources, October 17, 19, and 20, 1967, p. 36.

24. Randall Ripley, House Select Committee on Committees, Panel Discussions, Vol. 2 of 3, Part I of 3, June 1973, p. 52.

the chairman of the legislative committee or appropriations subcommittee. Even so revered a figure as Wilbur K. Carr, who served for forty-seven years in the State Department, much of the time as its principal executive officer, was packed off as Minister to Czechoslovakia when a new appropriations subcommittee chairman refused to do business with him.[25] Probably more executive branch officials have been fired or reassigned as a result of pressure from the Congress than by the president.

An executive agency's ability to withstand legislative committee pressures, assuming that it desires to do so, depends upon many factors. Most vulnerable are the agencies which are required to do one or a combination of the following: renew their legislative charters at specific time intervals; obtain authorizing legislation before appropriations can be made; obtain congressional directives to undertake surveys and legislative authorization for individual projects; keep committees "fully and currently informed" of pending action and supply copies of all correspondence; "come into agreement" with committees or committee chairman before disposing of real property, entering into leases or sales agreements, issuing rules or regulations, or comparable executive actions. Single-headed agencies are more resistant to pressure than are boards and commissions, and Cabinet departments have greater immunity than do independent agencies.

The annual authorizing bill has been seized upon by the legislative committees as a means for obtaining leverage over executive agencies and counteracting Appropriations Committee influence over administration. Until 1948 the practice was limited to the civil works program of the Army Corps of Engineers. In 1948 it was applied to the foreign aid program, and by 1974 it had been extended to cover over $48 billion of the administrative budget. The largest programs requiring both

25. Incident recounted in Katherine Crane, *Mr. Carr of State—Forty-seven Years in the Department of State,* St. Martin's Press, 1960, pp. 328–29.

basic authorizing legislation and appropriations annually are foreign aid, defense construction and procurement, atomic energy, space, and the National Science Foundation. In 1972, for the first time in the history of the republic, an entire executive department, the Department of State, was required to obtain an annual authorization for its programs.

The Congress would do well to subject the system of annual authorizations to a rigorous cost-benefit analysis. The costs are high and can be measured in public confusion and dissatisfaction (the average citizen does not recognize the subtle distinction between an authorization and an appropriation), program uncertainties and delays, late appropriations, and diversion of committees and executive branch officials from perhaps more productive endeavors. Long-range planning is not possible with one-year authorizations. Where the process degenerates into a form of "gamesmanship" between the legislative and appropriations committees it is not calculated to enhance the public image of Congress. The requirement ought to be employed selectively and only for those programs where the need for annual review and legislative authorization can be clearly demonstrated.

The last twenty years have been marked also by a rapid proliferation in the number of laws requiring executive agencies to "come into agreement" with committees before taking action, or subjecting specified executive actions to legislative veto by either or both houses of the Congress. Congressman Eliott H. Levitas was nearly successful in having a bill enacted in 1976 which would allow the Congress to veto almost any regulation issued by an executive department or regulatory agency.[26] Congress in response to Watergate has come to rely increasingly on the veto as a means for constraining the president and controlling the "unelected bureaucracy." In the period 1973–1977, 107 laws were enacted containing legislative and committee veto provisions, as contrasted with 140 such

26. *Congressional Quarterly*, July 24, 1978, p. 1623.

provisions in the previous forty years. Not only are proposed presidential actions subject to veto, but also through this device the Congress is able to bypass the president and directly control subordinate executive branch officers. The Congress, for example, retained the right to disapprove the schedule of expected family contributions to be made for higher education support recommended by the Commissioner of Education.

Presidents have consistently denounced these provisions as unconstitutional encroachments on executive authority, and many have been vetoed.[27] President Johnson in 1965 advised his Cabinet that any such provisions in the future would be vetoed. In signing the Flood Control Act of 1965 he stated:

> So just as I would not want to infringe on the power of the Senate or lessen the jurisdiction of the House or disregard the decisions of the Supreme Court, I do not want the Legislature—through two committees—to encroach upon the responsibilities of the President.

While welcoming strengthened congressional oversight of executive branch decisions, President Carter warned that the legislative veto was calculated to "do more harm than good." He argued that the veto "treats symptoms, not causes" and that "the vast effort to second-guess individual regulatory decisions could impede the crucial task of revising the underlying statutes." The multiplication of veto provisions was seen by President Carter as a threat to "the constitutional balance of responsibilities between the branches of government" and a major obstacle in the way of efforts "to make the administrative process quicker and simpler."[28]

27. For a discussion on legislative encroachment see Joseph P. Harris, *Congressional Control of Administration,* The Brookings Institution, 1964; John R. Bolton, *The Legislative Veto: Unseparating the Powers,* American Enterprise Institute for Public Policy Research, 1977; Harold Bruff and Ernest Gellhorn, "Congressional Control of Administrative Regulation: A Study of Legislative Vetoes," *Harvard Law Review,* Vol. 90, 1977.

28. *Congressional Quarterly,* July 24, 1978, *op. cit.*

The constitutional objections to provisions that blur the separation of executive-legislative functions, bypass the president's veto, and authorize action by a single house of the Congress are serious and will ultimately be resolved by the courts. But the provisions may be criticized on more pragmatic grounds. While ostensibly designed to control the bureaucracy, the provisions often enhance the power of the congressional and executive bureaucracies. Differences between the Congress and an executive agency are negotiated by the respective bureaucracies. Members of Congress have more important responsibilities and do not have the time to participate in the review. On the other hand, Bruff and Gellhorn's case studies reveal that the negotiations "imposed a greater burden on the Congressional staff than much legislation."[29] It is questionable whether it serves the long-run interests of the Congress to divert its members limited time and staff resources to routine reviews. Furthermore, as a direct or indirect participant in executive decisions, the Congress is in no position to exercise independent oversight.

As soul brothers, the executive agencies and legislative committees make common cause against the "third house of the Congress"—the Appropriations Committees. The National Institutes of Health and the Federal Bureau of Investigation are among the few who have had strong allies on the Appropriations Committees—an alliance that from time to time has resulted in more generous funding than requested in the president's budget. Lords of the executive establishment generally enjoy the cozy atmosphere of legislative committee hearings where they are received with courtesy and the deference due their office. They shun, wherever possible, meetings with appropriations subcommittees whose chairman upon occasion may accord them about the same amount of deference as shown by a hard-boiled district attorney to a prisoner in the dock. Congressman Albert Thomas deflated Budget Director

29. Harold Bruff and Ernest Gellhorn, *op. cit.*

Maurice Stans, a distinguished accountant, by referring to him as "a bookkeeper."[30] Before the House Appropriations Committee obtained new quarters, it was not uncommon for high officials to stand hat-in-hand for up to an hour in the corridors of the Capitol basement waiting to be summoned by their appropriations subcommittee.

Actions by the Appropriations Committees may override presidential directives or nullify laws enacted by the Congress itself.[31] The appropriations "rider" is frequently employed for these purposes. A rider prohibited the Department of Housing and Urban Development from using any of its funds to carry out Section 204 of the Model Cities Act of 1966. This section provided that applications for federal loans and grants for various public works projects be reviewed by area-wide agencies designated to perform metropolitan or regional planning. The rider canceled the delegations made to HUD and compelled the Bureau of the Budget to undertake a function which it was not well equipped to perform. Riders, at least theoretically, are subject to review by the Congress as whole and sometimes can be eliminated on a "point of order" as legislation in an appropriation act. There is no effective way, however, for the Congress to review or amend the directives contained in Appropriations Committee reports which may tell an agency what to do, when to do it, where to do it, and how to do it. Reports do not have the force and effect of law, but agencies ignore such directives at their peril. A committee report was used to rescind one of the most important sections of the District of Columbia Reorganization Plan only a few months after the Congress had allowed the plan to go into effect. The plan conferred upon the D. C. commissioner authority to reorganize the district government and to establish so many agencies and offices, with such names or titles as he

30. House Committee on Appropriations, Hearings on the Budget for 1960, January 20, 1959, p. 57.

31. Michael W. Kirst, *Government without Passing Laws,* The University of North Carolina Press, 1969.

shall from time to time determine. The committee directed that the commissioner obtain its "prior approval" before exercising his statutory authority, thus restoring an unsatisfactory arrangement which the plan was intended to eliminate. Modernization of the D. C. government had been estopped for fifteen years by the requirement that the Congress approve each transfer, no matter how minor. Senator Mike Mansfield attempted to soften the committee report by having Senator Robert C. Byrd (West Virginia) agree on the Senate floor that he wanted merely to be informed of "major changes in organization or financing plans." Senator Byrd would have none of it and stated:

> . . . I want to emphasize that I for one do not want to bind the Appropriations Committee by a colloquy which leaves only so-called major changes subject to congressional approval when there can be wide variations of interpretations as to what constitutes major changes. I do not mean to be exasive, nor do I want to appear to be unyielding or difficult. I want the Appropriations Committee to be informed of all such transactions, as they have been in the past. And, as far as I am concerned, that is what the language means.[32]

Committee jurisdictions are the most important single factor influencing program assignments among executive agencies. Congressional dynamics can be of equal significance in molding and shaping the choice of administrative instruments, advisory arrangements, delegations, and field structure.

Institutional types are judged by their relative accessibility to members of Congress, not by juridical concepts or abstract principles of organization. For members of Congress the executive branch is divided among the "president's men"—White House staff, heads of executive office units, and Cabinet secretaries—and "agencies of the Congress"—independent boards and commissions and the Army Corps of Engineers.

32. *Congressional Record,* November 8, 1967, p. S16080.

Administrators of independent agencies, such as the General Services Administration and Small Business Administration, sit uncomfortably in a no-man's land between the "president's men" and "agencies of the Congress" and are considered fair game for both sides. These distinctions are not based on law, except possibly for the independent regulatory commissions where the Supreme Court has limited the president's power, but from "understandings" tacitly accepted by the president and the Congress.

Least accessible to the Congress are members of the White House staff. As a matter of long-standing practice, White House staff do not testify before congressional committees. To his later regret, President Kennedy departed from this custom in allowing James Landis in 1961 to present a series of reorganization plans related to the regulatory commissions. When four of the seven plans were disapproved, it was construed as a personal rebuff to the president. Sherman Adams did testify, but in a personal capacity to explain charges that had been made against him, as did Wallace H. Graham, Harry Vaughan, Donald Dawson, and Peter Flanigan.

Congress was particularly frustrated by its inability to obtain information and testimony from the president's special assistant for science and technology. Senator John McClellan complained: "Unless legislative action is taken by the Congress to establish some medium through which reliable information and supporting technical data is made available to Congress by officials who are responsive to its needs, the committees of the Congress will continue to be denied information necessary to the legislative process in establishing policies in the fields of science and technology."[33] The reorganization creating the Office of Science and Technology in 1962 was in part the President's response to congressional demands for better access to his principal science adviser.

33. Senate Committee on Government Operations, Repot No. 1828 on S. 2771 to establish a Commission on Science and Technology, 87th Congress, 2nd Session, p. 9.

Presidents ask for trouble when they co-opt a congressional agent as a White House aide. The Congress regards such "two-hatted" arrangements as a violation of the rules of the game. Atomic Energy Commission Chairman Lewis Strauss invoked his position as a special adviser to the president on atomic energy affairs in flatly refusing to answer questions asked by the Joint Committee.[34] Lingering resentment from this incident was one of the factors that led the Senate to reject Strauss's nomination as secretary of commerce.

President Nixon's designation of the secretary of the treasury and the director of the Office of Management and Budget as assistants to the president, and the secretaries of HEW, HUD, and agriculture as presidential counsellors, was seen by some members of the Congress as a device for limiting congressional access to these officials. The director of the OMB, the heads of other executive office units, and the Cabinet secretaries spend much of their time meeting with members of Congress and testifying before committees. But Congress recognizes that it is subject to certain restraints when dealing with these officials. These restraints were noted by Senator J. William Fulbright in opposing the 1950 reorganization plan to transfer the Reconstruction Finance Corporation to the Department of Commerce:

> Under the accepted principles of our government, the Secretary of Commerce is a member of the Executive family. He looks primarily to the President for his policy and his influence. We all know he is removable at the discretion of the President. It is customary also, whenever a Cabinet nomination comes up here, whether we like him or not, it is generally understood that we confirm him, in contrast to some of the other agencies, the Federal Reserve or one of the others which we look upon more as a congressional agency. I think the Cabinet is in a little different

34. Morgan Thomas and Robert M. Northrop, *Atomic Energy and Congress,* University of Michigan Press, 1956, p. 174.

> position in relationship with the Congress than the heads of these independent agencies.[35]

Senator Fulbright acknowledged: "We rarely, if ever, call up the Secretaries of any of the major departments and question them and examine them like we do the heads of agencies."[36] He contended that the reorganization would tend to insulate the RFC from the committee's supervision and place "between us and the RFC a member of the President's Cabinet who is given supervision and policy guidance over that Board. I think the tendency would be to look upon it as not our responsibility anymore.[37] Senator Fulbright's views were confirmed by the committee in its report recommending disapproval of the reorganization plan. The report observed:

> This proprietary attitude of the Congress toward the Reconstruction Finance Corporation was emphasized time after time during the course of the hearings, invariably coupled with the fear that, were the corporation to be placed within the framework of an executive department, the affinity between the corporation and the Congress would increasingly become a thing of the past.[38]

The Congress does not concede, however, that a secretary's right to reign over a department necessarily carries with it the power to rule. Herbert Hoover discovered as secretary of commerce that the Congress "while giving us generous support for our new activities . . . refused to add to my personal staff."[39] Secretary Hoover employed two secretaries and three assistants at his own expense. The Congress continues to be grudging in granting to department heads the resources which they believe

35. Senate Committee on Expenditures in Executive Departments, hearing on Reorganization Plan No. 24 of 1950, June 14 and 15, 1950, p. 8.
36. *Ibid.*, p. 39.
37. *Ibid.*, p. 15.
38. Senate Committee on Expenditures in Executive Departments, Senate Report No. 1868, 81st Congress, 2nd Session, June 26, 1950, p. 10.
39. Herbert C. Hoover, *The Memoirs of Herbert C. Hoover, The Cabinet and the Presidency, 1920–1933,* The Macmillan Co., 1952, p. 43.

are required to coordinate and manage effectively the programs for which they are responsible. Some committees are more generous than others, but normally the first budget item to be cut is funds for the office of the secretary. Funds requested by the Department of Justice and other agencies to install the new Planning-Programming-Budgeting system, as directed by President Johnson, were specifically denied.

Limitations on congressional access to Cabinet members do not extend to their principal bureau chiefs. At one time, many bureau chiefs, for all practical purposes, were immune to secretarial authority. These chiefs were appointed by the president subject to Senate confirmation, often for fixed terms of office, and statutory powers were vested in them, not the secretary. The first Hoover Commission found that "statutory powers often have been vested in subordinate officers in such a way as to deny authority to the President or a department head."[40] Since 1949, the number of autonomous bureaus has been substantially reduced by a series of reorganization plans, but not wholly eliminated. The plans transferred the statutory functions of all subordinates to the department head. Quasi-autonomous status has been retained by such agencies as the Office of Education in the Department of Health, Education, and Welfare and the Comptroller of the Currency in the Treasury Department.

Even the Executive Office of the President has not been wholly immune from infiltration by the Congress. What some in Congress have termed a "congressional agency," the Office of Federal Procurement Policy was established within the Office of Management and Budget in 1974. The OFPP administrator is appointed by the president, by and with the advice and consent of the Senate, and the office's functions are vested in him, not the OMB Director. The administrator is

40. Commission on Organization of the Executive Branch of the Government, "General Management of the Executive Branch," a report to the Congress, February 1949, p. 4.

required to keep the Congress and its committees "fully and currently informed" and to transmit at least 30 days prior to the effective date proposed policies and regulations to the Government Operations Committees of the House and Senate. The bill's Senate sponsor, Senator Lawton Chiles, emphasized that the law made the administrator independently responsible for carrying out the office's duties and keeping the Congress informed.[41]

Nonorganizational devices are employed also to promote responsiveness to congressional direction. The Tenure of Office Act of 1867 provided that certain civil officers, appointed by and with the advice of the Senate, should hold office during the term of the president who appointed them and one month thereafter. This act was declared unconstitutional, but this did not prevent the Congress from providing that members of the Tennessee Valley Authority Board could "be removed from office at any time by a concurrent resolution of the Senate and House of Representatives."

Executive power can be offset by specifying terms of office coterminous with or exceeding that of the appointing official. Such was the congressional intent when in 1967 it changed the tenure of members of the Joint Chiefs of Staff, except the chairman, from two to four years.

The established chain of command can be circumvented by establishing a direct channel of communications between an executive agency or a subordinate bureau within an agency and the Congress. The Inspector General Act of 1978 requires the appointment by the president of inspectors general to conduct and supervise audits and investigations relating to programs and operations of the Departments of Agriculture, Commerce, Housing and Urban Development, Interior, Labor, and Transportation and the Community Services Administration, the Environmental Protection Agency, the Gen-

41. Judith H. Parris, "The Office of Management and Budget: Background Responsibilities, Recent Issues," Congressional Research Service, July 27, 1978.

eral Services Administration, the National Aeronautics and Space Administration, the Small Business Administration, and the Veterans Administration. It is the duty of each inspector general to keep the head of the agency within which his office is established and the Congress fully and currently informed concerning fraud and the serious problems, abuses, and deficiencies detected by him.

The Defense Reorganization Act of 1958 included a provision which President Eisenhower termed "legalized insubordination." The secretary of each service or any member of the Joint Chiefs of Staff was authorized to present to Congress, on his own initiative but after notifying the secretary of defense, "any recommendations relating to the Department of Defense that he may deem proper."[42] The administrator of the State Department's Bureau of Security and Consular Affairs is directed by law to "maintain close liaison with the appropriate committees of Congress in order that they may be advised regarding the administration of this chapter by consular offices." At the time of enactment, the words "appropriate committees of Congress" were read to mean Senator Joseph McCarthy. Congress instructed the commissioner of education in 1968 to make whatever changes might be necessary in his office of legislation to assure that it "can and will carry out the functions which are inherently associated with an agency's relationship with Congress."[43]

Statutory interdepartmental committees are condemned by James Rowe, Jr., as another device "striking directly at the jugular of Presidential responsibility."[44] These and statutory advisory committees can be used to limit presidential and secretarial discretion by controlling their sources of advice. Rowe correctly concludes that once an interdepartmental committee or advisory body "is given a statutory floor with defined powers

42. Harris, *op. cit.*, p. 27.
44. Rowe, *op. cit.*
43. *Congressional Record*, July 15, 1968, p. S8697.

and a separate staff, it too begins to look toward its creator, the Congress, for sustenance." Our foreign assistance programs have been profoundly influenced by the lead role given to the secretary of the treasury as chairman of the National Advisory Council on International Monetary and Financial Problems. Congress intended, and with some success, to assure that a tough-minded money man had the decisive voice in passing on foreign loans and in coordinating international monetary transactions, although the authority to make loans was lodged elsewhere. Reorganization Plan No. 4 of 1965 abolished nine statutory committees, including the NAC, but the president re-established the NAC by executive order with somewhat more limited powers. In the same year the Congress created the Water Resources Council by law. The Housing and Urban Development Act of 1968 created no less than three statutory advisory bodies—the National Advisory Commission on Low Income Housing, the Advisory Board on National Insurance Development Program, and the Flood Insurance Advisory Committee. This act also contains several provisions requiring the secretary of HUD to consult with such officials as the secretary of labor, secretary of agriculture, secretary of commerce, and the small business administrator before taking action.

Multi-headed agencies are classified indiscriminately by the Congress as "agencies of the Congress" without regard to nice distinctions between executive functions and quasi-judicial and quasi-legislative functions. Boards and commissions are unloved by everyone but the Congress. Plural executives may be inefficient administrators, but the Congress is more concerned with responsiveness than efficiency. Congress has gone along somewhat reluctantly with strong chairman plans for most commissions. It was once feared that a chairman designated by the president and with control over a commission's budget and personnel might open the door to presidential influence.

Reorganizations to replace boards and commissions with single administrators are opposed out of fear of disturbing the delicate balance of power between the executive and the Congress. It is too easy for a single administrator to become a "president's man." President Eisenhower was able to put through a reorganization plan in 1953 abolishing the board of directors of the Export-Import Bank, but the Congress in 1954 re-established the board. In objecting to the substitution of one commissioner for the three-member board of commissioners of the District of Columbia, Chairman John McMillan of the House District Committee did not argue about public administration theory. He put it bluntly:

> There are not many members of Congress here of the old school whom I have not helped somewhere along the line since I have been serving as chairman of the committee. I imagine that from now on if this plan is adopted, members of Congress will be required to get District of Columbia automobile tags, as you will no longer have the kind of reciprocity that you have now as a member of Congress from every state in the Union.[45]

Despite growing criticism, the commission form of government in the District of Columbia had endured unchanged from 1874 to 1967. The situation had deteriorated by then to a point where reform could no longer be postponed. Chairman McMillan's objections did not prevail.

Almost every member of Congress feels obliged at times to rise above principle. The urge is overwhelming when the issues involve the location or relocation of federal field offices or delegations of decision-making authority to the field.

Wrangling over proposed locations of Customs regional headquarters came close to defeating Reorganization Plan No. 1 of 1965 abolishing the offices of collector of customs, comptroller of customs, surveyor of customs, and appraisers of merchandise.[46] The plan itself did not specify regional head-

45. *Congressional Record,* August 9, 1967, p. H10190.

46. Dominic Del Guidice, "Reorganization of the Bureau of Customs: A Struggle for Status," in *Reorganization by Presidential Plan: Three Case Studies,* National Academy of Public Administration, 1971.

quarters locations, but an independent study by a group of management experts had recommended Boston, New York, Miami, New Orleans, San Francisco, and Chicago. To salvage the plan, Treasury bowed to congressional pressures and added regional offices in Baltimore, Houston, and Los Angeles—districts represented by influential members of the Committee on Government Operations and Appropriations Committee. The Government Operations Committee has jurisdiction over reorganization plans.

Decentralization makes an excellent theme for campaign speeches, but those who take campaign promises seriously run the risk of incurring congressional displeasure. Governors and mayors are competitors of senators and representatives. Once decisions are made outside of the nation's capital, local officials can deal directly with federal field staff and members of Congress are excluded from a key role in the decision-making processes. Constituents do not have to come to their Senator or Representative for assistance. What is worse, a local official may announce a federal project or grant before the member of Congress can issue a press release.

Franklin Roosevelt became painfully aware of senatorial jealousy of governors when he bypassed the Senate delegations and dealt directly with his former colleagues in the Governors' Conference. He told Frances Perkins: "Every governor, particularly in states where the governor's salary is about $3,000, looks forward to being a United States Senator. No United States Senator, even if he belongs to the same party, likes to be ousted by the superior prestige and patronage which the expenditure of federal money may get for the governor. Well, *that* is something to remember."[47]

The House Committee on Appropriations in 1967 warned "against overemphasis on regionalization." In the committee's view: "Many people fear that the regional offices will, to a great extent, become one more administrative layer that im-

47. Frances Perkins, *The Roosevelt I Knew,* The Viking Press, 1946, p. 172.

portant matters must clear, since there will always be the right of appeal to headquarters, and with regard to many decisions, headquarters will have to give final approval in the absence of an appeal. The committee feels that there is valid reason for this apprehension."[48] The committee denied requested increases to finance strengthening of HEW field staffs and decentralization of the office of education. In barring further regionalization the committee was reflecting not only the traditional congressional bias but also lobbying by state education agencies which preferred to deal directly with Washington rather than with their own state houses.

If we persist in treating separately those things which are inseparable, we will seek in vain those improvements in government structure which must be accomplished to maintain the effective functioning of our democratic system. More studies of executive branch organization, in isolation from the Congress, are bound to be exercises in futility. For this reason, a Citizens Committee for the Study of the U.S. Government, sponsored by the National Academy of Public Administration, urged that a bipartisan commission be established to examine the "*roles and relationships of the three branches in the making and execution of national policies.*"[49] The committee stressed that each element of the governmental system is interdependent with, and in some degree dependent upon, other elements.

In proposing reorganization of the congressional committee structure the Senate and House Select Committees on Committees largely ignored interrelationships with executive organization. Roger H. Davidson and Walter Oleszek, who served on the staff of the House Select Committee, report that the

48. House Committee on Appropriations, Departments of Labor and Health, Education, and Welfare Appropriations Bill, 1968. Report No. 271, 90th Congress, 1st Session, p. 4.

49. Italics supplied. "A Bicentennial Commission on American Government," a proposal by an Ad Hoc Citizens' Committee for the Study of U.S. Government, August 26, 1975.

committee "though not adverse to promoting better legislative-executive relationships, never gave the matter high priority."[50] The members of the House Committee deliberately rejected the concept of developing a structure parallel to that of the executive branch. Committee structure was viewed by both committees as something almost exclusively concerned with distribution of power within the Congress.

Admittedly, reform of congressional organization presents a unique complex of difficult issues which are not raised by executive reorganization. Every member of the Congress constitutes an independent sovereign entity subject to no authority other than the Congress as a whole or the voters in his or her constituency. Congressional structure must be capable of reconciling the needs of members and the needs of the Congress as an institution.

Existing arrangements result from compromises and historical accidents, not from conscious organizational philosophy or planning to achieve identified purposes. Committee jurisdictions reflect a series of pragmatic decisions designed mainly to provide an acceptable division of the workload and to secure committee assignments which enhance an individual member's ability to represent and serve his constituency. Inadequate attention has been given to the implications of these decisions for government policies, program-administration, and relationships with the executive branch.

In determining committee jurisdictions, the Congress should be aware that the kind of constituency that is being created can significantly influence policy outcomes and encourage or discourage alliances with executive agencies and interest groups. Constituencies can be established in such a way that a committee will be uninterested in or actually hostile to certain program objectives. If, for example, members seek assignments on the House Education and Labor Committee principally because of their interest in labor legislation, then, education is

50. Davidson and Oleszek, *op. cit.*, p. 9.

certain to be a matter of secondary concern. Care must be taken to assure that committees have reasonably consistent sets of program responsibilities, and that no single function is so dominant that it will determine committee membership and outlook.

Committee assignments should be viewed as something more than a means for distributing power within the Congress. If the government is to function effectively, congressional organization also must be compatible with that of the executive branch. Speaker Carl Albert was of the view that "up to a point" legislative committee jurisdictions should reflect the organization within the executive branch.[51] This does not imply that executive and legislative organization structures must be identical. A legislative body has different requirements from the executive.

Obviously any committee structure which fails to serve the needs of individual members and their constituents will be unacceptable. But compensating features should be built into the present system to balance the strong centrifugal forces representing the particular interests of professional and economic groups and regions. Such urgent problems as energy, rural poverty, and urban transportation should not be permitted to fall within the cracks of the present committee and subcommittee structure. If the Congress is to be something more than a representative and advocate of the diverse interests in our society, it must be capable of examining problems from a national perspective and reviewing and appraising the results of executive operations.

Sooner or later the Congress will be compelled to grasp the nettle. The existing *status quo* breeds frustration in the Congress, ineffectiveness in the executive branch, and rising dissatisfaction among the citizenry.

51. House Select Committee on Committees, Vol. 1 of 3, Part 1 of 2, May 1973 p. 15.

3

Executive Branch Organization: View from the White House

Andrew Jackson saw it as the president's "especial duty to protect the liberties and rights of the people and the integrity of the Constitution against the Senate, or the House of Representatives, or both together."[1] As the elected representative of *all* the American people, the president alone has the power and the responsibility to balance the national interest against the strong centrifugal forces in the Congress for the special interests of subject matter or region. His effectiveness in performing this pivotal role within our constitutional system depends in no small measure on his instinctive grasp of the political and strategic uses of organization type and structure.

Such insight is not likely to be gained within the halls of the Congress or in the military service. Perspectives, attitudes, and behavior patterns developed on Capitol Hill or in the Pentagon become a way of life. They are the key to understanding the style, values, and administrative habits of Presidents Truman, Eisenhower, Kennedy, Johnson, and Ford.

Five of our last seven presidents earned their public repu-

1. Quoted in Clinton Rossiter, *The American Presidency,* The New American Library, Inc., 1956, p. 92.

tations in the Congress. Whatever its other virtues as a breeding ground for presidents, the Congress is a poor school for executives and managers. The emphasis in a legislative body is on individuals, not institutions or organizations. Legislators do not think in institutional terms, except when some immediate constituency interest is threatened. The skills needed are those of the tactician, not the long-range strategist. Congress cannot respond to problems, other than by speeches, press releases, investigations, and, ultimately, by enacting laws and appropriating money.

Some senators are critical of what John Gardner calls "the vending-machine concept of social change. Put a coin in the machine and out comes a piece of candy. If there is a social problem, pass a law and out comes a solution."[2] Senator Abraham Ribicoff has acknowledged that "because we rely so heavily on the programmatic approach—passing a program whenever we discover a problem or a part of the problem—and rely so little on a systematic approach that would treat our major problems in a comprehensive manner—our efforts often are marked by confusion, frustration, and delay."[3] But the critics are unable to offer clear alternatives. The diffusion of power within the Congress and the inherent constraints of the legislative process do not foster concentration on long-range goals and allow anything other than a piecemeal approach to problem solving.

Within the Congress words are sometimes equated with deeds. Votes represent final acts. There is concern with administration, but it is focused principally on those elements which directly affect constituency interests or committee jurisdictions. Legislative proposals seldom are debated from the viewpoint of their administrative feasibility. Grubby details of planning, organizing, staffing, and developing the administra-

2. John W. Gardner, *No Easy Victories*, Harper & Row, 1968, p. 28.

3. Senate Committee on Government Operations, Subcommittee on Executive Reorganization, hearings on "Modernizing the Federal Government," January–May 1968, p. 2.

tive system to translate laws into working programs are for someone else to worry about. It is assumed that the executive branch, or in the case of grants-in-aid, state and local governments, have or can obtain the necessary competence to devise and install efficient delivery systems. If things go wrong, failure always can be attributed to the incompetence or stupidity of the administrators.

Congress is weak on follow-through, even though it has been devoting increasing attention to legislative oversight. Laws on the statute books are not news, except when investigations disclose scandals or serious abuses in their administration. The political pay-offs from measures to improve administrative efficiency or to promote administrative reform are minimal. To capture the headlines, studies must be launched into problems of the moment and new legislative proposals thrown into the hopper. An ambitious senator with an eye on the White House has an insatiable appetite for "ideas" which will keep him on the front pages and contribute to his national image.

For a president, long service in the Senate or House carries with it special disabilities. President Johnson saw the outside world through the eyes of the Congress, particularly the Senate. Congressional reaction on major issues was for him the most accurate and reliable expression of the national will. As a result, his sensitivity to evolving trends in public opinion and national concerns was markedly reduced.

The Johnson "system," which functioned admirably in the Senate, had fundamental weaknesses when installed in the White House. The essence of the Johnson system was a network of loyal henchmen who could be counted on to furnish timely information and help when needed, bilateral negotiations, and meticulous head counts before action. You moved when you had the votes, not before. Effective operation of the system placed a premium on secrecy. Premature disclosure of the majority leader's position would impair seriously his ability to harmonize the contending forces and arrive at a consensus.

Presidential leadership demands something more than the talents of an expert congressional power broker. People want to know where the president stands and what he stands for. Secrecy cuts off the communication flow within the executive branch and blurs the president's public image. Presidential greatness is not measured by his legislative batting average or his standing in the public opinion polls. A true gauge is his capacity for leadership—his ability to anticipate and articulate the nation's needs, hopes, fears, and aspirations. In the words of the first president: "For the more combined and distant things are seen, the more likely they are to be turned to advantage."[4]

Introduction of the congressional style and culture into the White House is in part an inevitable by-product of growing dependence by the Congress on the president for leadership and initiative in developing major legislative proposals and in setting the legislative timetable. This trend was visible before President Johnson, but, because he did nothing on a small scale, it became magnified and was brought more sharply into focus during his administration. President Johnson instructed his 1964 task forces that he wanted to be an activist president, "not a caretaker of past gains." So far as his domestic program was concerned, he conceived of activism primarily in terms of bold, innovative legislative proposals.

Activist presidents necessarily will continue to think in these terms, even those who have not graduated from the Congress. Major White House emphasis will and should be given to development of the legislative program. Indeed the Congress will insist upon it. Difficulties occur when the approach is not systematic and selective, and the enactment of administration bills in wholesale lots becomes the overriding objective.

Unlike a legislator, a president should view the passage of a law as a beginning, not an end. His responsibility does not

4. Quoted in Douglass Cater, *Power in Washington,* Vintage Books, 1964, p. 253.

cease when he has decided *what* to do. The less politically rewarding and often more complex task of determining *how* to do it must be undertaken by the executive, if programs are to produce results. Training in the Congress does not equip a president to deal with the *how* to, and he is predisposed to downgrade its importance. The tendency has been, as noted by Louis Brownlow, "to elevate the political consideration, the *what* to do, above the administrative consideration of how to do it," and "even on the rare occasions when administrative questions do rise to a level where they are subject to general and popular discussion, very frequently that discussion will go off at a tangent whose direction is determined by some political, even some partisan or pressure group, interest."[5]

Brownlow made this observation some thirty years ago. In the interim, the strengthening of the staff resources available to the president has not noticeably enhanced White House appreciation or understanding of administrative management. If anything, the growing preoccupation with the legislative program and legislative and political tactics reinforce the disposition to dismiss administrative and organization problems as annoying trivia.

Dwight Ink, a former assistant secretary of administration of the Department of Housing and Urban Development and onetime assistant budget director for executive management, reflects the frustrations shared by many administrators. Ink found that "When an effort is made to provide sound administration, these considerations have the lowest priority in the inevitable bargaining which is part of the enactment process. . . . Following enactment of a program, the White House and the administering department rush breathlessly forward to implementation with little time or attention given to its management."[6] Ink argues not "for perfecting planning before launch-

5. Louis Brownlow, *The President and the Presidency,* Public Administration Service, 1949, p. 91.

6. Dwight Ink, "A Management Crisis for the New President: People Programs," *Public Administration Review,* Vol. 28, No. 6, 1969.

ing programs" but for sufficient advance administrative planning "to provide reasonable assurance that the program can move forward rapidly under competent staff and with funds adequately safeguarded."

In the preface to their book with the provocative subtitle, *How Great Expectations in Washington Are Dashed in Oakland or Why It's Amazing That Federal Programs Work At All,* Jeffrey L. Pressman and Aaron Wildavsky observe: "Presidents and their advisers, department secretaries and their subordinates, local officials and groups in their communities complain that good ideas are dissipated in the process of implementation. . . . Complaints about implementation do not constitute serious efforts to grapple with the problem."[7]

If a president recognizes his own shortcomings he can offset them to some degree by astute use of his institutional staff, including the Office of Management and Budget, and his department heads. President Truman was fortunate in having as his budget directors men such as Harold Smith, James Webb, and Frank Pace, who were pre-eminently public administrators; and he listened to them. Presidents Kennedy and Johnson had no less capable budget directors, but their expertise and interest were in fiscal and economic policy, and program analysis and development, not administration.

Reorganization Plan No. 2 of 1970 was designed to reemphasize the management role of the Office of Management and Budget (the successor to the Bureau of the Budget) and provide the president with substantially enhanced institutional staff capability in areas of executive management other than the budget—"particularly in program evaluation and coordination, improvement of executive branch organization, information and management systems, and development of executive talent."[8] Whatever its intentions, the reorganization

7. Jeffrey L. Pressman and Aaron Wildavsky, *Implementation,* University of California Press, 1973, p. xiii.

8. Message of the President of the United States transmitting Reorganization Plan No. 2 of 1970, House Document No. 91–275, 91st Congress, 2nd Session.

plan has not restored the Office of Management and Budget, as an organization, to its position as the "President's principal arm for the exercise of his managerial function." The office has not re-established the monopoly the Bureau of the Budget once exercised as the "unique supplier of presidential services" and adviser on legislation and government organization.[9] Indeed, shortly after the reorganization plan went into effect, John Ehrlichman staked a claim to jurisdiction over the president's reorganization program by establishing, without the knowledge of the Office of Management and Budget, a Domestic Council subcommittee on organizational problems.[10]

Under President Nixon the director of OMB was housed in the White House and functioned as an assistant to the president, not as the head of an office. At its senior levels the OMB was politicized and officials with predominantly business orientations were interposed between the career staff and the White House. The turnover of political appointees was so frequent that one senior career OMB official stated: "The top management of this place is like a carousel. I don't know from week to week who my next boss will be." Career staff access to senior levels within OMB was limited with the result that "knowledgeable staffers with 'institutional memory' could not inform new policy-makers, for example, the 'square wheel' they thought to be a remarkable innovation had been tried twice before and found wanting, and why it had failed."[11]

Jimmy Carter's transition team urged that OMB be "depoliticized," but he ignored their advice.[12] As his first OMB

9. For analysis of the change in the Bureau of the Budget's role see Allen Schick, "The Budget Bureau That Was: Thoughts on the Rise, Decline and Future of a Presidential Agency," *Law and Contemporary Problems,* School of Law, Duke University, Vol, 35, Summer 1970.

10. Harvey C. Mansfield, "Reorganizing the Federal Executive Branch: The Limits of Institutionalization," *Law and Contemporary Problems,* School of Law, Duke University, Vol. 35, Summer 1970.

11. Louis Fisher, *Presidential Spending Power,* Princeton University Press, 1975, p. 56.

12. *Washington Post,* November 4, 1976.

director he appointed a personal crony and political adviser, Bert Lance. Lance rarely communicated directly with the career staff and was characterized by the *National Journal* as an "absentee director."[13] Lance added another political layer on top of those created by Nixon—two new positions of executive associate director. Career staff are now insulated from the White House by four layers of political appointees.

As now structured, OMB cannot serve effectively as the president's "management conscience" and organization strategist. It has lost the "neutral competence" which has enabled it to serve effectively both Democratic and Republican presidents. Hugh Heclo is correct in noting that neutral competence "entails not just following orders but having the practical knowledge of government and the broker's skills of the governmental market place that makes one's advice worthy of attention. Thus neutral competence is a strange amalgam of loyalty that argues back, partisanship that shifts with the changing partisans, independence that depends on others."[14]

President Roosevelt recognized that the White House staff is not immune to a virulent species of Parkinson's disease. Work will expand in proportion to the number of people available to do it. The president needs help, but he does not need helpers who monopolize his time and try to interpose themselves between him and his department heads. President Ford was estimated to spend 50 percent of his time with White House staff, even though he desired to maintain an open office.[15] When James H. Rowe, Jr., one of the original assistants with a "passion for anonymity," asked President Roosevelt for an assistant, his request was politely but firmly denied. Roosevelt told him that if he was unable to do his job without

13. Joel Havemann, "OMB—Writing the Budget in the Post Lance Era," *National Journal,* October 1, 1977.

14. Hugh Heclo, "OMB and the Presidency—the Problem of 'Neutral Competence,'" *The Public Interest,* No. 38, Winter 1975.

15. Stephen J. Wayne, *The Legislative Presidency,* Harper & Row, 1978, pp. 54–55.

assistance, he was not doing what the president wanted him to do.

Rowe was impressed by Roosevelt's deep understanding of government organization and "what in it was good for Presidents," and his insistence that "the White House not do everything." He pushed as much on the departments as he could and wanted only vital matters to come to him and then only for a last quick look.[16]

Roosevelt drew a sharp distinction between staff who served him as president and those whose first duty was to the presidency. Rowe was assigned responsibility to assist in the process of reviewing and developing recommendations on enrolled bills, but with precise instructions that his job "was to look after the President," and the Budget Bureau's to protect the interests of the presidency.[17] The personal, political interests of an incumbent president and the interests of the presidency as an institution are by no means identical, although it may be hard at times for White House staff to see the difference. Continuity is essential for protection of the institution, and this is something no White House staff can provide.

Roosevelt emphasized that his administrative assistants were to be "personal aides to the President and shall have no authority over anyone in any department or agency, including the Executive Office of the President." Executive Order No. 8248, September 8, 1939, establishing the divisions of the Executive Office of the President, directed: "In no event shall the administrative assistants be interposed between the President and the head of any department or agency or between the President and any one of the divisions in the Executive Office of the President." The executive order reflected the President's Committee on Administrative Management's view that assistants to the President "would not be Assistant Presidents in

16. Letter to the author from James H. Rowe, Jr., dated February 17, 1969.
17. *Ibid.*

any sense" and should remain in the background, "issue no orders, make no decision, emit no public statements."[18]

President Nixon did not rescind or modify Executive Order No. 8248. Shortly after his inauguration he explained that his personal staff would function exclusively as "information gatherers," not as major policy advisers or "freewheeling" operators.[19]

The contrast between the White House office prescribed by executive order and envisaged by President Nixon in 1969 and that described by H. R. Haldeman, John Ehrlichman, John Dean, and other witnesses before the Senate Select Committee on Presidential Campaign Activities could not be more dramatic. From analysis of the testimony and evidence it would appear that President Nixon's principal assistants acted on the following assumptions:

—The president's constitutional powers, including his inherent powers, are delegable and may be legitimately exercised by his principal assistants acting in his name.

—The president must operate on the basis that staff come to him only when called.

—As surrogates of the president, the principal assistants must be "self-starters" because "in the Nixon White House there is no one else who is going to have the time to supervise, make assignments, decide what should be looked into. It would be impossible for the President, or any one person in his behalf, to keep informed of everything being done by the staff, even in areas of major current interest or concern."

18. Report of the President's Committee on Administrative Management, Government Printing Office, 1939, p. 5.

19. See column of Rowland Evans and Robert Novak, *Washington Post,* January 16, 1969.

—Department and agency heads must obey orders from the White House even in those areas where statutory powers are vested in them and they are legally accountable for the actions taken. Agency heads should understand that when a request comes from the White House, they must accomplish it without being told how to do it.[20]

There has been no more striking or significant development in the past quarter of a century than the growth in the size and power of the president's personal household. Those who anticipated that President Carter would reorganize the Executive Office of the President and drastically reduce the size and power of the White House office have been doomed to disappointment. Despite his pledge to reduce the White House staff by nearly one third,[21] cuts below the levels reached in the Ford and Nixon administrations have been more illusory than real and represent in the main the shifting of positions from one box to another. The 1978 budget provided for a White House complement of 460 permanent positions, a reduction of 40 from the Ford administration's last year. Thomas E. Cronin, among others, has noted that "the Presidency has become a large bureaucracy itself, rapidly acquiring many dubious characteristics of large bureaucracies in the process: layering, overspecialization, communication gaps, inadequate coordination, and an impulse to become consumed with short-term operational concerns at the expense of thinking systematically about the consequences of varying sets of policies and priorities and important long-range problems."[22]

Tensions between political "dilettantes" and civil service "experts" are inevitable, as Max Weber observed in his classic

20. Senate Select Committee on Presidential Campaign Activities, hearings May–August 1973, pp. 1682, 2514–17, 2599.

21. *Ibid.*, p. 201.

22. Thomas E. Cronin, "The Swelling of the Presidency," *Saturday Review*, February 1973.

essay on bureaucracy, but these tensions are heightened when the competing White House bureaucracy is staffed with inexperienced outsiders with little knowledge of the federal government. President Carter has surrounded himself with assistants who are "predominantly White males, young, from Georgia and veterans from his political campaigns."[23] For most of them Washington is a foreign and hostile terrain. The *Congressional Quarterly* correctly described President Nixon's White House staff as a "campaign staff."[24] This description applies equally to the Carter staff.

What has come into being is a presidential court with all the trappings and intrigues associated with an ancient monarchy. The Johnson court is vividly characterized in George Reedy's book, *The Twilight of the Presidency,* as a "mass of intrigue, posturing, strutting, cringing and pious commitment to irrelevant windbaggery."[25] Members of the White House staff possess no power in their own right and depend for status, prestige, and influence on the favor of the president. Consequently, staff compete with each other, other units in the Exexcutive Office of the President, and Cabinet secretaries for information and presidential access.

No one will quarrel with the need for some growth in the size of the White House staff. The world of Jimmy Carter is not the world of Franklin D. Roosevelt. Some would argue that the centralization of power in the White House is a necessary and inevitable response to the incompatible and contradictory demands made upon the government, the consequences of the technological revolution, the increasing number of federal programs cutting across established jurisdictional lines and the frequency of jurisdictional disputes, the need to control departmental and bureau satrapies which are

23. Don Bonafede, "Something Old, Something New, Something Black and Spanish, Too," *National Journal,* January 22, 1977.

24. *Congressional Quarterly Almanac,* 1969, p. 1182.

25. George E. Reedy, *The Twilight of the Presidency,* New American Library, 1970, p. xii.

responsive only to their constituencies, the decline of the Cabinet as an institution, and the supineness of the Congress.

But there are dangers. One of the prime lessons of Watergate is that large "do-it-yourself" staffs can isolate the president and, if they mirror his personality too closely, accentuate rather than compensate for his weaknesses. Most important, a large, ambitious, and able staff can create for the president an illusion of self-sufficiency, where none exists. Congressman Morris K. Udall summed it up well when he said:

> Certainly no loyal American would begrudge any President the expertise or manpower needed to cope with the pressing problems of the nation and the world. But a serious problem does arise when the White House staff begins to replace both the functions of the Cabinet and the career civil service. . . .
>
> The personal staff of Richard Nixon, with its overwhelming size, shadowy functions and obvious influence has undermined the traditional decision making rules and interrelationships of other branches of our government. Not only has this affected the powers of the Congress but it has unquestionably eroded the responsibilities of the Cabinet and the stabilizing controls of the Civil Service. The checks and balances mechanisms are thrown out of kilter.[26]

Few studies of the presidency have failed to quote with approbation Charles G. Dawes's statement that "Cabinet members are the natural enemies of the President." They rarely, however, quote the first budget director in full. What Dawes said was that "Cabinet members are vice presidents in charge of spending, and as such they are the natural enemies of the President."[27] Dawes obviously was speaking from the perspective of budget director. Cabinet members may be the natural

26. House Committee on Post Office and Civil Service, Committee Print No. 20, April 24, 1971, pp. 2–3.

27. Kermit Gordon, *Reflections on Spending*. The Brookings Institution, 1967, p. 15.

enemies of the budget director, or White House staff, but they are the president's natural allies. A president may not like his Cabinet members; he may disagree with them and suspect their loyalty; but he cannot destroy their power without seriously undermining his own.

Sudden awareness of his dependency on the executive establishment and the bureaucracy can produce severe cultural shock in a president fresh from the Congress, or for that matter, from the Pentagon or a state house. A president is not self-sufficient. The Congress can perform its constitutional functions without the executive establishment and the bureaucracy. A president cannot.

It is the agency heads, not the president, who have the men, money, materiel, and legal powers. With a few exceptions, such as foreign assistance, disaster relief, and economic stabilization activities, funds are appropriated to the agencies and authority to execute the programs vested by law in agency heads. As a general rule, the president cannot enter into a contract, make a loan or grant, initiate a public works project, or hire and fire federal employees other than those appointed by him. The president's authority to approve or modify regulations issued by agencies has been challenged on the grounds that such power has not been expressly granted to him by law.[28] To work his will in the Congress and outside community, a president must have at his disposal the trade goods controlled by the agencies and be able to enlist the support of their constituencies.

The occupant of the "most powerful office on earth" quickly learns the harsh truth. His executive power has a very frail constitutional foundation—the power to appoint officers of the United States. Appointing authority may be so hedged about with restrictions as to limit severely his discretion. He can fire officers performing administrative duties, but here again his

28. Timothy B. Clark, "When the President Tries to Regulate," *National Journal,* December 16, 1978.

power is limited. Dismissal of a high official is a measure of last resort which can be utilized only under extreme provocation.

A president does not enforce his will by dictate. His instructions are not obeyed automatically. Jesse Jones admitted that when the president "asked me to do something which in my opinion we could not or should not do—and that happened only a few times—we just did not do it."[29] Harry Truman believed that the principal power possessed by a president was "to bring people in and try to persuade them to do what they ought to do without persuasion. That's what I spend most of my time doing. That's what the powers of the President amount to."[30]

An alliance—which is what the executive branch really is—is by definition a confederation of sovereigns joined together in pursuit of some common goal. Some members may be more powerful than others, but they are nonetheless mutually interdependent. Individual purposes and goals are subordinated only to the extent necessary to hold the alliance intact. Each member will find it necessary at times to act contrary to the interests of the alliance when compelled to do so to protect his own vital interests. Unless a president is able to convince his departmental allies that they need him as much as he needs them, inevitably they will gravitate to another power base.

The executive branch is no more a monolith than the Congress. There are multiple power centers, and the president must employ all of the authority and ingenuity at his command "to evoke the prime loyalty of the divers parts of the great governmental machine, each part being also animated by loyalty to its particular purpose."[31] Presidents Nixon and Carter's visits during their first weeks in office to each of the executive departments represented something more than a symbolic gesture.

29. Jesse H. Jones, *Fifty Billion Dollars: My Thirteen Years with the RFC (1932–1945)*, The Macmillan Co., 1951, p. 262.
30. Rossiter, *op. cit.*, p. 149.
31. Brownlow, *op. cit.*, p. 64.

Intellectually presidents recognize that their own power is not entirely separable from that of their department heads. President Carter was almost paraphrasing the words of Richard M. Nixon when he said that his Cabinet members would play "a much larger and more autonomous role."[32] He promised that his would be a "Cabinet government" and that there would never be an instance while he was president "when the members of the White House staff dominate or act in a superior position to the members of our Cabinet."[33]

But presidents operate under rigid time restraints. What they want, they want now. They are impatient with solutions that go beyond the next congressional election, and their maximum time span is four years. They say they welcome disagreement and dissent, but cannot understand why Cabinet members do not share presidential perspective. The fiefdoms are fractious, and the machinery of government moves too slowly to suit their purposes. Their experience in the Congress has given them neither the knowledge nor the aptitude to energize the executive establishment, so as far as possible they attempt to bypass and neutralize it.

Executive departments and the bureaucracy are called upon to behave in a way that is contrary to their very nature. McGeorge Bundy reflected a typical White House view when he said: "Cabinet officers are special pleaders" and "should run their part of the government for the Administration—not run to the Administration for the interests of their part of the government."[34] One might as well echo Professor Henry Higgins's plaint in *My Fair Lady,* "Why can't a woman be more like a man?" as ask "Why can't Cabinet members act more like presidents?" Those who accept the differences can enjoy them and put them to proper use.

32. Neal R. Pierce, "The Democratic Nominee—'If I were President,'" *National Journal,* July 17, 1976.

34. Senate Committee on Government Operations, *op. cit.,* p. 282.

33. Dom Bonafede, "Carter Sounds Retreat from 'Cabinet Government,'" *National Journal,* November 18, 1978.

The bureaucracy is damned as "uncreative" because it is unable to satisfy the White House appetite for immediate solutions to complex social and economic problems and dramatic imaginative proposals for the legislative program. "Slow moving," "unresponsive," "disloyal" are among the milder epithets used to describe the bureaucracy. Bundy is dismayed because "the contest between the President and the bureaucracy is as real today as ever, and there has been no significant weakening in the network of triangular alliances which unite all sorts of interest groups with their agents in the Congress and their agents in the bureaucracy."[35]

As an entity, the bureaucracy is no better equipped to manufacture grand designs for government programs than carpenters, electricians, and plumbers are to be architects. But if an architect attempted to build a house, the results might well be disastrous. What the White House identifies as bureaucracy's inherent deficiencies are often its strengths. Effective functioning of the governmental machine requires a high degree of stability, uniformity, and awareness of the impact of new policies, regulations, and procedures on the affected public. If the post office at the outset refused to handle mail which did not include the zip code, the Department of Defense each year revised *in toto* its procurement regulations, the Department of Health, Education, and Welfare discarded all previous standards applicable to grants-in-aid, the public outcry against innovation would shake the Congress and the White House.

The bureaucracy all too frequently is not asked for its advice on the "how to," where it does have the knowledge and experience to make a contribution. Those who raise administrative problems may be considered "obstructionists." It is reported that Joseph Califano, Jr., overrode the objections of high officials of the Department of Housing and Urban Development who wanted more time to plan and organize the Model Cities

35. *Ibid.*, p. 281.

program.[36] The difficulties and delays encountered in launching the program might have been reduced if HUD's cautions had not been overriden.

Institutional staff in the OMB and elsewhere in the Executive Office of the President are viewed in a somewhat more favorable light, but they do not come off scot-free. As the president's abominable "no man"and management conscience, the OMB in particular can be a source of irritation. Some White House staff during the Johnson administration successfully pressured the Budget Bureau to devote more of its resources to developing constructive program proposals and coordinating operations. The bureau always has played a significant role in both areas, but on a highly selective basis, and only when there was no other logical place to make the assignment. Unless extreme care is exercised, OMB may be placed in a position of a program advocate and a defender of its own operations, thus compromising its objectivity and effectiveness as a protector of the "presidency" and a bastion against the unremitting pressure brought on a president by representatives of narrow, partisan interests.

Under Johnson, the White House staff took over from the Bureau of the Budget the main responsibility for coordinating development of the president's legislative program. Where until 1961, except for a few major proposals, initiative for developing the legislative program was left to the agencies subject to the Budget Bureau's aegis, the White House assumed direct control, with the Budget Bureau acting as its agent. Development of the legislative program, together with the flood of special messages that now traditionally follow the State of the Union, budget, and economic messages, has been converted into one of the most effective "action-forcing processes" and thus provided White House staff with the sinews of power.

36. Patrick Anderson, "Deputy President for Domestic Affairs," *The New York Times Magazine,* March 3, 1968.

The legislative program now competes with the budget for presidential attention during the months from October to January. While one obviously has a direct impact on the other, at times the two have proceeded in separate orbits.

The task force was invented as a device for undercutting the power of the agencies and the bureaucracy in the legislative development process. The 1964 task force leaders were told "we don't want agencies to dictate personnel or agenda!" and urged to select any members from the agencies before the president announced formation of the task forces at a cabinet meeting. Agency heads were to be informed, but they were not to be allowed to have institutional representatives on the working groups.

Bill Moyers, who was in charge of the 1964 task forces, was conscious of the need to link together the several different constituencies that would be served or alienated by the recommendations—"the world of bureaucracy which would be finally responsible for implementing the ideas, . . . the world of expertise outside the government," and the White House.[37] Moyers arranged to have a Budget Bureau staff officer serve as executive secretary of each of the fourteen odd task groups.

Moyers looked upon the task forces as more or less of a one-time exercise to pump some new life into a lagging domestic program. He foresaw that an overdose of task forces could result in a situation where "departments by reacting so much to initiative from the White House lose their role as innovators and become dependent almost exclusively upon Presidential and White House staff initiatives."[38]

The 1964 task forces skimmed the cream. Unless there is careful preparatory staff work, the off-the-cuff musings of "experts" around the table are not calculated to produce meaningful results. When confronted with a highly complex problem,

37. "The White House Staff vs. the Cabinet: Hugh Sidney Interviews Bill Moyers," *Washington Monthly*, February 1969.
38. *Ibid.*

the best they can usually produce is a nonanswer—a proposed new organization or reorganization.

The post-Moyers Johnson White House shared neither his solicitude for maintaining linkages nor his cautions about indiscriminate use. Task forceitis ran rampant. At least forty-five task forces were organized in the fall of 1966. Papers were circulated on an "eyes only" basis and when agency people were included on the task forces they were reluctant to tell even their bosses about what they were doing. The task force operation bred a miasma of suspicion and distrust without producing very much that was useable.

While the White House may not consider a Cabinet member's participation in the development of a legislative proposal essential, the president will hold him to account for assuring its enactment by the Congress. So far as the president is concerned, a Cabinet member's primary responsibility is to mobilize support both within and outside the Congress for presidential measures and to act as a legislative tactician. Major questions of policy and legislative strategy are reserved, however, for decision by the White House staff.

To perform in this role, a department head must maintain the loyalty of his subordinates and strengthen his alliances with congressional committees and interest groups, which in turn raises questions about his allegiance to the president and confirms White House distrust. John Ehrlichman complained that Cabinet officers "go off and marry the natives."[39] Senior Carter staff maintain that Cabinet secretaries were given too much leeway at the start of the administration and must be put on notice that "we expect them to work with the President in a positive way."[40] "Loyalty" and "ability to work with White House staff" were the primary tests employed by President Carter in determining who would be retained in his Cabinet. The net result is that more and more, those respon-

39. *Washington Post,* August 24, 1972.
40. Dom Bonafede, *op. cit.*

sible for carrying out policies are being excluded as "special pleaders" from the development of the policies which they are to administer. The ill-concealed unhappiness of several Nixon Cabinet members was not surprising.

Joseph W. Bartlett, former Undersecretary of Commerce, noted the difficulties posed for Cabinet officers by the "baffling ambivalent" White House attitude. White House staff demand "unquestioning obedience" to orders, but the president expects secretaries to maintain "at least the public image of independence" and the capability to enlist their constituencies in support of presidential proposals. Bartlett observed: "In short, a Cabinet officer who is loyal to the President and his deputies but feels constrained to retain some independence must anticipate trouble in carrying water on both shoulders."[41]

No president can afford to allow his Cabinet, the Congress, or outside constituencies to restrict his choice of counselors or the devices he employs to obtain advice. He must be no less zealous in preventing his own staff from doing so.

Each component of the governmental system has its own special function. Each has its strengths and each has its weaknesses. The White House staff is no exception. The most critical and difficult job facing a president is to learn the system and to assure that each component is properly utilized and exploited to its full potential.

Perhaps a president's most important lesson is to learn the strengths and limitations of his personal staff. There are many things which the White House staff cannot do or will do poorly. They do not have technical competence and do not have the time to acquire it. Errors may occur when staff usurp the functions of technicians. These can be embarrassing.

Authorship of a proposal necessarily narrows the staff's vision and judgment. The advice they give the president and

41. Joseph W. Bartlett and Douglas N. Jones, "Managing a Cabinet Agency: Problems of Performance at Commerce," *Public Administration Review,* Vol. 34, No. 1, January–February 1974.

their evaluation of conflicting opinions inevitably will be colored by their own biases. They are disposed to discount objections and to exaggerate potential benefits. The president cannot rely upon them to report accurately and promptly on their projects that go sour. A president has too many advisers who are protagonists of special interests. He does not need them in his own household.

Members of the staff do not have to explain or justify their proposals before the Congress. White House staff do not testify. The fact that one ultimately has to undergo cross-examination by the Congress is a healthy tempering influence and compels an official to anticipate the questions that are going to be asked. It is too easy for a staffer to gloss over the unanswered questions.

Unless decisions are fed into the institutional machinery, there will be no effective follow-through. President Johnson's senior aide, Joseph Califano, conceded: "We are not equipped to maintain day-to-day relationship with only one program—no matter how important."[42] If a White House aide picks up the ball and runs with it, no one will be around to retrieve the ball when it is dropped.

Moyers is right when he observes that power is the president's greatest resource and "is not something that he is likely to invest in people whose first allegiance is not to him."[43] Moyers does not seem to appreciate, however, that a president can conserve his power by delegating decision-making *authority* to agency heads. The distinction between power and authority is vital. When authority is delegated, the president can employ his power selectively and let others absorb the heat of the initial contact.

Presidential power is a precious commodity and is not inexhaustible. It retains its potency only so long as it is applied

42. Bernard J. Frieden and Marshall Kaplan, *The Politics of Neglect,* The MIT Press, 1975, p. 112.

43. *Washington Monthly,* February 1969.

to issues of immediate presidential importance. White House staff have no power of their own and whenever they exercise power they are draining the president's limited resources. The Watergate record graphically demonstrates the consequences of allowing the presidency to speak with many voices. Furthermore, the president cannot disavow acts by White House aides even when they are acting on their own. All their mistakes become the president's mistakes.

According to John Ehrlichman, "jurisdictional conflicts between Cabinet officers and departments, levels of government all now find their way to the White House by some law of governmental gravity."[44] The assumption, however, that "White House clout" is always necessary to settle such disputes is questionable. If the White House enters a dispute prematurely, there is no appeals mechanism short of the president himself. It is far preferable to use the Office of Management and Budget, or some other executive office agency, to sort out the issues and act as a shock absorber. When the differences are crystallized, the White House is in a better strategic position to step in and pronounce final judgment on the unresolved issues.

The answer does not lie in having the presidency secede from the executive branch and in constituting it as an independent branch of the government. The Nixon administration moved in this direction by attempting to run the whole government from the White House. The Carter administration appears also to be moving in this direction.

What the President *does not do* may be as important what he does do. If the strong pressures to escalate decisions upward remain unchecked, the organization structure becomes top-heavy, slow-moving, and unresponsive. Over-centralization of decision-making in the White House encourages buck-passing and stifles initiative and creativity by those officials

44. Senate Select Committee on Presidential Campaign Activities, *op. cit.*, p. 2516.

who are closest to the people and best acquainted with their needs and problems. When it is coupled with secrecy and all but chosen White House confidants are excluded from meaningful participation in the process, the results can be close to disastrous.

White House involvement inevitably produces a chain reaction which has repercussions throughout the executive establishment. Decisions are sucked up to the top, with the result that department heads may be compelled to deal with matters which might best be left to their bureau chiefs, and Washington bureau chiefs with matters which ought to be delegated to the field. Cabinet members are reluctant to delegate authority when their actions are subject to close White House scrutiny.

A president should carefully pick and choose the issues which merit his personal participation in the give and take of policy formulation. This does not imply that he should allow himself to become the captive of completed staff work to the point where his only option is to say yes or no. It does imply a need for a keen sense of timing as to when presidential participation will not cut off debate at too early a stage and discrimination to avoid over-exposure and dilution of presidential influence.

President Truman deliberately limited his attendance at National Security Council meetings because he believed that his presence would inhibit frank and open discussion.[45] If a president says at a council meeting, "I think thus and so," the others will take their cue from him.

A president's most important challenge is to harness the energy produced by diversity in support of the national good, not to try to eliminate it. The bureaucratic bastion cannot be reduced by bombarding it with a fusillade of White House directives ordering it to be more creative and more efficient. The perspectives of the president's chief lieutenants cannot be

45. Sidney W. Souers, "Policy Formulation for National Security," *The American Political Science Review,* June 1949.

broadened or redirected by concentrating more and more power in the president's own household. More effective means for meeting the challenge are at a president's disposal, if he has the knowledge to use them and is willing to pay the cost.

The perspective of Cabinet members depends in part on what the president demands from them. Their sights can be raised by assignments which compel them to subordinate their more narrow concerns, although obviously those with strong constituencies will find it difficult to abandon them completely. From time to time presidents have used Cabinet members as ministers without portfolio. Secretary of Commerce Herbert Hoover, Attorney General Robert Kennedy, and Secretary of Defense Robert McNamara are notable examples, and sought their advice on matters outside their immediate departmental jurisdictions. The principal and perhaps only advantage of formal Cabinet meetings held on a regular schedule is that they contribute to a sense of common purpose and collective responsibility. The Cabinet may be nothing more than a symbol, but the value of symbols is not to be underrated.

A president should be as alert to safeguard the powers and prestige of his department heads as those of his own office. To the extent that the status and authority of any department head are downgraded, he is less able to resist the pressures brought upon him by his constituencies, congressional committees, and the bureaucracy.

Kermit Gordon has cited instances where the Budget Bureau "sometimes works in quiet collusion with an agency head who wants to make a sound but unpopular decision which would strain his relations with a bureau chief or the agency's clientele; the Bureau, exploiting its more secure sanctuary, will make no denial when word is passed to the protesting parties that the objectionable action was pressed on the agency by the Bureau of the Budget."[46] The White House and the

46. Gordon, *op. cit.*, p. 16.

Executive Office should not be permitted to become refuges for timid administrators. Yet confidence that in a crunch they can count on White House support fosters department heads' loyalty to the president and gives them the courage to take unpopular actions. Proposed reorganizations almost always require this kind of support. The secretary of the treasury, for example, cannot publicly advocate transfer of the Coast Guard to a Department of Transportation without jeopardizing his future relationships to the Coast Guard by making it feel "unwanted." Whatever his personal views, he is obliged to protest for the record, even though he is quite prepared to be overruled.

Frontal assaults on the bureaucracy and entrenched constituencies can yield, at best, temporary gains, and the cost may well be excessive. A president is not powerless to bring about significant transformations in the bureaucracy and in the balance of power among constituencies, but his approach must be indirect. To secure lasting results, a president has to take positive action to alter the bases of bureaucratic and constituency power-personnel systems and organization structure—so as to adapt them to the nation's long-range goals and requirements. The task is fraught with hazards, but it can be done if the president exercises leadership and exploits fully the powers at his command. The likelihood of success is enhanced if actions are planned within the context of a well-conceived and realistic organization strategy. It is in the development of a sound and realistic organization strategy that recent presidents have failed most conspicuously.

In the words of Morton H. Halperin: "Every President needs to know how bureaucratic interests interact, in order to be the master rather than the prisoner of his organization, and also in order to mold the rational interests of the bureaucracies into the national interest as he sees it."[47]

47. Morton H. Halperin, "Why Bureaucrats Play Games," *Foreign Policy*, No. 2 Spring 1971.

Personnel systems are the nerve center of bureaucracy. It is idle for presidents to complain that the State Department is a "bowl of jelly," and then do nothing to reform the Foreign Service system, which makes the State Department what it is. The Department's career professionals have condemned the recruitment and promotion system for stifling "the creative dissent and responsible questioning of alternatives which could have helped the organization adapt to changing times."[48]

Jimmy Carter was the first modern president willing to tackle the thorny and politically unrewarding task of overhauling the Civil Service system. He pledged: "Civil service reform will be the centerpiece of government reorganization during my term of office."[49] A major objective of his reform proposals was "to provide incentives and opportunities for managers to improve the efficiency and responsiveness of the Federal Government." Their enactment would "mean less job security for incompetent Federal employees, but conscientious civil servants will benefit from change that recognizes and rewards good performance."[50]

Important milestone that it is, the Civil Service Reform Act of 1978 cannot be expected to produce miraculous overnight changes in bureaucratic behavior. Alan K. Campbell, director of the Office of Personnel Management, recognizes that the enactment of legislation represents "just the beginning," not the end.[51] Reorganization of the Civil Service Commission into an Office of Personnel Management and Merit System Protection Board, authorization of a mobile and flexible Senior Executive Service, establishment of new performance appraisal systems, and the other provisions of the Civil Service Reform

48. *Diplomacy for the 70's: A Program of Management Reform for the Department of State,* U.S. Government Printing Office, 1970, p. 306.

49. Message to the Congress on Civil Service Reform, March 2, 1978.

50. Text of address by President Carter to the National Press Club, March 2, 1978.

51. U.S. Civil Service Commission, *Introducing the Civil Service Reform Act,* U.S. Government Printing Office, 1979.

Act merely provide the opportunity to take the preliminary first steps toward the ultimate goal. Civil service reform is a complex process with minimal political payoff. Whether or not the hoped for results are achieved will depend in large measure on the White House's ability and willingness to maintain interest and genuine support for the unglamorous but vital tasks that lie ahead.

Organization and reorganization can be used to change program emphasis and to modify the power balance among constituencies. But as Hugh Heclo has observed: "Reorganization plans or techniques like management by objectives and zero-based budgeting are all executive proclamations that presume rather than create changes in subordinates' behavior. Instituting new management techniques and making them part of the bureaucracy's standard operating procedure lie at the end of state-craft, not the beginning."[52] If he is to be successful in promoting desired change, a president must have an organization strategy. A miscellaneous collection of reorganization proposals, which may by design or otherwise include some of tremendous strategic significance, does not add up to an organization strategy.

James Webb demonstrated in the National Aeronautics and Space Administration what could be done with organizational restructuring as an "element of leadership."[53] In his efforts to maintain management initiative and drive, Webb "deliberately employed fairly frequent organizational restructuring. . . ."

Reorganization and restructuring are important, but they can be overemphasized. Califano exaggerates the difficulties when he asserts: "Any President may have one or two shots at it in his career, but that's all, maybe one that's already under

52. Hugh Heclo, *A Government of Strangers: Executive Politics in Washington,* The Brookings Institution, 1977, p. 220.

53. Foreword to *Preliminary History of the National Aeronautics and Space Administration During the Administration of Lyndon B. Johnson,* National Aeronautics and Space Administration, January 15, 1969.

way when he comes in and one he gets up himself."[54] There is no contesting the fact, however, that major reorganizations do call for a heavy investment of presidential capital. The same results can be sometimes achieved at considerably less cost by building sound organizational concepts into the design of new programs. It is here that the lack of organizational strategy has hurt the most. Without agreed upon organizational concepts and goals, policies will be related solely to short-term tactical objectives.

At times the White House may give the impression of dashing off simultaneously in several different, and contradictory, directions. President Nixon signed "with pleasure" the Rural Development Act of 1972, although it was designed to undercut his proposal to transfer rural development programs to a new Department of Community Development. The act establishes a Rural Enterprise and Community Development Administration within the Department of Agriculture. He apparently saw no inconsistency in recommending at one and the same time the establishment of independent agencies for cancer and environmental protection and the reorganization of government programs in four "goal-oriented" superdepartments to reduce the number of "fragmented fiefdoms."

In his message on the "Quality of American Government" President Johnson specifically cited the proliferation of categorical grant programs as a cause of red tape, delays, inconvenience to state and local officials, and diffusion of the channels through which federal assistance to state and local governments can flow. He requested the Bureau of the Budget to develop basic plans for consolidating narrow categorical grants into more broadly based program grants.[55] This message was delivered to the 90th Congress. Nonetheless, the administration itself sponsored proposals for fifteen or more categorical

54. Meg Greenfield, "Joe Califano: Lessons of Experience on Decentralization," *Washington Post,* December 16, 1968.

55. Lyndon B. Johnson, Message to the Congress on "Quality of American Government," House Doc. No. 90, 90th Congress, 1st Session.

programs in the same Congress, including rat control, rehabilitation services, occupational safety, juvenile delinquency, child health, and so forth.

When Franklin D. Roosevelt was president he had a personal organization strategy. Roosevelt played with federal agencies as if they were pawns in a chess game, moving them wherever it would best strengthen his strategic position. He delighted in violating the organizational commandments laid down by the orthodox theorists. Organization for him was "fun," something which could not be said of any of his successors. Only Roosevelt could have written to his budget director:

> I agree with the Secretary of the Interior. Please have it carried out so that fur-bearing animals remain in the Department of the Interior.
>
> You might find out if any Alaska bears are still supervised by (a) War Department (b) Department of Agriculture (c) Department of Commerce. They have all had jurisdiction over Alaska bears in the past and many embarrassing situations have been created by the mating of a bear belonging to one Department with a bear belonging to another Department.
>
> F.D.R.
>
> P.S. I don't think the Navy is involved but it may be. Check the Coast Guard. You never can tell![56]

Roosevelt relied heavily on competition among agencies and checks and balances to keep final authority in his own hands.[57] Innovative programs were cultivated with care so they could grow strong roots before being transferred to old-line agencies which might stunt their development. Staff for the New Deal agencies was recruited from outside the Civil Service. At the same time, Roosevelt knew how to use his de-

56. Memorandum for the Director of the Bureau of the Budget, July 20, 1939.
57. For a description of the Roosevelt mode of operations see Louis W. Koenig, *The Chief Executive,* Harcourt, Brace & World, Inc., 1964, pp. 166–68.

parment heads and encouraged rather than deplored their dedication to departmental programs.

In fostering competition, Roosevelt was not organizing to produce conflict. Competition and conflict are not the same thing. One is constructive; the other is destructive. This difference is misunderstood by those who believe incorrectly that Roosevelt was promoting conflict for its own sake.

Roosevelt's organization strategy was formulated before he entered the White House. As assistant secretary of the Navy, he advocated strongly a national budget system under the President's direction and urged that department heads should be given complete authority in all matters over bureau chiefs. Rexford G. Tugwell cited this Roosevelt statement as providing

> something of a preview of his sophistication, as he entered the Presidency, in such matters. . . . As many still living can testify, one of the most obsessive preoccupations of Roosevelt as President was to be reorganization of the government. . . .[58]

Roosevelt knew in general terms what he wanted from his Committee on Administrative Management. The committee's primary focus was to be on "what gives the President more effective managerial control," rather than on the traditional goals of economy and efficiency.[59] Roosevelt instructed the committee to "not get lost in detail" and waste its time on constructing a neat and orderly organization chart. When Brownlow and Gulick discussed the committee's draft report with the president, they found that their recommendations were in accord with Roosevelt's own thinking. The president's Committee on Administrative Management performed an in-

58. Quoted in A. J. Wann, "Franklin D. Roosevelt and the Bureau of the Budget," *Business and Government Review,* University of Missouri, March–April 1968.

59. Richard Polenberg, *Reorganizing Roosevelt's Government,* Harvard University Press, 1966, p. 17.

dispensable service, but its contribution consisted mainly in providing a conceptual framework for the president's organization strategy. Unless a president has an organization strategy, he runs a considerable risk in establishing an outside commission on federal organization which may devise its own strategy without regard for the president's interests and objectives.

President Truman had an organization strategy, but it was that supplied to him by the first Hoover Commission. The Hoover Commission reports provided a conceptual framework for the organizational philosophy developed by Herbert Hoover during his years as president and secretary of commerce, and did not stem from Truman's own thinking. There is no evidence, however, that the return to orthodoxy symbolized by many of the commission's recommendations was in conflict with Truman's views.

Of the forty-one reorganization plans transmitted by President Truman under the Reorganization Act of 1949, nine dealt with relatively minor matters and had little if any strategic significance. Most of the others did have a unifying theme—a theme which tied together the recommendations of the first Hoover Commission and made them a consistent whole. While expressed in terms of the orthodox dogmas, they complemented the recommendations of the President's Committee on Administrative Management and were Rooseveltian in their concepts of presidential power. The fourteen reorganization plans vesting in department heads the functions previously vested in subordinate officers, and transferring "executive functions" to regulatory commission chairmen designated by the president were calculated to eliminate some of the impediments to the effective exercise of presidential and secretarial power. The Congress reacted by disapproving the plans reorganizing the Treasury Department, Interstate Commerce Commission, Federal Trade Commission, and Federal Communications Commission.

Truman did accomplish the first restructuring of executive

departments since 1913. At his initiative, steps were taken toward unification of the armed services and this led to formation of the National Military Establishment in 1949. The powers of the new secretary of defense as head of the establishment were compromised seriously in order to accommodate the deep-seated and often bitter differences among the Army, Navy, and Air Force. Truman twice failed in attempts to elevate the Federal Security Agency to Cabinet rank. The idea for a Department of Welfare or Department of Health, Education, and Security did not originate with Truman but with the president's Committee on Administrative Management.

Truman was not given to theorizing about organization, but, as in other areas, his intuitive responses exhibited a keen understanding of the issues. He was quick to sense threats to the powers of the presidency. His adroit maneuvers scotched the schemes of those who wanted to assure Defense domination of the National Security Council by housing the Council in the Pentagon, where office space already had been prepared, and by designating the secretary of defense as chairman in the president's absence.[60] Truman's forthright veto of the bill creating the National Science Foundation took courage and his veto message forecast the problems which would result if public powers were yielded to private institutions.

President Eisenhower shared Truman's orthodoxy, but not his intuition or convictions about the powers of the presidency. A President's Committee on Government Organization composed of Nelson Rockefeller, Milton Eisenhower, and Arthur Flemming, was organized prior to the inauguration and remained more or less active throughout the Eisenhower administration. Neither Eisenhower nor the committee produced a coherent organization doctrine.

Except for the 1953 reorganization of the Department of

60. Senate Committee on Government Operations, Subcommittee on National Policy Machinery, "Organizing for National Security," Vol. 2, Studies and Background Materials, p. 421, and footnote, p. 422.

Defense and the establishment of the Department of Health, Education, and Welfare, Eisenhower's fourteen reorganization plans represented either follow-up on Hoover Commission recommendations or dealt with minor items. President Eisenhower passed on the most controversial proposals coming from his Advisory Committee—a First Secretary of Government, an Office of Executive Management, a Department of Transportation, and transfer of the Army Corps of Engineers' civil functions to the Department of the Interior—as a legacy to President Kennedy.

President Eisenhower was willing to say the right things, but he was less willing to act. Draft veto messages occasionally became signing statements, as is evidenced by signing statements deploring legislation requiring executive agencies "to come into agreement" with congressional committees, or circumventing the president's veto authority.[61] He did veto a few of these so-called "encroachment" bills. President Eisenhower hailed the Farm Credit Act of 1953, which for all practical purposes made the farm credit system independent of the president, as "another milestone in our march toward an agriculture which is productive, profitable, responsible and free from excessive regulation."[62] He had some second thoughts when the board later defied his instructions, but, nonetheless, approved "despite some misgivings" the Farm Credit Act of 1956 which relaxed the few remaining controls over the farm credit institutions.[63]

President Eisenhower warned about the growing influence of the military-industrial complex, but apparently he did not recognize the role of institutional arrangements in fostering that influence. In any event, he did nothing to curb the power of the industry advisory committees which flourished and mul-

61. See, for example, the signing statements of the 1956 Defense Appropriation Act and the Small Reclamation Act of 1966.

62. Statement of President Eisenhower on signature of H.R. 4353, August 6, 1953.

63. Statement of President on H.R. 10285, July 26, 1956.

tiplied during his administration and sometimes arrogated to themselves effective decision-making authority.

President Kennedy evinced little interest in organization structure and administration, and his orientation was almost entirely toward individuals and programs. He appointed a panel of advisers on government organization, but never used them collectively, and rarely as individuals, except for Neustadt. The main thesis of Sorensen's book, *Decision-Making in the White House,* which stems from his experience in the Kennedy administration, is that there is too much preoccupation with "form and structure" and too little with "the more dynamic and fluid forces on which Presidential decisions are based."[64]

Kennedy was unwilling to send forward a reorganization plan unless he was assured that it was noncontroversial. His reaction to the letter from the Atomic Energy commissioners proposing their own demise was that he would support a bill if introduced by the Chairman of the Joint Committee. President Kennedy chastised the Budget Bureau when a 1963 amendment to the Reorganization Act prohibiting the use of reorganization plans to create executive departments was construed as a defeat for the president and advised the bureau in no uncertain terms that *he* had never asked for extension of the act. The reorganization authority was allowed to lapse and was not restored until Lyndon Johnson took office.

Kennedy sent forward ten reorganization proposals, four of which relating to regulatory commissions were disapproved. None were designed to strengthen the president's powers, and the creation of the Office of Science and Technology was in the main a response to pressures from the Congress for access to the president's science adviser. His one major reorganization effort, establishment of a Department of Urban Affairs and Housing, met with a crushing defeat.

64. Theodore C. Sorensen, *Decision-Making in the White House: The Olive Branch and the Arrows,* Columbia University Press, 1963, p. 3.

Lyndon Johnson's all-encompassing concern with every aspect of government policies, programs, and operations included government organization and reorganization along with everything else. For him, important reorganization measures—such as those establishing the Department of Transportation, Department of Housing and Urban Development, and reorganizing the District of Columbia government—were trophies to be hung on his wall next to the other landmark bills enacted during his administration. Johnson could react boldly to attempts by the Congress to encroach upon the president's constitutional powers and did not shrink from direct confrontations over such issues. His position on provisions requiring committee consent to executive actions or bypassing the president's veto authority was unequivocal, and he was less inclined to compromise than any of his predecessors.

President Johnson's thinking about government organization was traditional. His messages invariably made proper obeisance to the gods of "economy and efficiency" and overlapping and duplication. He stressed that he would take steps to "modernize and streamline" the government with the objective of assuring that federal programs are "administered effectively and at minimum cost to the taxpayer."[65]

Johnson's reorganization program and decisions on organization issues reflected little if any unity of purpose. His approach was episodic, pragmatic, and sometimes gave the appearance of being improvised on the spur of the moment.

Lyndon Johnson was a master legislative tactician, not a strategist. To facilitate the passage of an administration measure in the Congress, he was quite prepared to rise above organizational principles and was not disturbed in the least by inconsistencies. We have cited previously examples of the discrepancies between Johnson's words and Johnson's deeds, notably with respect to categorical grants.

65. Memorandum from Joseph A. Califano, Jr., to the heads of executive departments on reorganization proposals, January 15, 1966.

Several Johnson reorganizations did have a significant strategic impact. The transfer of water pollution control responsibilities from Health, Education, and Welfare to Interior was motivated by a desire to obtain a change in program emphasis and to wean Interior away from its narrow Western orientation. The District of Columbia reorganization made the District of Columbia government somewhat less susceptible to domination by the House and Senate District committees. The plans relating to the Public Health Service, customs, locomotive inspection, statutory interagency committees, mass transit, and narcotics accomplished subtle alterations in the balance of power with respect to the affected programs and afforded an opportunity to re-examine and reorient program objectives.

Opportunism can be self-defeating as shown by Johnson's controversial proposal to merge the Commerce and Labor departments—probably his worst fiasco. A combination of circumstances, the impending resignation of Secretary of Commerce Connor, White House irritation with both the Commerce and Labor departments, and, perhaps most of all, the search for a "surprise" to liven up the 1967 State of the Union Message inspired the idea. White House staff had unearthed the 1964 task force recommendation for a Department of Economic Development which would absorb the Department of Commerce, Office of Economic Opportunity, Small Business Administration, and at a later date, the Department of Labor. The president agreed to the merger, but not the rationale. By recommending simply the consolidation of the two departments and preserving the words "Labor" and "Commerce" in the title, the president hoped to avoid alienating the two constituencies involved.[66] The Budget Bureau was told that it could not refer to economic development or economic planning and had to develop a new justification out of whole cloth *after* the recommendation had gone to the Congress.

Neither the justification nor the details had been thought

66. *Washington Monthly, op. cit.*

through prior to the State of the Union Message. Labor and business opposition probably would have been sufficient by itself to doom the proposal. Defeat was guaranteed by an indiscriminate dragnet operation to identify functions which could be transferred to the Commerce and Labor Department. This triggered immediately the powerful defensive mechanisms within the departments and the bureaucracy.

Consolidation of the Labor and Commerce departments had a superficial logic, but not much more. Absent an intention to create a Department of Economic Development, the arguments for the reorganization were strained indeed. It is certainly open to doubt that merger of his organized labor and business constituencies would have been to the president's advantage. Interlocking arrangements between organized labor and organized business rarely have been in the public interest. Some within the administration feared that the proposed merger represented a step toward a new mercantilism.

At the very time when government programs increasingly called for a high degree of teamwork and unity in program design and execution, the Johnson administration did not oppose and sometimes supported measures which gave stimulus to the powerful centrifugal forces working within the federal structure. Its principal institutional innovation was the twilight zone agencies—the Urban Institute, the private Federal National Mortgage Association, and the National Housing Partnerships—which are insulated against effective public control and diminish the president's powers.

President Johnson devoted more personal time and attention to government organization than any president since Roosevelt. Measured by customary standards his accomplishments were fantastic—two new executive departments and the first reorganization of the District of Columbia in almost a century, all within the space of two years. The times, however, called for strategy adapted to a radically different mix of organizational problems, and this Lyndon Johnson was unable to provide.

4

Nixon's New American Revolution

For Richard M. Nixon the major cause of ineffectiveness of government was not a matter of men or money. It was "principally a matter of machinery."[1] Government reorganization was to be the means for bringing about "a new American Revolution." President Nixon's concept of government as a machine was at odds with that of Franklin D. Roosevelt, who stressed that "reorganization is not a mechanical task, because government is not a machine, but a living organism."[2]

President Nixon apparently did not believe that accomplishment of the "New American Revolution" called for the development of revolutionary doctrines. The forging of "new institutions to serve a new America" was to be achieved by strict application of the orthodox dogmas. As in the case of the "New Federalism," the new, in fact, represented a return to the old.

What President Nixon described as "the most comprehensive and carefully planned . . . reorganization since the executive was first constituted in George Washington's administration 183 years ago"[3] professed to be a nonpartisan

1. President's Message on Reorganization, March 25, 1971.
2. President's Message on Administrative Organization, January 12, 1937.
3. President's Message on Reorganization, March 29, 1972.

measure without political implications and to contain nothing that would offend the fundamentalists. In his several reorganization messages President Nixon repeatedly reaffirmed his faith in the orthodox doctrines: economy and efficiency as the objective of organization and administration; organization around major goals or purposes; policy administration dichotomy; rigid separation of powers; limited span of control; and straight lines of authority and accountability with each subordinate expected to obey the orders of his superior.

President Nixon argued that the organizational principles he advocated had been "endorsed" by the Brownlow and Hoover commissions, but the underlying philosophy has its roots in Max Weber's ideas about bureaucracy and power relationships. Weber is concerned with the special type of power relationship he calls domination. As explained by Nicos P. Mouzelis, "domination refers to a power relationship in which the ruler, the person who imposes his will on others, believes that he has a right to the exercise of power; and the ruled consider it their duty to obey his orders. . . . Domination, when exercised over a large number of people, necessitates an administrative staff which will execute commands and which will serve as a bridge between the ruler and the ruled."[4]

It is with respect to the career civil service or the bureaucracy, to use Nixon's code word, that Nixon parted company with Brownlow. The President's Committee on Administrative Management recommended that "the merit system be extended upward, outward and downward to include all positions in the Executive Branch of Government except those which are policy-determining in character."[5] President Nixon considered that President Eisenhower had committed a major error in failing to clean out the "Democrat-infested" federal bureaucracy. He was resolved to replace Democratic civil ser-

4. Nicos P. Mouzelis, *Organization and Bureaucracy,* Aldine Publishing Co., 1968, pp. 15–16.
5. Report of the President's Committee on Administrative Management, 1937.

vants with Republican civil servants.[6] Nixon's viewpoint is reflected in an internal White House memorandum which complains that "the lack of key Republican bureaucrats at high levels precludes the initiation of policies which would be proper and politically advantageous."[7]

Distrust of the bureaucracy was a recurring theme in almost all of Richard Nixon's public statements. "Ossified" and "obstructive" are typical of the adjectives applied to the civil service. When he signed the legislation establishing the Special Action Office for Drug Abuse, the president threatened that "heads would roll" if "petty bureaucrats" thwarted the efforts of the office director.[8] John Ehrlichman was not exaggerating when he described relationships with the bureaucracy as "guerrilla warfare."[9] As it ultimately evolved, the major objective of Nixon's organization strategy was to contain and neutralize the bureaucracy. This became clear in his March 1972 reorganization message which stated:

> Notwithstanding the famous sign on President Truman's desk—'the buck stops here'—there will be no stopping of the buck, no ultimate clarification of blame and credit, and no assurance that voters will get what they contracted for in electing Presidents, Senators, and Congressmen until the present convoluted and compartmentalized Washington bureaucracy can be formed anew and harnessed more directly to the people's purposes.

President Nixon did not come into office with a preconceived organization strategy. He did not see in organizational and procedural reform—reorganization, decentralization, and revenue sharing—a vehicle for achieving his political goals.

6. Rowland Evans, Jr., and Robert D. Novak, *Nixon in the White House*, Random House, 1971, p. 12.

7. Senate Select Committee on Presidential Campaign Activities, June–July 1973, Book 4, p. 1683.

8. Douglas M. Fox, "The President's Proposals for Executive Reorganization: A Critique," *Public Administration Review*, Vol. 33, No. 5, September–October 1973.

9. Senate Select Committee on Presidential Campaign Activities, *op. cit.*, Book 6, p. 2518.

Government reorganization was something that could be left to businessmen who would solve the government's management problems by applying sound business techniques. In 1969 he established an Advisory Council on Executive Organization, chaired by Roy L. Ash, then president of Litton Industries, to study and recommend reform of the government structure. All the council members, except former Texas governor John B. Connally, were businessmen without significant government experience. Evans and Novak reported that the president's eyes would glaze during the council's periodic reports. Only a strong protest from Mr. Ash gained an appointment with the president to discuss the council's proposals for reorganization of the Executive Office of the President.[10]

Management of domestic affairs was something that Nixon at first thought could be left to the Cabinet. He told an interviewer: "All you need is a competent Cabinet to run the country at home. You need a President for foreign policy; no Secretary of State is really important; the President makes foreign policy."[11] There was to be no Sherman Adams or Joe Califano in the Nixon White House. All the president had to do was put the right people in charge and let them do the job.[12]

The initial reorganization plans transmitted to the Congress by President Nixon broke no new ground and were relatively noncontroversial. Reorganization Plan No. 1 of 1969 provided for a strong chairman designated by the president for the Interstate Commerce Commission—thus applying to the ICC the pattern of organization adopted for all other major regulatory commissions. Reorganization Plan No. 1 of 1970 created an Office of Telecommunications Policy in the Executive Office of the President as recommended by the Jackson Subcommittee and the House Committee on Government Operations.

Reorganization Plan No. 2 of 1970 which changed the name of the Bureau of the Budget to the Office of Management and

10. Evans and Novak, *op. cit.*, pp. 238–240.
11. *Ibid.*, p. 11.
12. *Washington Post*, January 20, 1969.

Budget and established the Domestic Council reflected the thinking of the Ash Council and Haldeman and Ehrlichman, not the president. Ehrlichman reacted negatively to the Ash Council draft, but changed his mind after he secured modifications designed to enhance his power.[13] The Ash Council intended that the Domestic Council be a small agency with a highly qualified professional staff which would (1) help define national goals and objectives; (2) synthesize policy alternatives into consistent domestic programs; (3) provide policy advice on pressing domestic issues; and (4) consider policy implications on ongoing programs. To avoid the necessity of Senate confirmation, it was recommended that the council's executive director be an assistant to the president, but it was expected that the designated assistant would testify before congressional committees in his capacity as executive director.

John Ehrlichman wanted the Domestic Council to be a part of his personal apparatus, a power base comparable to Henry Kissinger's National Security Council staff. He insisted that (1) the plan be revised to eliminate the provision for staff appointments within the career civil service; and (2) the Congress be advised that under no circumstances would the executive director be available for questioning. The latter qualification came close to defeating the plan.

Congressman Chet Holifield objected bitterly to the "90-man faceless, formless group" made up of "a group of people that apparently are political appointees, they have not been confirmed, and they can do many things and can remain hidden in the things that they do."[14] The House Committee on Government Operations voted against approval of the reorganization because, among other objections, the executive director of the Domestic Council and his staff would not be ac-

13. Evans and Novak, *op. cit.*, p. 240.

14. House Committee on Government Operations, Subcommittee on Legislation and Military Operations, Reorganization of Executive Departments (Overview), June–July 1971, p. 226.

countable to the Congress and would be "beyond the power of the Congress to question."[15] The plan survived on a close House vote. Reorganization Plan No. 2 of 1970 is mainly significant because it marks the beginning of the trend toward formalizing the transfer of power to the president's personal staff. The director of OMB also was given a status comparable to that of John Ehrlichman when he was housed in the White House and designated as assistant to the president.

With the 1971 State of the Union Message, structural reform moved from the wings to center stage. In defining his "six great goals," President Nixon stated: "I shall ask not simply for more new programs in the old framework, but to change the framework itself—to reform the entire structure of American government so we can make it again fully responsive to the needs and wishes of the American people." Included among the major goals were revenue sharing and a bold plan, modified from the blueprint prepared by the Ash Council, for abolishing the constituency- and clientele-oriented Departments of Agriculture, Commerce, Labor, and Transportation and distributing their functions among four "goal-oriented" super Departments of Community Development, Economic Affairs, Human Resources, and Natural Resources.

Herbert Roback, staff director of the House Committee on Government Operations, explained the shift in emphasis from substantive programs to structural reform as the logical outgrowth of fiscal conservatism. According to Roback, "reorganization fits nicely with fiscal conservatism since it requires no significant budgetary outlays. In that sense, reorganization is policy on the cheap, an inexpensive commitment to progress."[16]

A desire to promote "progress" without significant budget-

15. House Report No. 91–1066.

16. Herbert Roback, "Problems and Prospects in Government Reorganization," Selected Papers of the National Academy of Public Administration, No. 1, January 1973.

ary costs obviously made the reorganization plan attractive. But the strategic objectives of the proposal were far more subtle and aimed at nothing less than a fundamental change in the balance of power within the federal system. It is something of a measure of Nixon's and his advisers' naïveté and administrative inexperience that they assumed initially that Cabinet officers were mere extensions of the presidency and had no competing loyalties. Discovery of the triangular alliance among departments, congressional committees, and clientele groups, known to any reasonably sophisticated observer of the Washington scene, came as a rude and nasty shock. Obscured within the sixteen pages of full-blown rhetoric and theoretical justification contained in the March 25, 1971, reorganization message is the following key sentence: "When any department or agency begins to represent a parochial interest, then its advice and support inevitably become less useful to the man who must serve *all* of the people as their President." Administration spokesmen conceded privately that a major purpose was to break "the linkages of professional groups and bureaucracies."

Even such an astute analyst as *New York Times* columnist Tom Wicker failed to grasp the full import of the Nixon plan. Wicker characterized the reorganization proposal as "the most brilliant stroke of Mr. Nixon's administration" and "squarely in line with the President's campaign pledges and the managerial tradition on which Republicans pride themselves."[17] Political scientists and public administration experts were somewhat more cautious but generally supported the proposed Departments of Community Development and Natural Resources as constructive measures to achieve long overdue reforms.[18] Enthusiasm in the Congress and among constituencies which would be deprived of their bases within the executive branch was considerably more restrained.

17. *The New York Times,* January 24, 1971.
18. See House Committee on Government Operations (overview), *op. cit.*

Given the political difficulties of enacting any single departmental reorganization, the very dimensions of the Nixon plan raised serious problems of credibility.[19] Some congressmen viewed it as a "grandstand play" which was not to be taken seriously. Nixon's legislative tacticians miscalculated in thinking it "easier to win large wars than small ones." By uniting in opposition such unlikely allies as farmers, labor unions, highway contractors, poor people's organizations, and congressional committee chairmen fearing loss of jurisdictions, the "New American Revolution" faced almost overwhelming odds.

Compromises had been incorporated in the Nixon grand design in an effort to placate the U.S. Army Corps of Engineers and the protectors of the pork barrel. Presidents Harding, Hoover, and Eisenhower and the Hoover Commission Task Force recommended that the civil functions of the Corps of Engineers be transferred as an integral unit to the Department of the Interior.[20] On the pretext of retaining an essential training capability in the Corps, an argument disputed by President Eisenhower among others, Nixon provided for only a partial transfer to the proposed Department of Natural Resources. He recommended that the Corps retain responsibility for project construction, operation, and maintenance.[21] Further concessions to the Corps and the Department of Agriculture incorporated in the 1973 proposal for a Department of Energy and Natural Resources cannot be reconciled with President Nixon's stated purpose of establishing "a center of responsibility for natural resources, energy and water policies" and "a single key official" on whom the president could rely to carry out natural resource policies and programs.[22] The

19. Herbert Roback, "The Congress and Super Departments," *The Bureaucrat*, Spring 1972.

20. Papers Relating to the President's Departmental Reorganization, March, 1971, pp. 160–161.

21. *Ibid.*, p. 168.

22. *Ibid.*, p. 162.

Corps and the Soil Conservation Service would retain responsibility for preparation of feasibility reports, project design, construction, operation, and maintenance, but the secretary of energy and natural resources would be made responsible for project approval, budget requests, and justifications. The proposed reorganization does not eliminate but perpetuates fragmentation of executive responsibilities for energy and natural resource programs.

The solicitude shown for pork barrel programs did not extend to the social and economic programs identified with the New and Fair deals and President Johnson's "Great Society." If the bureaucracy was the primary target of the "New American Revolution," certainly the "Great Society" programs and comparable measures designed to assist and provide access for the disadvantaged were a secondary target. The poverty agency, the Office of Economic Opportunity, was to be retained as a symbol but stripped of its major programs, which would be transferred to the Departments of Community Development, Economic Affairs, and Human Resources. The Small Business Administration was to be abolished, and responsibility for loans to small businesses and minorities lodged in an Administration for Business Development in the Department of Economic Affairs along with services to big business. Also to be abolished was the Farmers Home Administration whose programs to assist small farmers were to be split up among the Departments of Community Development, Natural Resources, and Economic Affairs.

The House Committee on Government Operations conceded a need for executive branch reorganization, but expressed doubts about the feasibility of super departments modeled on corporate conglomerates. It noted that the organizing principle for conglomerates is profitability, not functional similarity or common goals.[23] In the committee's view

23. House Committee on Government Operations, "Executive Reorganization: A Summary Analysis," House Report No. 92–922, March 1972, p. 26.

the attempt to organize around "basic goals" presented serious difficulties because: "Such goals, characteristically, are broad, overlapping and open-ended. Furthermore, they can be formulated in different ways, so that alternative or additional organizational patterns could be readily devised."[24]

Administration witnesses were hard pressed to identify the basic goals for the disparate programs (business loans, labor-management relations, transportation, etc.) to be lodged in the Department of Economic Affairs. The Department looked like a last-minute creation to accommodate the pieces left over from the other reorganizations. George P. Shultz, then OMB director, acknowledged that "to a certain extent it is true that everything is related to everything else. . . . So some sort of breakdown within the total picture is necessary, and the problem is to design a reasonably small number of packages and to find dividing lines that make sense in terms of their effectiveness in generating policy in managing the results of the legislative process."[25]

The ultimate defeat of the "New American Revolution" could not be blamed entirely on its enemies, powerful as they were. Administration support was at best lukewarm. On the very day that the Undersecretary of Agriculture J. Phil Campbell was dutifully testifying before the House Committee that the Department of Agriculture ought to be abolished as a constituency and clientele-oriented department, the president, disturbed by the political repercussions of declining farm prices, announced that the plan had been abandoned and that the Department of Agriculture would be retained as the spokesman for farmers. The position that what was good for farmers was not good for organized labor or other interest groups logically could not be sustained. The president's failure to veto the Rural Development Act of 1972 placed the supporters of the bill to create a Department of Community De-

24. *Ibid.,* p. 25.
25. House Committee on Government Operations (overview), *op. cit.,* p. 154.

velopment in an awkward position and made it easier for the Rules Committee to kill the legislation.

Enthusiasm may have cooled because of growing awareness that the sources of bureaucratic power would not be reduced significantly by rearranging the big boxes on the organization chart. The real power centers in the federal structure are the bureaus. Breaking up the constituency-oriented departments might make the secretaries more responsive to the White House, but not necessarily the bureaus. Most secretaries today have difficulty in managing and controlling their departments and without a strong, relatively cohesive constituency their power would be reduced further.

Even if it had succeeded, the "New American Revolution" never would have amounted to more than a paper revolution. This could not be said of the new Cabinet and White House staff relationships established by President Nixon on January 5, 1973, "to revitalize and streamline the Federal Government in preparation for America's third century." As a panel of the National Academy of Public Administration reported to the Senate Select Committee on Presidential Campaign Activities, if it were not for the accidental discovery of the Watergate break-in, the American state might well have been transformed into "Max Weber's ideal type of monocracy, ruled from the top through a strictly disciplined hierarchical system" with impeachment the only means of holding a president accountable.[26]

By White House press release the president created a corporate type of structure with a rigid hierarchy in which

—Access to the president was limited to five assistants to the president (a more accurate description would be assistant presidents).

—Four assistants to the president would act as presi-

26. Frederick C. Mosher and others, *Watergate: Its Implications for Responsible Government,* Basic Books, 1974, p. 11.

dential surrogates with responsibility "to integrate and unify policies and operations" in the following areas: domestic affairs (Ehrlichman); foreign affairs (Kissinger); executive management (Ash); and economic affairs (Shultz).

—Access to the assistants to the president would be limited with some exceptions, to three counsellors (to be housed in the Executive Office Building) for human resources (secretary of HEW), natural resources (secretary of agriculture), and community development (secretary of HUD). An anonymous "think-piece" supplied by the Administration to the Senate Committee on Government Operations indicated that within his assigned area a counsellor would: be informed and make judgments on budget matters; control key personnel positions and manpower strength; provide policy direction on legislation and legislative strategy; and review speeches, testimony, press releases, and internal policy statements.

In effect the president had converted the executive branch into a three-tiered structure with the assistants to the president at the top and department and agency heads (other than those designated as counsellors) at the bottom. The clear intent was to transfer to the president's immediate staff effective control over executive branch policies and programs and to reduce Cabinet officers to an essentially ministerial role. In the words of John Ehrlichman: "There shouldn't be a lot of leeway in following the President's policies. It should be like a corporation, where the executive vice presidents (the Cabinet officers) are tied closely to the chief executive, or to put it in extreme terms, when he says jump, they only ask how high."[27]

White House control over the departments would be main-

27. *Washington Post,* August 24, 1972.

tained directly through key deputies appointed by and reporting to assistants to the president. The *Washington Post* disclosed that over a hundred people formerly employed by the White House, Office of Management and Budget, and Committee to Re-elect the President had been reassigned to departments and occupied such strategic positions as undersecretary (HEW, Interior, Transportation), deputy director OMB, Federal Aviation administrator, and director of the National Parks Service.[28] Politically endorsed appointees recruited by the deputy director of OMB and operating under his general supervision replaced the departmental assistant secretaries for administration, most of whom had been in the career civil service. Assistant secretaries for administration, with their control of budgets, management services, and personnel, were regarded as potentially powerful instruments of control—"an instant bush telegraph into the jungle."[29] President Ford's transition advisers, headed by Secretary of the Interior Rogers C. B. Morton, were highly critical of the OMB role and recommended that steps be taken to prevent OMB from boring holes "below the waterline in the departments."[30]

No doubt as a result of the Watergate disclosures and the resignation of top White House aides, the press was advised in a very low key announcement on May 10, 1973, that the president was reinstituting "a direct line of communication with the Cabinet" and discontinuing the "experiment" with counsellors, except on an informal basis.[31]

President Nixon's organization strategy stemmed from certain ideological biases and his unique interpretation of the president's role within our constitutional system. While he nowhere precisely articulated his philosophy of government, if one puts the bits and pieces together certain basic premises emerge:

28. *Washington Post,* July 19, 1973.
29. *The New York Times,* December 23, 1972.
30. *Washington Post,* August 23, 1974.
31. *Weekly Compilation of Presidential Documents,* May 11, 1973, pp. 662–63.

—As "the President of all the people," the president does and should occupy a superior position to that of the Congress which represents narrow parochial interests.
—As the sole definer and protector of the "national interest," the president has the implied constitutional authority and moral obligation to take such actions as he deems necessary to carry out his responsibilities.
—Protection of the national interest as defined by the president requires undivided loyalty to the president and unquestioning obedience to his orders.
—Department and agency heads function as presidential delegates and powers vested in them by law are, in fact, powers stemming from the president as chief executive.
—Loyalty to the office of the presidency and loyalty to the incumbent are indivisible.
—The bureaucracy or civil service represents the principal threat to presidential power. Members of the civil service cannot be trusted because they are either disloyal or have divided loyalties.

Richard M. Nixon was a self-proclaimed Gaullist. Aaron Wildavsky pointed out that Nixon shared with de Gaulle "a plebiscitary view of the Presidency," one in which the presidency exists wholly apart from other institutions and is at one with the people.[32] This plebiscitary view was reinforced by the "mandate" of November 1972.

The organization strategy developed after the 1972 election was aimed squarely at the vitals of bureaucratic power. Political appointees too narrowly identified with programmatic and constituency interests, or with an independent power base,

32. Aaron Wildavsky, "Government and the People," *Commentary,* August 1973.

were purged. The transition between the first and second terms was as extreme as most transitions from one political party to another.[33] The bureaucracy was neutralized and isolated by (1) leaving major departments "headless" by co-opting the secretaries as assistants to the president and White House counsellors, thus preventing "capture" by the natives; (2) depriving it of resources through revenue sharing and impoundment; and (3) cutting lines of communication by interposing regional councils under White House and OMB control between departments and their agents in the field. The departments were to be allowed to wither away with the White House assuming direct operational responsibility.

The testimony and evidence presented to the Senate Select Committee on Presidential Campaign Activities underscore the serious and disturbing constitutional questions raised by the centralization of power in the White House, the fractionalization of presidential power among assistants to the president, and the assumption that statutory powers of executive agencies automatically vest in the president and his principal assistants.

The Nixon strategy reflected a profound misunderstanding of the executive establishment and its culture and personality. Emmet J. Hughes observed most perceptively: "And the President who dreads this legion of careerists, as a conspiracy bent on his embarrassment or frustration, fails to perceive the realities as completely as the President who wastes dreams on a vision of mobilizing them in an army eager to do battle for his own political success."[34]

33. Frederick C. Mosher, *op. cit.*, pp. 8–9.

34. Emmet J. Hughes, *The Living Presidency*, Coward, McCann & Geoghegan, 1973, p. 186.

5

Carter's "Bottom-Up" Reorganization

If nothing else, President Jimmy Carter shares with Richard M. Nixon a profound distrust of the bureaucracy and faith that bureaucrats can be brought to heel through structural change. As used by President Carter, reorganization appears to be a code word symbolizing citizens' hostility toward intrusive government and frustration with the bureaucratic system. President Carter again stressed this anti-bureaucracy theme in his 1979 State of the Union message in which he stated: "With the support of the Congress, we have begun to reorganize and get control of the bureaucracy."

Jimmy Carter ran for president on a platform of government reorganization. He promised that he would duplicate the success he had in Georgia by drastically reducing the number of agencies and by making the bureaucrats more efficient and responsive. He told the Democratic Platform Committee: "Our government in Washington now is a horrible bureaucratic mess. . . . We must give top priority to a drastic and thorough reorganization of the Federal bureaucracy, to its budgeting system and to the procedures for analyzing the effectiveness of its services."[1] In New Hampshire he advised

1. *Congressional Quarterly,* October 16, 1976, p. 3009.

voters: "Don't vote for me unless you want to see the executive branch of government completely reorganized."[2]

Outsider Jimmy Carter was at a serious disadvantage in debating fundamental issues of foreign and domestic policy with his more experienced rivals for the Democratic nomination. Government reorganization was a safe issue, as long as he avoided specifics, and it was an advantage not to be identified too closely with the existing "bureaucratic mess."

Except for one lapse when he pledged to reduce 1,900 federal agencies to 200, Carter refused to go into the details of his reorganization proposals. Jules Witcover, who covered Carter's primary campaign, concluded that "he was unable or unwilling to be more specific."[3] The 1,900 figure remained an unexplained mystery for some time and apparently included 1,189 advisory committees.

Jimmy Carter as a candidate appeared to recognize that he ran grave political risks by talking about reorganization in other than general terms. As Vice President Walter F. Mondale was to say at a later date: "Organizing the government is very much like cutting the Federal budget. Everyone is for it in principle, but the difficulties and controversies arise when you get specific."[4]

If candidate Jimmy Carter had a well-articulated organization strategy and precise reorganization objectives, these have yet to be revealed by President Jimmy Carter. In his book *Why Not the Best?* Carter argues against an incremental approach and concludes that reorganization proposals are doomed unless "they are bold and comprehensive."[5] President Carter's approach to government reorganization has not been bold or comprehensive. Instead the President's Reorganization

2. Quoted in John R. Dempsey, "Carter Reorganization: A Midterm Appraisal," *Public Administration Review,* Vol. 39, No. 1, January–February 1979.
3. Jules Witcover, *Marathon,* New American Library, 1978, p. 221.
4. Rochelle Stanfield, "The Reorganization Staff is Big Loser in Latest Shuffle," *National Journal,* March 10, 1979.
5. Jimmy Carter, *Why Not The Best?,* Bantam Books, 1976, p. 172.

Project has adopted "an incremental, people-centered, bottom-up approach."[6] The "bottom-up approach" was proclaimed as an innovative method of analyzing organization structure as it affects people directly, and not looking at it from the top down as was done in previous reorganization studies.[7]

The reorganizers appeared to assume that the people would be able to tell them what should be reorganized, or at least give them the clues as to the trouble spots. By letter of June 24, 1977, Richard A. Pettigrew, assistant to the president for reorganization, invited citizens to submit comments on reorganization issues to "assist both in guiding initial studies and in identifying additional reorganization priorities." Approximately 2,000 replies were received. According to staff, none were useful and a number were typical crank letters. Few citizens are concerned with or directly affected by the structure of federal agencies or the subtleties of bureaucratic politics.

Jimmy Carter has been called, perhaps unfairly, "the first process President."[8] But up to now the President's Reorganization Project clearly has emphasized the *how* above the *what* and *why*. Innovations appear to be limited to the methods and tactics of conducting reorganization studies.

No unifying theme or set of innovative organizational principles can be discerned from analysis of Carter's proposals for Departments of Energy, and Education, as well as for civil service reform and consumer protection. The same can be said for his reorganization plans for the Executive Office of the President, International Communication Agency, Equal

6. Statement by Richard A. Pettigrew, Assistant to the President for Reorganization, at meeting of the American Society for Public Administration on "Reorganizing the Federal Establishment," Washington, D.C., December 1–2, 1977.

7. Richard A. Pettigrew, "Improving Government Competence," *Publius,* Vol. 8, No. 2, Spring 1978.

8. Thomas E. Cronin, "The Carter Presidency," *National Journal,* Reprint Series, "The Carter Presidency: The White House at Mid-Term," 1978–79.

Employment Opportunity Commission, Federal Emergency Management Agency, and Employment Retirement Income Security Act. Except for civil service reform, none can be related specifically to Carter's goal of energizing and controlling the bureaucracy.

Overall reorganization objectives are described in almost meaningless generalities—streamlining the government and making it more competent to serve the people. Specific proposals are justified mainly by reference to orthodox doctrines: elimination of overlapping and duplication, consolidation of related functions, improved economy and efficiency, and more effective planning and coordination.

Absence of organization "principles" is regarded as a virtue, not a vice, by the Carter reorganizers. Harrison Wellford, executive associate director of the Office of Management and Budget for reorganization and management, emphasized: "We're not operating under the assumption that the government is so simple that it can be reorganized according to one or two basic principles."[9] The pragmatic and *ad hoc* approach to reorganization was explained by OMB Director James T. McIntyre, Jr., as (1) concentrating on solving problems; (2) looking for the least disruptive remedies to identified problems; and (3) following a process committed to openness and public and congressional involvement.[10]

Congressmen John W. Wydler, Thomas N. Kindness, and Arlan Strangeland were highly critical of the absence of a "defensible administrative theory" in objecting to President Carter's first reorganization plan restructuring the Executive Office of the President.[11] In their dissent they wrote: "Aside from this highly dubious 'shell game' of showing more or

9. Jean Conley and Joel Havemann, "Reorganization—Two Plans, One Department Down, Much More to Come," *National Journal,* December 3, 1977.

10. Senate Committee on Governmental Affairs, hearing on nomination of James T. McIntyre, Jr., to be director of the Office of Management and Budget, March 16, 1978, p. 39.

11. House Report No. 95–661, 95th Congress, 1st session, p. 60.

fewer employees in any particular part of an organization chart, a reader will search in vain for any indication of a basic premise underlying the plan. This is one of its most serious shortcomings."

Without a well-conceived presidential organization strategy and agreed upon organization concepts, reorganization proposals are highly vulnerable to attack on political grounds. Reorganizations attract many enemies and almost no friends. A major Carter mistake was to deal with reorganization as if it were a purpose in itself divorced from policy and program development.

The comprehensive plans developed over two years by the President's Reorganization Project to consolidate fragmented programs in four areas—economic and community development, natural resources, food and nutrition, and trade—into four Cabinet departments were shot down in whole or in part by the White House staff. The proposals were written off as politically naïve. Senior White House aides "raised serious questions about the wisdom of advancing such controversial proposals at a time when the Administration will be battling with the Congress on many other fronts."[12]

The plans for a Department of Development Assistance, a Food and Nutrition Department, and a Trade Department were dropped altogether. The plan for a Department of Natural Resources emerged in an emasculated form without the water resource functions and finally was abandoned because of strong opposition by key members of the Congress.

In light of the political heat generated by the congressional committees, clientele groups, and others whose turf was threatened by proposed reorganizations, President Carter was advised "to point to civil service reform, declare victory in reorganization and withdraw from the field."[13]

12. Rochelle Stanfield, "The Best Laid Reorganization Plans Sometimes Go Astray," *National Journal*, January 20, 1979.
13. *Ibid*.

Organizational errors made in the initial program design rarely can be undone by subsequent reorganizations, or can be undone only at considerable cost. Presumably, the expertise developed by the President's Reorganization Project would have been useful to the White House staff concerned with program development, but it was seldom utilized. As in past administrations, decisions have been dictated by political expediency. HEW Secretary Joseph A. Califano, Jr., admitted that when he served in the Johnson White House "often we didn't know where to put a program . . . and we didn't particularly care where it went; we just wanted to make sure it got enacted. That's one reason why the government is disorganized now."[14]

The Carter administration's credibility as experts in government organization is shaken when the president cannot decide whether the secretary of HUD, commerce, or treasury should be given control of a proposed National Development Bank. A compromise vesting administration of the Bank in a triumvirate consisting of the three secretaries obviously carried within it the seeds of future organization problems. The bank proposal has since been abandoned.

The incremental, people-centered, bottom-up approach to reorganization implies an absence of presidential direction and leadership. For President Carter reorganization appears primarily to represent fulfillment of a campaign commitment, not an opportunity to alter the distribution of power within the government in ways which would support accomplishment of his long-range programmatic goals and strengthen the institution of the presidency.

The President's Reorganization Project is a project, or series of projects, not a program. Project teams have been organized to undertake organization studies in discrete functional areas such as border law enforcement, disaster preparedness, edu-

14. Timothy B. Clark, "The Power Vacuum Outside the Oval Office," *National Journal*, February 24, 1979.

cation, economic analysis, food and nutrition, and small agency reduction. None have been assigned responsibility for examining the total government system and identifying problems cutting across functional lines or common to all agencies. Consequently, critical issues have been ignored by the project staff. These include the proliferation of institutions and legislative provisions undermining presidential power, such as government-sponsored enterprises and nonprofit enterprises, exemptions from the president's budget, annual authorization of executive departments, and the legislative veto. The piece-meal incremental approach inevitably has yielded piece-meal results.

If Carter's reorganizations are evaluated individually, his record is quite impressive and compares favorably with that of most other presidents. Civil service reform is a significant achievement, as is the reorganization creating the Department of Energy. The Reorganization Project has also contributed to management improvement in other areas such as cash management, paperwork reduction, and regulatory reform. However, measured against President Carter's expressed goal of energizing and controlling the bureaucracy and making a substantive change in the government's behavior and outlook, his reorganization program thus far must be judged a failure. Ronald C. Moe, Specialist in American National Government, Congressional Research Service, has concluded: "On balance, the President's reorganization effort has resulted in more, not fewer, agencies and in more agencies and programs being placed outside direct accountability to the President."[15]

There appears to be little understanding of what can and cannot be accomplished by structural change. The one exception is civil service reform where reorganization was linked with a fundamental revision of the civil service system and basic laws and regulations. Abolition of the Civil Service Com-

15. Ronald C. Moe, "The Reorganization Efforts at Mid-Term," Congressional Research Service Report No. 79–56, January 20, 1979, p. 10.

mission and creation of the Office of Personnel Management and Merit System Protection Board, while justified on their own merits, could not have been expected to produce anything more than marginal progress.

The results at midterm are disproportionate to President Carter's huge investment of political capital, time, and staff resources. Preoccupation with reorganization has diverted attention from more critical systemic problems, particularly the development of control systems and arbitrary constraints such as personnel ceilings which deter effective administration without producing compensating benefits. Reorganization is a means to an end, not an end in itself. Development of an organization strategy and reorganization proposals should *follow,* not precede, the establishment of the president's program goals and priorities.

6

The Executive Establishment: Culture and Personality

Until the Congress declared by law in 1978 that all presidential records were federal property, a president's office files were deemed to be his private property and were taken with him when he left the White House.[1] In theory at least, an incoming president started with a clean slate. Obviously a president's freedom is circumscribed by the need for continuity, political commitments, tradition, and accepted norms of presidential behavior, but within these limits he retains considerable discretion to organize and staff his household as he sees fit, determine his work priorities, and develop his own style and interpretation of the presidential role. In Woodrow Wilson's words, each president has the freedom "to be as big a man as he can."[2]

Department heads seldom start with a clean slate. Generally they must adapt to the institution, rather than the institution to them. There are likely to be daily reminders that they are merely temporary custodians and spokesmen for organizations

1. H. G. Jones, *The Records of a Nation,* Atheneum, 1969, p. 160.

2. Quoted in Richard E. Neustadt, *Presidential Power,* John Wiley & Sons, Inc., 1960, p. 5.

with distinct and multi-dimensional personalities and deeply ingrained cultures and subcultures reflecting institutional history, ideology, values, symbols, folklore, professional biases, behavior patterns, heroes, and enemies. The individual style of department heads must not do violence to the institutional mystique, and the words they speak and the positions they advocate cannot ignore the precedents recorded in the departmental archives. Most department heads are free only to be as big as the president, the bureaucracy, the Congress, and their constituencies will allow them to be.

A Cabinet member is confronted with all the problems of an actor type-cast to take over the lead role in a long-run classical drama. The audience expects the part to be played in a certain way and will react hostilely to departures from the main lines of characterization set by generations of previous actors. Responses different from those in the prepared script are highly disturbing to the bureaucracy and the principal constituencies in the Congress and the outside community upon whom a department head must rely for support. It would be as unthinkable for a secretary of agriculture to question the innate goodness of the rural way of life and the inherent virtues of the family farm as it would be for an OMB director to be against economy and efficiency.

Whatever his background and individual bent, a secretary of the treasury, for example, is obliged to play the part of a "sound" money man. Given the setting in which he performs, it would be very difficult for him to do otherwise. One only has to walk into the ancient Treasury Department building adjoining the White House to sense the atmosphere of a conservative financial institution. The money cage at the main entry way, the gilt pilasters, the gold-framed portraits on the walls, all reinforce the Treasury "image." As the leader of a rugged "outdoors-type" department, a secretary of the interior is not out of character when he climbs mountains, shoots the Colorado River rapids, and organizes well-publicized hiking and jogging expeditions. Identical conduct by the secretary of the treasury would shake the financial community to its core.

Program transplants which are alien to the institutional culture and environment seldom take root and are threatened with rejection. Franklin Roosevelt recognized this risk when he vetoed the Brownlow Committee's suggestion that federal loan programs be placed under the Treasury. Roosevelt advised Brownlow: "That won't work. If they put them in the Treasury, not one of them will ever make a loan to anybody for any purpose. There are too many glass-eyed bankers in the Treasury."[3]

A department head who cannot adapt to the institutional environment also runs the risk of rejection. Appointment by the president and confirmation by the Senate are no guarantee of institutional loyalty. Former Attorney General and later Chief Justice Harlan F. Stone is reported to have said of FBI Director J. Edgar Hoover: "If Hoover trusted you, he would be absolutely loyal; if he did not, you had better look out; and he had to get used to his new chief each time."[4] Among bureau chiefs, Hoover was unique in power and influence, but not in his attitude toward his nominal political superiors.

Cabinet members have much in common with the university president who observed ruefully: "Universities may have presidents, but presidents don't have universities." The plain truth is that such powerful subordinate organizations as the Federal Highway Administration, Army Corps of Engineers, Public Health Service, National Park Service, and Forest Service constitute the departmental power centers and are quite capable of making it on their own without secretarial help, except when challenged by strong hostile external forces. Often they can do more for the secretary than he can do for them.

3. A. J. Wann, *The President as Chief Administrator—A Study of Franklin D. Roosevelt,* Public Affairs Press, 1968, pp. 103–4.

4. Francis Biddle, *In Brief Authority,* Doubleday & Co., Inc., 1962, p. 257.

Institutional loyalty is not as crucial when the secretarial role is discrete and separable from that of department head. The secretaries of state, treasury, and at times, defense tend to function more as staff advisers to the president than as administrators of complex institutions. Their effectiveness and influence are only coincidentally related to their access to institutional resources. Upon occasion, presidents have utilized Cabinet officers essentially as ministers without portfolio, notably the postmaster general and attorney general, offices which have been occupied by political party chairmen, campaign managers, legislative strategists, or others who were appointed to serve in a noninstitutional capacity as presidential advisers.

For the secretaries of agriculture, commerce, energy, health, education, and welfare, housing and urban development, interior, labor, and transportation, as well as the heads of the major independent agencies, the secretarial or agency head and institutional roles cannot be divorced. Without the loyalty, or at least neutrality, of their principal bureau chiefs, these officials can be little more than highly ornamental figureheads. As such, they are powerless to advance the president's objectives either within their agencies or with their constituencies. The paradox is that a president ultimately may be best served by an agency head who is willing to risk occasional presidential displeasure to defend his agency's territory and vital interests. Once he has established his credibility within his agency, he can be much more effective in achieving his own goals and mobilizing support for the president's program.

The political executive is the proverbial man in the middle —what James E. Webb identifies as "the main point of impact in the relationships between the endeavor and its environment."[5] Based on his experience as NASA administrator, Webb recognizes that a department head has twofold and sometimes conflicting responsibilities:

5. James E. Webb, *Space-Age Management,* McGraw-Hill Book Co., 1969, p. 128.

> . . . he has to represent within the endeavor the outside environmental factors—the Federal Government, the President and the administration in all its facets, the Congress, and the national public; he has to make sure that the endeavor's goals and activities are responsive to the requirements and desires of the environment under conditions of rapid change and uncertainty.
>
> At the same time, the executive represents the entire endeavor as against the environment. He has the ultimate responsibility for securing from the environment the support necessary for gaining and sustaining momentum, for safeguarding against dysfunctional forces seeking control and influence, for—in short—keeping the endeavor viable and on course toward its goals.
>
> The executive can do none of these inside or outside tasks alone. He must bind his associates to his objectives and to his team, even though they may hardly understand all the forces that are at work.[6]

While presidents are not unmindful of the need to fit the man to the institution, the time has passed when presidents felt bound to appoint secretaries of labor from the ranks of organized labor or "dirt farmers" as secretaries of agriculture. However, these kinds of restraints do persist for some sub-Cabinet posts. President Nixon conceded the right of the National Science Board to nominate the director of the National Science Foundation, although this was the very issue that caused President Truman to veto the original National Science Foundation Act.[7] President Nixon was doing nothing more than acknowledging overtly what had been the actual practice since 1948. No president has named a director who did not have the board's approval, even though there is no statutory bar to his doing so. President Nixon was unwilling to press for his choice of an assistant secretary of Health, Education, and Welfare for Health and Scientific Affairs in the face of strong objections by the American Medical Association.

6. *Ibid.*
7. *Washington Post,* April 29, 1969.

The restraints applicable to Cabinet appointments are of two kinds. Custom still requires that the secretary of the interior be from the West or Middle West and that the secretary of agriculture, if not a "dirt farmer," be from an agricultural state and have a farm background and preferably a land grant college education. The attorney general must be, of course, a lawyer, and the secretaries of commerce, labor, and treasury must be individuals who have the confidence of their respective constituencies—organized business, organized labor, and the financial community. The second and overriding restraint, however, is the need to find someone who is *simpatico* and subscribes to the basic institutional outlook, goals, and values. To appoint a known critic of an agency's program, as President Eisenhower did in naming John Hollister as foreign aid administrator, or to select a Henry Wallace or a Harry Hopkins as secretary of commerce, is almost the equivalent of a presidential vote of "no confidence" in the agency's program.

The degree to which the original Nixon Cabinet members were cut from much the same cloth as their Democratic predecessors was no accident. The differences represented those which were found within any professional or institutional family, and not those with rank outsiders. This is not to minimize the fact that family differences may be real and bitter, but they seldom are carried so far as to jeopardize institutional survival. Party labels tend to mean less than social and economic status and background, education, professional and constituency ties, and geographic origins.

Secretaries of Labor Shultz and Wirtz were from Chicago and traveled in much the same labor, business, and academic circles. Secretary Shultz served as adviser to the Department of Labor under both the Kennedy and Johnson administrations and was not unknown to the departmental bureaucracy. Shultz probably had more in common with the Democrat whom he succeeded than he had with most of his Cabinet colleagues. The same could be said of Secretary of the Treasury Kennedy, whose predecessors included investment banker and fellow Republican Douglas Dillon and Secretary of Commerce Stans, who represented much the same part of the business community as such corporate executives as Secretaries Connor and Smith who served under President Johnson. Secretary Kennedy also served as an adviser to the Johnson administration and was well acquainted with the upper echelons of the Treasury bureaucracy.

Republican Secretaries of Agriculture and Interior, Nebraskan Clifford Hardin and Alaskan Walter Hickel, conformed closely to the prototypes for their departments, as did the Democrats, Minnesotan Orville Freeman and Arizonan Stewart Udall. Secretary Hardin spoke for a somewhat different faction of the agricultural establishment than Secretary Freeman, but as the chancellor and former dean of agriculture of a land grant college, he was entirely at home in the Department of Agriculture with its deeply rooted land grant college traditions. While President Nixon's appointees as secretaries of state, defense, HUD, HEW and transportation, attorney general, and postmaster general were drawn from communities different from their Democratic counterparts, none was identified with elements adverse to established departmental interests. In selecting his Cabinet members, President Carter was also sensitive to constituency and bureaucratic interests, and appointments adhered to traditional criteria.

As one descends the hierarchical scale, the distinctive departmental colorations come into focus even more sharply. Undersecretaries and assistant secretaries are less likely than secretaries to be generalists or people with broad political background. Sub-Cabinet appointments tend to mirror the diverse clientele groups, dependencies such as defense contractors, construction companies, educational institutions, and professional organizations which constitute an agency's constituency.

His examination of the personal and career characteristics of

800 men who served as assistant secretaries from 1933 to 1961 has led Dean E. Mann to emphasize the marked differences among departments and agencies. He groups sub-Cabinet appointments within seven categories: State and Defense, professionals and professional amateurs; Treasury, the specialists; Justice, politics and the law; Post Office, politicians and businessmen; Interior and Agriculture, politics, pressure groups, and policy; Commerce and Labor, clientele politics; Health, Education, and Welfare, politics and expertise; and the independent agencies, a mixed bag.[8] If one were to update Mann's categories, there would have to be added the professions, educational institutions, and state and local government constituents who are now heavily represented in such departments as HUD, HEW, and Transportation, as well as in some of the old-line departments.

A biographical profile of federal political executives prepared by David Stanley, Dean Mann, and Jameson Doig revealed significant differences among departments with respect to geographic origins and education as well as other personal characteristics.[9] As might be expected, the highest concentration of political executives from the West was to be found in Interior, and from the Middle West in Agriculture. Interior and Agriculture executives also tended to be from communities under 100,000. On the other hand, big-city boys from the East monopolized the top jobs in such agencies as Treasury, Defense, the military departments, and Commerce. The study also identified important social and educational distinctions. While a high percentage of political executives were graduates of "name" prep schools such as Groton, Choate, and Exeter, Agriculture and Interior, true to their bucolic image, did not have a single prep school alumnus among their political executives.

8. Dean E. Mann and Jameson W. Doig, *The Assistant Secretaries,* The Brookings Institution, 1965, pp. 32–60.

9. David T. Stanley, Dean E. Mann, and Jameson W. Doig, *Men Who Govern,* The Brookings Institution, 1967.

The process by which political executives are fitted to their institutions often produces people who talk the same language as the members of their oversight congressional committees. A city-bred prep school product would be as out of place before the Agriculture Committees, as an Easterner would be before the Interior Committees. This rapport facilitates smooth working relationships, but it does not always operate to the president's advantage, particularly when he is seeking basic program changes which challenge entrenched departmental and constituency interests.

Hubert Humphrey may have complained with some justice that "Every once in awhile one gets the view down here in Washington that the respective departments are members of the United Nations, and that each has a separate sovereignty."[10] But if all department heads were cast from the same mold and always spoke in unison with the president, could our pluralistic political system as we now know it survive? It may be doubted that either the national interests or, in the final analysis, those of the president himself would be best served if departments were headed by agnostics who did not believe in the goals and values of the institutions they administered.

Admittedly there are dangers in the present system. Institutional myths and symbols may be worshiped for their own sake long after they have lost their original meaning. Institutional loyalties may be internalized with the result that programatic goals are displaced, and institutional, professional, or bureaucratic survival and aggrandizement become the overriding objectives. These dysfunctional influences are latent in almost all organizations. Most susceptible are agencies with obsolete, static, or contracting programs or those that are highly in-bred, such as the military, Foreign Service, and Public Health Service.

Organizational behavior can be modified and redirected by substituting new program goals, redesigning administrative

10. Speech before National Housing Policy Forum, February 14, 1967.

systems, altering standards for recruitment and promotion, reorganization, training, and indoctrination. To be effective as a "change-agent" takes what few secretaries possess—leadership, a profound knowledge of institutional mores and programs, and, above all, time. Turnover among secretaries is high and few serve for a full presidential term. President Nixon exceeded President Grant's record of twenty-six Cabinet appointees in eight years with thirty in five years. One fact is clear, however. Presidents seldom evaluate Cabinet appointees in terms of their potential as change-agents. As we have seen, appointments generally go to conformists.

In selecting their Cabinets, presidents tacitly acknowledge what the orthodox organization theorists ignore—each major agency and its component elements symbolize certain widely-held social values and bring a unique perspective to the councils of government. What has been described as the "machinery of Government" is not a machine with interchangeable parts. The Hoover Commission remedies for the manifest ills besetting the executive branch—removal of legal impediments to presidential and secretarial control over their subordinates and a neater arrangement of the boxes on the organization chart—are simple and logical but treat the symptoms rather than the disease.

Attempts to solve structural defects without knowledge or understanding of the institutional psyche or the environmental factors that condition organizational behavior are bound to fail and may produce severe traumas. Reorganizations are major surgery and should not be prescribed as a cure for personality problems. If reorganizations are indicated, under no circumstances should a physician trained only in anatomy be allowed to operate.

Government agencies are social institutions. Social psychologists would concur in the opening sentences of the official Labor Department history which read: "In fifty years an institution, just as a person, takes on a character and develops attitudes which distinguish it from all others. The Department of Labor is no exception."[11] Such common expressions as "the military mind" and the "Navy way" recognize that institutions do have an individual personality and outlook, but we rarely associate this phenomenon with civilian agencies. While each of the major departments has its own special character, these personality traits may or may not be shared fully by its principal subordinate bureaus. Attorney General Robert Kennedy's failure to understand the unique culture and language of the FBI, what Victor Navasky calls "Bureau-speak," constituted a major obstacle to achieving Kennedy administration goals of promoting civil rights and combating organized crime.[12] Deviations occur most frequently among the professional officer corps and in bureaus with limited missions and narrow constituencies. The Bureau of the Budget once was advised bluntly that the "Secretary of State does not necessarily speak for the State Department" when it cited conflicts between the secretary's views and those advocated by a foreign service representative. There is a Department of Agriculture culture, but there is also an Extension Service culture, REA culture, Soil Conservation Service culture, and Forest Service culture. These are not always compatible and sometimes produce conflicts.

According to social psychologists, "social systems are anchored in the attitudes, perceptions, beliefs, motivations, habits, and expectations of human beings."[13] A major unifying force in any organization is what Chester Barnard terms "associational attractiveness."[14] Men seek favorable associational conditions from their viewpoint and tend to gravitate to organ-

11. U.S. Department of Labor, *The Anvil and the Plow,* Washington, 1963.
12. Victor S. Navasky, *Kennedy Justice,* Atheneum, 1971. For a discussion of bureaucratic culture, see Morton H. Halperin, *Bureaucratic Politics and Foreign Policy,* The Brookings Institution, 1974.
13. Daniel Katz and Robert L. Kahn, *The Social Psychology of Organization,* John Wiley & Sons, Inc., 1966, p. 33.
14. Chester I. Barnard, *The Functions of the Executive,* Harvard University Press, 1942, p. 146.

izations which share their personal values and norms and where they can work comfortably with colleagues of the same professional, educational, and social backgrounds. For this reason, career executives do not transfer freely from one department to another. In 1975 approximately two thirds of the career executives had worked in the same agency since reaching the middle grade. Only 12 percent of supergrade executives had worked in three or more agencies after attaining the middle grade.[15] Whatever movement there is normally takes place within the foreign affairs, science, intelligence, and budgeting communities, where interagency relationships are particularly close or within the established professions such as law, engineering, and accounting.

The American Civil Service is distinguished from the classical European bureaucracies by its identification with program and professional objectives. Primary loyalty is given to the profession, program, bureau, and department, probably in that order, and not to the Civil Service career system. The exceptions again are the Foreign Service, Public Health Service, and Environmental Science Service which adhere more closely to the classical bureaucratic pattern. In those cases, loyalty is given to the service rather than to the program or to the department. The corps systems are characterized by rank-in-man (Civil Service grades depend on job classification), entry at junior levels with a commitment to a career within the service, periodic rotation in job assignments, and, perhaps most important, selection and promotion based on the judgment of one's senior officers. Like the military officers corps, these are "closed systems." Interference by politicians or other outsiders in the selection and promotion processes is viewed as the "gravest impropriety."[16]

15. Hugh Heclo, *A Government of Strangers: Executive Politics in Washington,* The Brookings Institution, 1977, p. 117.

16. A typical example is Admiral King's reactions to Secretary Forrestal's tampering with the established promotion processes in the U.S. Navy. See Ernest J. King and Walter M. Whitehill, *Fleet Admiral King—A Naval Record,* W. W. Norton & Co., Inc., 1952, p. 635.

We can find almost all stratas of American society and all geographical areas represented in the United States government, but their distribution among the various agencies, bureaus, and services is by no means uniform and there are striking divergences. An undersecretary of state could write in 1923 "that no man who was not possessed of a large income should be admitted to the diplomatic service."[17] While personal wealth is no longer a criterion, the concept of the Foreign Service as a "gentleman's club" persists. George Kennan has deplored efforts to dilute the Foreign Service elite by opening up the doors to Civil Service employees or others who did not meet the club's traditional standards. Kennan told the Jackson Subcommittee:

> I am frank to say that I cannot conceive of an effective foreign service otherwise than as a gentlemen's service, not in the sense that it would be based on distinctions of birth or social status, but in the sense that reliance would be placed at all times on the honor and the sense of obligation of the individual officer himself, and he would be treated with the confidence and consideration customary in circles where high standards of honor and responsibility are assumed to prevail.[18]

A gentlemen's club has an appeal for a special type of individual. The very small proportion of college seniors interested in Foreign Service careers were found by Frances Fielder and Godfrey Harris to have remarkably similar personal backgrounds.[19] They came from higher-income groups than their contemporaries, and included relatively few from minority races or religions. Their college education had been concen-

17. Katherine Crane, *Mr. Carr of State—Forty-seven Years in the Department of State,* St. Martin's Press, 1960, p. 261.

18. Senate Committee on Government Operations, "Organizing for National Security," Hearings, Vol. 1, p. 807.

19. Frances Fielder and Godfrey Harris, *The Quest for Foreign Affairs Officers —Their Recruitment and Selection,* Carnegie Endowment for International Peace, 1966.

trated in the liberal arts field. Those students who specialized in business administration and management or in technical, scientific, or professional fields were not attracted to the Foreign Service.

Even more striking was the distribution by educational institution of the 3,815 applicants for the Foreign Service in 1961. Fully, 30 percent of the applicants came from a handful of mostly "prestige" institutions with the Universities of California, Georgetown, Harvard, Princeton, and Yale ranking among the five highest in the number of undergraduate applicants. The top five at the graduate level were Columbia, California, Harvard, Johns Hopkins, and Georgetown. Measured by successful applicants, the ranking was Princeton, Dartmouth, Yale, Georgetown, and Harvard.[20]

The percentage of Foreign Service officers from the big three—Harvard, Yale, and Princeton—has declined from 34.9 percent in 1924–1932 to 16.8 percent in 1961. Nonetheless, the percentage of career minister appointments going to Harvard, Yale, and Princeton alumni has gone up during the period since 1946, from 25.3 percent (1946–1953) to 38.2 percent (1954–1961).[21]

The Foreign Service appeal also varies considerably in accordance with geography. The Middle Atlantic states are heavily over-represented and produce approximately one third of all Foreign Service officers. No less than 44.6 percent of the officer appointees in 1960–1961 came from the Middle Atlantic states and New England as compared with 13.2 percent from the Pacific and Rocky Mountain states, and 5 percent from the South.[22]

Efforts to broaden the base of the Foreign Service have not been notably successful. That inbreeding is a source of concern

20. *Ibid.*

21. David R. Segal and Daniel H. Willick, "The Reinforcement of Traditional Career Patterns in Agencies Under Stress," *Public Administration Review,* Vol. 28, No. 1, 1968.

22. Fielder and Harris, *op. cit.,* p. 25.

even for some members of the service itself is evidenced by the interim report of the American Foreign Service Association's Committee on Career Principles published in 1967. The report cites the "closed nature of the foreign service" as a major cause of "organizational ineffectiveness," and isolation from "outsiders with new or unorthodox ideas" as a natural consequence of the desire to "maintain a guild-like structure."

Once the military also was thought of as a gentlemen's profession. Personal conduct of both the Foreign Service officer and the professional soldier is strongly motivated by a sense of honor and duty. Yet those who find associational attractiveness in military service have little in common with our diplomats. Morris Janowitz stresses that "the out-of-doors existence, the concern with nature, sport, and weapons which is a part of rural culture, have a direct carry-over to the requirements of the pre-technological military establishment."[23] The military profession has provided career opportunities which were not otherwise available to rural residents.

Unlike members of the Foreign Service, professional military officers are overwhelmingly of rural and small town origin. Almost 70 percent of our military leaders in 1950 had rural backgrounds. Whereas the Middle Atlantic and New England states are over-represented in the foreign service, the South is over-represented among the military elite. Janowitz cites 46 percent of Army general officers and 44 percent of Navy officers of flag rank as having Southern affiliations.[24]

The training given in the service academies has a direct bearing on the service culture and standards of behavior. Academy education emphasizes personal honor and the distinctive qualities which are essential for membership in the military brotherhood. Academy graduates have a virtual monopoly of the general officer or comparable posts, except for

23. Morris Janowitz, *The Professional Soldier—A Social and Political Portrait,* The Free Press of Glencoe, 1960, p. 85.

24. *Ibid.* All data is from Janowitz.

approximately 25 percent of Army Major and Brigadier Generals who are not West Point products.[25]

The U.S. Coast Guard shares many of the characteristics of the Army and Navy. A majority of cadets are from small towns and suburbia. Only 3.8 percent of the class of 1974 at the Coast Guard Academy were raised in a large city and over 50 percent came from communities with populations of less than 25,000. The Academy draws primarily from "middle class" and "upper middle class" socioeconomic groups, and the overwhelming majority of cadets classify themselves as "political moderates."

To a greater degree than the other military services, the Coast Guard stresses technical competence. The Coast Guard perceives itself as an organization in which engineering has primacy. The broadening of the Academy curriculum in 1965 to include social science, oceanography, and management sciences upset the traditionalists who believed the primary emphasis should continue to be on training in engineering.[26]

The military services have not consciously given preference to individuals with rural backgrounds. Until 1966, farm or ranch background was a specific requirement for employment in such Department of Agriculture agencies as the Soil Conservation Service and Farmers Home Administration. The Department of Agriculture has its equivalent of the service academies in the land grant colleges. The Joint Committee of the Department of Agriculture and Land Grant Universities on Education for Government Service was established in 1936. The committee's major purpose is to consider "matters relating to the educational background, training, and courses of study needed by college students to qualify for employment with the U.S. Department of Agriculture."[27]

25. Segal and Willick, *op. cit.*

26. Gary Russell, "The Bureaucratic Culture and Personality of the U.S. Coast Guard," unpublished master's thesis, The University of Connecticut, 1974.

27. Secretary of Agriculture, Memorandum No. 1412, Revised, March 14, 1968.

Most of the Department of Agriculture's elite, including scientists and most secretaries, have been exposed to land grant college training and the traditions of those institutions. Agriculture supergrades are nearly monopolized by those holding bachelor's and advanced degrees from land grant colleges. The principal producers of Agriculture supergrades in order of ranking are Iowa State, Minnesota, Michigan State, Wisconsin, California, and Illinois. In contrast, Treasury senior career staff earned their academic degrees predominantly from local District of Columbia institutions such as George Washington and Georgetown, and Harvard, Chicago, Columbia, and City College of New York.

Whatever their other virtues, the old "cow colleges" were not known for producing social theorists and critics. One of Henry Wallace's aides observed: "There was a wide difference in the accustomed thought and training of most Land Grant college graduates and most liberally educated urbanites. . . . Land Grant college graduates were extraordinarily landlord minded in the main."[28] Some of our foremost academic institutions are land grant colleges, and the number of colleges which continue to give primary emphasis to technical training in the agricultural and mechanical arts is dwindling. The liberalization of land grant college curricula may well mean that the next generation of the Agriculture Department elite will be more disposed to question traditional producer-oriented policies.

The West, North Central, and Mountain regions are disproportionately represented at the supergrade levels in the Department of Agriculture, and, as might be expected, the Department of the Interior also draws heavily on the Mountain region for the supergrades. The Middle Atlantic region is substantially over-represented among HEW supergrades and, to a lesser extent, the South Atlantic region.

28. Ross B. Talbot and Don F. Hadwiger, *The Policy Process in American Agriculture,* Chandler Publishing Co., 1968, p. 237.

In some respects the postal service is the most narrowly based of all federal institutions. Most employees enter at the bottom (only 2 percent do not) and spend their whole careers in a single post office. Eight out of ten postal workers enter and retire from the service at the same grade level, PFS-5. Supervisory personnel, other than postmasters, are selected from the ranks of carriers and clerks, but, as a rule, promotional opportunities are limited to a particular post office or, as in Seattle, the postal region. Minority groups supply nearly 22 percent of all postal employees, in marked contrast to the rest of the federal bureaucracy. The Post Office is the most highly unionized federal agency. Over 620,000 of its employees, approximately 87.5 percent, belong to one or more of twelve labor unions and employee associations.[29]

To speak of the federal bureaucracy as if it were a homogeneous entity is obviously most misleading. About the only thing that some federal employees have in common is that they are paid by the U.S. Treasury. Each group or subgroup has identifiable characteristics which motivate its behavior. A congenial or tolerable organizational environment for one group may be highly repellent to another. There is limited movement among the groups, but this is in part due to people seeking their right niche, as well as promotion opportunities. A small number have transferred by lateral entry from the Department of Agriculture and Defense establishment to the Foreign Service, but we doubt that any diplomat has ever considered seriously transfer to such agencies as the Post Office or Soil Conservation Service.

Most agencies conduct "orientation" programs for new employees, and several, notably the Forest Service and Marine Corps, have devised sophisticated techniques for making true

29. The President's Commission on Postal Organization, *Toward Postal Excellence,* U.S. Government Printing Office, 1968, pp. 14–18 and Study 3, "Postal Manpower."

believers out of their recruits.[30] Formal indoctrination is seldom necessary, however. Professional employees who remain with an agency for any length of time in part "co-opt" themselves. It is true that people shape an institution. But an institution also shapes its personnel.

The kinds of people an agency attracts, its organization, policy positions, and responses to environmental influences are conditioned by a complex of tangible and intangible forces. To understand an agency's organization and behavior, one must first know its history, program patterns, administrative processes, professional hierarchies, constituencies, and budget structure.

Many agency traits are acquired; others are inherited. For example, the Atomic Energy Commission's internal organization structure was modeled on that of the Tennessee Valley Authority, which furnished the commission's first chairman, David Lilienthal. The policy of hiring private concerns to manage and operate atomic energy facilities was initiated by the U.S. Army Corps of Engineers when it ran the Manhattan Project and could have been reversed by the Commission only at the risk of major disruptions to the program. While the AEC subsequently developed an elaborate rationale to justify the policy of contracting out its work, the Corps of Engineers was doing nothing more than conducting its business as usual when it commenced the practice.[31] The Corps traditionally has performed its civil functions through contractors, who provide much of its political muscle, and was not organized and staffed to construct and operate atomic energy facilities with its own personnel, even if it had believed that direct operations would be preferable.

30. For a description of the Forest Service techniques see Herbert Kaufman, *The Forest Ranger—A Study in Administrative Behavior,* The Johns Hopkins Press, 1960.

31. See Ninth Semiannual Report of the Atomic Energy Commission, January 31, 1951.

Government officials have an instinctive drive to reproduce the organizations, systems, and procedures with which they are most familiar. When asked to develop a self-financing plan for the rural electrification program, Agriculture inevitably proposed an exact duplicate of the farm credit banks. The regulatory commissions invariably insist that new regulatory programs be administered by multi-headed bodies. NASA is a missionary for project managers, Community Services Administration for community organizations which provide for maximum feasible participation of the poor, and HEW for grants to single-state agencies. Sometimes the motivation is self-protection. David Lilienthal believed that TVA would be vulnerable as long as it remained the only institution of its kind and, therefore, he wanted the TVA model to be duplicated in other parts of the country. Organizational eccentricities are often directly traceable to the institutional biases of the legislative draftsmen and first administrators.

It does not take much digging for an organization archeologist to uncover evidence of prior civilizations and cultures within the executive branch. The Department of the Interior was once the catch-all department of internal affairs before it was transformed into a natural resources and conservation agency, and its Bureau of Indian Affairs and Office of Territories represent vestiges of this earlier period. Through historical and political accident, the Maritime Administration remains as a symbol of the Commerce Department's lost transportation mission. Designation of the secretary of the Army to supervise the Panama Canal continues a precedent established when President Roosevelt asked the secretary of war to act as his representative in overseeing the construction of the interoceanic seaway. At the time, the War Department was the government's public works agency and, in addition, was responsible for United States territories and possessions. The latter functions were transferred to the Department of the Interior in 1939.

Organization structure may provide clues to dimly remembered public controversies and catastrophes. The Forest Service might well be in the Interior Department today if the historic dispute between Secretary Ballinger and Gifford Pinchot had not left conservationists with a nearly pathological distrust of the department. A collision of two commercial airliners over the Grand Canyon brought about the removal of the Federal Aviation Agency from the Department of Commerce. Organization location may stem from such ephemeral factors as the personality or background of a former secretary. President Kennedy wanted a southerner to administer the Community Relations Service and enforce the public accommodations laws and mainly for this reason gave the job to Secretary of Commerce Luther Hodges, who was from North Carolina. It was only with some difficulty that President Johnson was able to transfer the Community Relations Service to the Department of Justice after Secretary Hodges was succeeded in office by Secretary Connor, a northerner.

There are discernible differences between departments created in response to outside pressures (Agriculture, Commerce, and Labor) and those established primarily at executive initiative (Health, Education, and Welfare, Housing and Urban Development, and Transportation). Clientele groups have a somewhat less proprietary interest in the latter departments. They are more concerned with protecting their pet bureaus from departmental domination, as evidenced by statutory provisions according special status to the Office of Education, Federal Housing Administration, Federal Highway Administration, and Federal Aviation Administration.

Labor unions also have a proprietary interest in certain agencies and bureaus and will oppose reorganizations which threaten union jurisdictions. Lars H. Hydle, president, American Foreign Service Association, objected to Reorganization Plan No. 2 of 1977, creating the Agency for International Communications, because it would transfer State Department employees represented by his organization to a bargaining unit represented by another union.[32] Proposed transfer of Immigration and Naturalization Service inspectors to the Customs Service raised comparable jurisdictional issues. The implications of public service unions and collective bargaining for government organization and reorganization are only beginning to be recognized.

The influence of an organization structure of historical memory, clientele, and union pressures cannot be wholly eliminated. Greater discretion exists with respect to the choice of means for accomplishing program objectives. There is as yet insufficient recognition of the significance of program design as a determinant of institutional behavior. Research in this area is practically nonexistent. Regardless of where they are located on the organization chart or their program objectives, agencies engaged in common types of activities, such as lending and insurance, regulation, or public works, require people with comparable professional skills and backgrounds and share much the same professional and institutional values.

Government loans and insurance probably would be employed less frequently than they are to accomplish basic social and economic objectives if it were known that these programs have a built-in conservative bias. The professional elites in a lending agency are bankers or those with banking or financial experience. Bankers judge their success by the number of loans made and the repayment record, not by what they have contributed to the achievement of vague goals. Congress and the president are disposed to apply the same standard since it is very difficult to measure whether and to what extent government loans have, in fact, improved the relative position of small business in our economy, fostered regional development, or assisted developing nations.

The Federal Housing Administration has mirrored the professional values and prejudices of the real estate men and mort-

32. Subcommittee of House Committee on Government Operations, hearings on Reorganization Plan No. 2 of 1977, October 18 and 21, 1977, p. 99.

gage bankers who originally staffed the agency. The Douglas Commission found that "the main weakness of FHA from a social point of view has not been what it has done but in what it has failed to do—in its relative neglect of the inner cities and of the poor, and especially black poor."[33] Insurance was denied to the poor and blacks because they were considered to be bad credit risks. There was evidence of an agreement among the FHA, lending institutions, and fire insurance companies, to block off certain central city areas within "red lines" and not to loan or insure within them. FHA's policies were entirely justified, if a remarkably low default rate were the sole criterion of program effectiveness.

Exactly the same tendencies have been exhibited by the farm credit banks, as illustrated by the following exchange between R. B. Tootell, governor, Farm Credit Administration, and Congressman Dante Fascell:

> *Mr. Fascell.* Is a nonbankable finding a prerequisite to an FCA loan?
>
> *Mr. Tootell.* It is not, sir.
>
> *Mr. Fascell.* By regulation or law, it is not?
>
> *Mr. Tootell.* By none of those things. If it were, we would be placed in the position, I am sure, where our banks would be solvent enterprises for only a limited period of time.
>
> *Mr. Fascell.* You mean by that you have to get in the fight for the cream of the money market in order to make your operation go?
>
> *Mr. Tootell.* Well, we have to get our share of sound business.
>
> *Mr. Fascell.* You have to get your share of straight, good banking business?
>
> *Mr. Tootell.* Yes, we call it banking business.
>
> *Mr. Fascell.* That is what it is.[34]

33. National Commission on Urban Problems, "Building the American City," report to the Congress and the President, December 12, 1968, p. 100.

34. House Committee on Government Operations, hearings on H.R. 8332 to amend the Government Corporation Control Act, February 24, 1958, p. 178.

A quite different set of professional norms are introduced by the regulatory process. The financing institution is the banker's domain, but the lawyer reigns supreme over the regulatory agencies. Lawyers approach problems as "cases" and rely primarily on precedent and highly formalized adversary proceedings to produce fair and just solutions. The lawyer's criterion for success is the number of cases won or the decisions sustained on appeal. The regulatory approach has obvious limitations, if what is called for is positive government leadership and initiative in protecting the public interest and maintaining the economic health and vigor of the regulated industries.

Public works also have drawbacks as a means for accomplishing social and economic objectives because of the dominance given to the engineering profession. Project approval may depend more on sound engineering design than on extraneous social values. Under the accelerated public works program, projects tended to be awarded to communities with well-drafted plans on the drawing boards rather than to those which needed them the most. By nature, engineers like to build things and are not social and economic planners.

Each profession seeks to mold and shape the decision-making process so that issues will be presented and resolved in accordance with its professional standards. Harold Orlans has found that "once a particular profession becomes entrenched in an agency or institute, it is not easily dislodged. Thus, research programs and institutes often concentrate on the methods and theories of one profession (even of one school within a profession) rather than employing whatever methods and theories are most pertinent to the problems at hand."[35] It was no coincidence that Department of Defense and Bureau of the Budget economists devised the Planning-Programming-Budgeting system which gives the economist, rather than the

35. Harold Orlans, "The Political Uses of Social Research," *Annals of the American Academy of Political and Social Sciences,* Vol. 384, March 1971.

program analyst or accountant, the key role in the budget process.

Professions are characterized by their "relative insularity" and "imperial proclivities."[36] Jockeying for position among various professions or for position among sects within professions is a prime cause of structural disequilibrium. Each profession wants to be represented at the apex of the departmental structure, preferably with its spokesman reporting directly to the secretary. Scientists propagandize for assistant secretaries for science or science advisers; accountants for comptrollers; lawyers for general counsels at the assistant secretary level; archivists for autonomous archival services. None wants to be subject to officials trained in alien disciplines.

The accounting, medical, and legal professions dominated the second Hoover Commission task forces on budget and accounting, medical services, and legal services and procedures. Their influence is evidenced by recommendations that comptrollers be established in all agencies and an assistant director for accounting in the Bureau of the Budget; an assistant secretary for health be created in HEW; and legal staffs of each department and agency be integrated under an assistant secretary for legal affairs or a general counsel. Congressman Holifield, a commission member, expressed concern about the report on "Budget and Accounting" because it "tends to exalt the role of the accountant in Government just as the Commission Report on Legal Services tends to exalt the role of the lawyer in Government."[37]

Arguments for status and autonomy are rationalized by an appeal to a "higher loyalty." Government lawyers are by no means the only profession to claim that its members are answerable to the people of the United States and their profes-

36. *Ibid.*

37. Commission on Organization of the Executive Branch of Government, report on "Budget and Accounting," June 1955, p. 70.

sions as well as to their immediate administrative superiors. Lawyers contend that "they must have a degree of independence from administrative control which will enable them to serve as lawyers in Government and not merely as employees of Government."[38]

Scientists argue that national policy for science is a matter to be determined primarily by scientists themselves. Alan T. Waterman, director of the National Science Foundation, testified: "In any recommendations . . . concerning a research effort of the country, any agency, public or private, should defer to the judgment of the active and capable research scientists in the field."[39]

A Brookings Institution study opposed a Department of Health, Education, and Welfare because it doubted "whether power over professional matters should be vested in a lay department head."[40] The fact that health, education, and welfare were separate professions, each with its distinctive body of knowledge and techniques, and that the bureau chiefs were leaders in their respective professions, meant for Brookings that anything other than a housekeeping and coordinative role for the secretary would be inappropriate. If a secretary attempted to do something to which the organizations of state, federal, and local professionals were opposed, he would have a difficult fight on his hands.[41] The Brookings Institution was correct in anticipating that establishment of a Department of Health, Education, and Welfare would not diminish significantly the power of the professional guilds.

Most HEW secretaries prefer not to get involved in disagreements among professional groups. Such modest legislative

38. Commission on Organization of the Executive Branch of Government, report on "Legal Service and Procedures," March 1955, p. 17.

39. W. Henry Lambright, *Governing Science and Technology*, Oxford University Press, 1976, p. 146.

40. Commission on Organization of the Executive Branch of the Government, task force report on "Public Welfare," January 1949, p. 11.

41. *Ibid.*, p. 6.

proposals as one giving a secretary discretion to waive the single-state agency provision upon a governor's request are approached with extreme caution. Under these provisions, state agencies other than those designated by federal law are ineligible to administer grant-in-aid funds. The designated agency is generally a "professional" agency such as the Health or Education Department.

Wilbur J. Cohen, at the time assistant secretary of HEW, testified in 1965 that the proposal was undesirable because "it did not protect a Secretary or a Governor from being pressured by professional or other groups" and would expose the secretary to "these kinds of sharp differences of opinion, which provoke strong feelings of professional personnel in the health, education and welfare field." Cohen concluded: "If you want good administration you have ultimately to get the support of the professional people, the State people, and the local people, or it makes little sense to change the administrative structure and lose the support of the people whom you actually have to count on to administer something."[42] Contrary to the advice from many of his principal subordinates, Secretary Gardner withdrew HEW's objection to this legislation and it was enacted in 1968.

Professional guilds are by no means confined to the Department of Health, Education, and Welfare. No less powerful guilds include the National Conference on State Parks, Society of American Foresters, American Association of State Highway Officials, National Association of Housing and Redevelopment Officers, Interstate Conference of Employment Security Agencies, and the Society of American Archivists. Federal officials are very active in these organizations. The guilds constitute a form of private government and are regularly consulted about proposed federal policies and regulations, often before they are discussed with the secretary. Secretaries have almost

42. Senate Committee on Government Operations, hearings on S. 561, Intergovernmental Cooperation Act, March 31, 1965, pp. 196, 197, 199.

no option but to approve when presented with pacts reached after several months of negotiations with a guild.

Organization issues may be sensitive because they spring from jurisdictional disputes among professional guilds or splinter groups within professions. Engineers and biomedical specialists vied for control of the environmental health program. The debate over organization was at its root a debate over whether environmental health was primarily a disease problem or an engineering problem. It was the surgeon general's view that "it is an engineering job to get pollutants out of the environment, but it is a biomedical job to know how much lead in the environment will not cause harm to human beings."[43] Business economists have demanded that the Council of Economic Advisers be reconstituted so as to break the virtual monopoly now held by academic economists over council appointments.[44]

In specifying that council members were to be persons "exceptionally qualified to analyze and interpret economic developments," the Congress did not intend to limit appointments to academic economists. On the contrary, as indicated by Senator Guy Cordon and others during the floor debates on the Full Employment Act of 1946, it was expected that the "exceptionally qualified" would be drawn from each of the "three great divisions of effort in this country, namely, agriculture, management or industry, and labor."[45] While two of President Truman's three original appointees to the council had Ph.D.'s in economics, they had backgrounds which identified them with business, labor, and agriculture. One council member, Leon Keyserling, was a lawyer.

Whatever the congressional intent, "exceptionally qualified" has, since President Truman, been interpreted as syn-

43. *Congressional Quarterly*, January 24, 1969, p. 170.

44. Statement by William H. Chartener, Assistant Secretary of Commerce for Economic Affairs, *Washington Post*, September 27, 1968.

45. Edwin G. Nourse, *Economics in the Public Service*, Harcourt, Brace and Co., 1952, p. 353.

onymous with an economics professorship at a major university. Of the twenty-nine economists who served on the council from 1949 to 1974, only two, Leon Keyserling and Herbert Stein, never held professorial rank. Except for Gary L. Seevers, who was appointed by President Nixon in 1973, the others were full professors at the time they were named to the council. Most were selected from a handful of elite institutions such as Harvard, Yale, Columbia, Michigan, and Chicago.

Few developments have had more significance for public administration than the rapid growth in the proportion of professional and technical employees since World War II. This trend is not limited to the federal government. Frederick Mosher estimates that about one third of all government employees are engaged in professional and technical pursuits, more than three times the comparable proportion in the private sector.[46] Mosher defines profession to include both the general professions (i.e., law, medicine) and the predominantly public service professions (i.e., foresters, social workers, educators.)

The consequences of increasing professionalization for federal organization structure are only beginning to be perceived. Professional concepts of status and autonomy are difficult to reconcile with orthodox doctrines of economy and efficiency, hierarchy, span of control, and straight lines of authority and accountability. The most sacred tenets of the orthodox theology are being openly challenged. Educators insist that "education is a unique activity—so different in its essential nature that it withers in an atmosphere of control to which most state activities can accustom themselves."[47] Archivists argued that "no mere concept of administrative efficiency could be per-

46. Frederick C. Mosher, *Democracy and the Public Service,* Oxford University Press, 1968, p. 103. For a discussion of the role of lawyers, economists, engineers, accountants, and scientists see "Symposium on Professions in Government," *Public Administration Review,* Vol. 38, No. 2, March–April 1978.

47. Malcolm Moos and Francis E. Rourke, *The Campus and the State,* The Johns Hopkins Press, 1959, p. 6.

mitted to deflect the object for which historians had labored so long," an independent National Archives.[48] From time to time scientists, lawyers, doctors, and other professionals have voiced similar heresies.

Mosher warns of the danger that "the developments in the public service of the mid-century decades may be subtly, gradually, but profoundly moving the weight toward the partial, the corporate, the professional perspective and away from that of the general interest."[49] In and of itself, professionalization is a major force for dividing the executive branch into separate narrow compartmentalized units. When professionalization is mixed with the centrifugal forces generated by clienteles, dependents, congressional committees, the politics of fund-raising, and collective bargaining, the pressures for further balkanization of the executive branch become nearly irresistible.

Clientele groups and dependencies fear agencies with divided loyalties. They want agencies to represent their interests and theirs alone. Some years ago, rumors of a pending reorganization of bank supervisory agencies inspired this banner front-page headline in the *United States Investor:* NATIONAL BANKS NEED SPOKESMAN: OFFICE OF THE COMPTROLLER OF CURRENCY SHOULD BE PRESERVED.[50] It is clear from positions taken on banking legislation that the comptroller of currency still speaks for the national banks, although few present-day comptrollers would express it as baldly as the comptroller's annual report in 1923: "The Comptroller of the Currency should, in the governmental organization, be the representative and partisan of the national banks."[51] President Truman's plan to strengthen the secretary of the treasury's control of the comptroller of the currency was defeated.

Certain agencies are admittedly partisans and representa-

48. Jones, *op. cit.*, p. 21.
49. Mosher, *op. cit.*, p. 210.
50. *United States Investor,* February 23, 1946.
51. Comptroller of the Currency, *Annual Report,* 1923, p. 18.

tives of particular interests within our society, and some were deliberately established for that purpose. President Truman thought it entirely proper that the Department of Commerce should be "a channel to the White House for business and industry" and regretted that organized labor did not use the Department of Labor in the same way.[52] President Nixon cited the need for preserving the Department of Agriculture as a "vigorous advocate" of farm interests when he abandoned his plan to abolish the department in order to divide its functions among the proposed Departments of Community Development, Economic Affairs, Human Resources, and Natural Resources.[53]

Clientele interests rarely focus, however, at the departmental level. The department is valued mainly as a symbol. Departmental constituencies, even for acknowledged partisans such as Agriculture, Commerce, and Labor, represent a diversity of interests and may speak with conflicting voices. That there is a contest for access and power among the diverse elements in each constituency is demonstrated by the struggles between the Farm Bureau, the Grange, and the Farmer's Union, and, before the merger, the American Federation of Labor and the Congress of Industrial Organizations.

Pressures are most intense when constituencies are narrowly based and united by a common interest in preserving tangible economic privileges granted to them by federal law. It is the independent agency or the bureau which is most likely to be seized upon as the vehicle for safeguarding and advancing these interests.

Congress does not encourage departmental scrutiny of bureaus with close constituency ties. Secretary of Agriculture Benson, for example, had his knuckles rapped for invoking his statutory powers to approve REA loans of over $500,000. Sen-

52. Harry S Truman, *Memoirs of Harry S Truman,* Vol. 1, Doubleday & Co., Inc., 1955, p. 110.

53. *The New York Times,* November 12, 1971.

ator Humphrey denounced the secretary for "downgrading" the Rural Electrification Administrator "to the detriment of the REA program." He called upon the secretary to cease and desist his "interference with the REA administrator's authority," or the Congress would take appropriate action.[54]

The REA's power in part derives from the strength of the organization representing the beneficiaries of REA loans—the National Rural Electric Cooperative Association. Each of the agencies dispensing federal largesse has its personal lobby: the Corps of Engineers has the Rivers and Harbors Congress; the Bureau of Reclamation, the National Reclamation Association; the Soil Conservation Service, the National Association of Soil and Water Conservation Districts. The Department of Agriculture's precedent in organizing its own support organization, the Farm Bureau, has been followed by many other agencies.

These groups are very jealous of the special relationship with their government sponsor. Interlopers are not treated kindly. Programs which may dilute the sponsor's single-minded concern with their interests are vigorously opposed. The Farm Bureau attempted to throttle at their birth the agricultural adjustment, farm security, and soil conservation programs which threatened the Extension Service–land grant college monopoly consummated by a 1914 agreement with the secretary of agriculture. Unless courted continually with suitable favors, an interest group may turn on its patron. The Department of Agriculture learned to its sorrow that the price of Farm Bureau allegiance was complete subservience.

Administrative systems are no more neutral than organization arrangements. Professional, dependency, and bureaucratic interests may be as much affected by *how* a program is administered as by *where* it is administered. The far-reaching policy implications of TVA's decision to channel its agricultural programs through the land grant colleges are brilliantly

54. *Congressional Record,* July 31, 1958, p. 14385.

documented in Philip Selznick's *TVA and the Grass Roots.* TVA became firmly locked into the Farm Bureau–Extension axis.

Federal agencies may be more responsive to the middle man or their administrative agents than they are to the ultimate consumers of goods and services. The Department of Health, Education, and Welfare, which channels most of its funds through state agencies, is subject to quite a different set of influences than are the Small Business Administration and Veterans Administration, which provide services directly to the people. The Department of Housing and Urban Development, which deals with urban agencies, responds differently than the Department of Agriculture, which administers its programs through land grant colleges, chosen instruments such as Soil Conservation districts, and elected farmer committees. The Corps of Engineers is wholly dependent on its contractors —in contrast to the Tennessee Valley Authority which, as a matter of long-standing policy, does almost all its own work.

Difficulties occur when agencies and their clienteles develop a vested interest in the way things are done. New approaches are resisted for no other reason than that they require major modifications in existing administrative patterns or complicate constituency relationships. John Gardner has observed that, if agencies become prisoners of their systems and procedures, "the rule book grows fatter as the ideas grow fewer. Almost every well-established organization is a coral reef of procedures that were laid down to achieve some long-forgotten objective.[55] We can see the results when the Department of Justice is reluctant to assume administrative responsibility for the law enforcement assistance program because it does not know how to fit a grant program into its administrative structure. The Department of Health, Education, and Welfare is as reluctant to assume responsibility for nongrant programs or

55. John Gardner, *No Easy Victories,* Harper & Row, 1968, p. 44.

direct grants to cities. The Atomic Energy Commission was practically incapable of operating anything except by contract, and went so far as to contract out administration of the city of Oak Ridge. This has become a major problem for the Department of Energy which has had to assimilate the AEC functions.

Original purposes may be submerged in an overlay of myths, sentiment, and slogans. The farmer committee system is venerated as the most perfect expression of the principles of "grass-roots" democracy. Forgotten are the system's humble beginnings as the offspring of a marriage of convenience between New Deal idealism and old-fashioned agricultural politics. The system was inaugurated at a time when the Farm Bureau and its state and local government allies were making a determined effort to capture the new action programs providing cash benefits to farmers. Whatever his public explanations, it is clear that Secretary Wallace was motivated as much by a desire to establish an effective counterweight to the Farm Bureau's political power as he was by ideological considerations. Soil conservation districts under elected boards were organized with much the same objective in mind.[56]

The farmer committee system has achieved its political purposes admirably, although not exactly in the way contemplated by Secretary Wallace. Committees have developed a base of power independent of the secretary which has enabled some of them to ignore his directives with impunity. As our first large-scale experiment in participatory democracy, farmer committees teach lessons which could have been studied with profit by those who designed the poverty program.

Grass-roots democracy in practice has proved to be highly

56. For origins of the farmer committee system and soil conservation districts see John M. Gaus, "The Citizen as Administrator" in *Public Administration and Democracy,* edited by Roscoe Martin, Syracuse University Press, 1965, pp. 175–76; Robert J. Morgan, *Governing Soil Conservation,* The Johns Hopkins Press, 1965, pp. 317, 318, 353, 354; Morton Grodzins, *The American System,* Rand McNally & Co., 1966, pp. 351, 352, 356.

undemocratic. Fewer than 23 percent of the eligible voters participated in elections for the more than 26,000 Agriculture Stabilization and Conservation Community committees in 1961. In a significant number of communities the number of people elected was as large or larger than the number of people voting.[57] Voter apathy has made it possible for committee careerists to gain and hold on to committee memberships and to operate the system for the primary benefit of the dominant economic groups within the community. A March 1965 report of the U.S. Civil Rights Commission documented the charges that the committees in the South consistently deprived Negro farmers and less prosperous white farmers of the benefits to which they were entitled under federal programs.

A committee appointed by Secretary Freeman in 1962 to review the farmer committee system uncovered evidence of serious administrative deficiencies. In an effort to bring some order and uniformity into the system, the Agriculture Department in Washington has inundated the committees with an increasing flood of rules, regulations, and procedures. This has resulted in the worst kind of centralization. Fewer rules and regulations are required where there is effective central control.

Nonetheless, except for political scientist Morton Grodzins and former Secretary Charles F. Brannan, the review committee's faith in grass-roots democracy remained unshaken. To deny the validity of the farmer committee system would be almost to deny faith in the fundamental virtues of the honest yeoman. The committee concluded that "farmers have confidence in the administration of farm programs on their behalf by their neighbors," and, therefore, "the farmer committee system should be strengthened and kept in the hands of elected bona fide farmers."

Clientele-oriented policies also may be engraved in stone.

57. U.S. Department of Agriculture, "Report of the Study Committee on Farmer Committee System," November 28, 1962.

Devotion to these "historic" policies endures in the face of changing circumstances and challenges by presidents and prestigious study commissions. The U.S. Army Corps of Engineers adheres rigidly to the policy first enunciated in 1787 that inland waterways should be regarded "as public highways open to use of the public generally without restriction," although every president since Franklin Roosevelt has recommended the imposition of user charges. It was the Corps' unswerving dedication to this policy, rather than admiration for its engineering skills, that caused user organizations to lobby for Corps of Engineers' control of the St. Lawrence Seaway. The campaign did not succeed, but the House Committee report directed that the St. Lawrence Seaway Corporation utilize the services of the Corps of Engineers for design, construction, maintenance, and operation of the seaway and emphasized that in approving tolls it was "not digressing from the firm and long-standing toll-free policy established with respect to inland waterways."[58]

Findings by the 1961 Commission on Money and Banking, the 1962 Advisory Committee to the Comptroller of the Currency on banking, and the 1963 President's Committee on Financial Institutions, that the practice of nonpar banking constituted "an imperfection in our banking system" did not persuade the Federal Deposit Insurance Corporation to modify its traditional policies. The board of governors of the Federal Reserve System and the FDIC consistently have taken diametrically opposed positions on this issue. A vast majority of the 1,500 odd nonpar banks which levy exchange charges in settling checks drawn upon them are small banks insured by FDIC which are not members of the Federal Reserve System. FDIC regards the small nonmember banks which it supervises directly as its special clients. Exchange charges are an anachronism going back to the time when check clearance involved a physical transfer of funds. The practice now has no

58. House Report No. 1215, 83rd Congress, 2nd Session.

other justification than the income it provides for small banks.

Interest groups have fascinated a generation of American scholars.[59] Political pluralists consider competition among interest groups as an integral and indispensable element in the democratic process. Those who deem all interest groups by definition to be evil and picture government agencies as marionettes dangling from strings manipulated by "special interests" are indulging in gross oversimplifications. The relationship between an agency and its constituency is based on a mutuality of interests—a mutuality generally established by the provisions of laws enacted by the Congress. The government agency often does the manipulating, not the reverse. The Forest Service, for example, maintains a roster of "key-men" who can be called upon in time of need for succor.[60] Other agencies maintain similar networks of individuals and organizations.

Interest groups are not monoliths. Their power is essentially negative. They are most effective in blocking actions—modification of the 2 percent interest rate on REA loans, transfer of the Maritime Administration to the Department of Transportation, imposition of user charges. These issues do not generate internal disputes. It is far more difficult to obtain unanimity when new proposals are being advanced, for then the sharp differences which exist in any organization quickly come to the surface.

Once systems are developed and patterns of organization behavior are established, in most instances they cannot be altered significantly by interdepartmental reorganizations. This is

59. See E. Pendleton Herring, *Public Administration and the Public Interest*, McGraw-Hill Book Co., 1936; David Truman, *The Governmental Process*, Alfred A. Knopf, 1964; Harmon Zeigler, *Interest Groups in American Society*, Prentice-Hall, Inc., 1964; Grant McConnell, *Private Power and American Democracy*, Alfred A. Knopf, 1967. Theodore J. Lowi, *The End of Liberalism*, W. W. Norton Co., 1969.

60. Donal V. Allison, "The Development and Use of Political Power by Federal Agencies: A Case Study of the U.S. Forest Service," May 1965 (unpublished thesis, University of Virginia).

particularly true when bureaus, such as the U.S. Employment Service, are moved intact from one department to another. Reorganizations may result in scarcely more than a new name on the letterhead. Where changes are produced, they are seldom those anticipated or intended by the proponents of the reorganization.[61] *Vin ordinaire* cannot be transformed into champagne merely by shifting the location of the bottle in the wine cellar.

The behavior of adult institutions can be changed. But this requires nonorganizational measures which enlarge the agency's constituency, compel redesign of the administrative system, and call for a different mix of professional skills. Enactment of the Elementary and Secondary Education Act of 1965 was the stimulus needed to bring about basic reforms in the Office of Education. Internal reorganization of the Office of Education was a response to a radically different complex of program responsibilities.[62]

The *first* organization decision is crucial. The course of institutional development may be set irrevocably by the initial choice of administrative agency and by the way in which the program is designed. Unless these choices are made with full awareness of environmental and cultural influences, the program may fail or its goals may be seriously distorted.

Herbert Hoover believed that the simple physical grouping of functions "cheek-by-jowl" in departments organized by major purposes automatically would make it possible to eliminate overlaps and produce coordinated policies. This hypothesis assumes that department heads are or should be chief executives, as the term is used in business or military organizations with authority reaching down through every step of the organization.

61. Harold Seidman, Dominic Del Guidice, and Charles Warren, *Reorganization by Presidential Plan: Three Case Studies*, National Academy of Public Administration, 1971.

62. Stephen K. Bailey and Edith K. Mosher, *ESEA: The Office of Education Administers a Law*, Syracuse University Press, 1968.

Luther Gulick defined the work of a chief executive by the acronym POSDCORB: planning, organizing, staffing, directing, coordinating, reporting, and budgeting.[63] In major or minor degree, department heads do perform all of these functions, but POSDCORB by itself provides an inadequate and unrealistic description of a secretary's job. Statutes which contemplate that a department head will "control" his agency are equally unrealistic.

A department head's job is akin to that of a major university president and is subject to the same frustrations. His principal duties involve matters which are unrelated to the internal administration and management of the institution. So far as his subordinates are concerned, he is the institution's ceremonial head, chief fund raiser, and protector of institutional values and territory. An informal check reveals that a department head may spend 25 percent or more of his time in meetings with members of the Congress and appearances before congressional committees, and probably an equivalent amount of time in public relations work such as speech-making and cultivating agency constituencies. One administrator reported that he was required to keep thirty-five full committees and seventy-five subcommittees informed of his agency's activities.[64] Another block of time is devoted to White House conferences and meetings of interagency and advisory committees. Minimal time is left for managing the department, even if a secretary is one of the rare political executives with a taste for administration.

A department head's managerial role is primarily that of a "mediator-initiator." In the words of Clark Kerr, former president of the University of California, who was referring to university presidents, "he must be content to hold the constituent

63. Luther Gulick, "Notes on the Theory of Organization" in *Papers on the Science of Administration,* edited by Luther Gulick and L. Urwick, Institute of Public Administration, 1937.

64. Michael J. Malbin, "You Can Please Some of the Senators Some of the Time," *National Journal,* January 15, 1977.

elements loosely together and to move the whole enterprise another foot ahead in what often seems an unequal race with history."[65] He has opportunities to set directions and exercise significant influence only when new programs are being developed or when major increases in expenditures are being requested for old programs. Normally a department head has neither the time nor the inclination to concern himself with on-going operations which appear to raise no problems.

The prime quality required of a department head, and most often lacking, is political leadership. Hugh Heclo correctly diagnosed the problem when he wrote:

> A political executive who does not know what he wants to accomplish is in no position to assess the bureaucracy's performance in helping him to do it. Likewise, an executive whose aims bear little relation to the chances for accomplishment is in an equally weak position to stimulate help from officials below. By trying to select goals in relation to available opportunities, political appointees create a strategic resource for leadership in the bureaucracy.[66]

In 1948 the Bureau of the Budget found that "The outstanding weakness in Federal Administration today lies in deficiencies in administrative leadership, coordination and control at the top of Federal departments and agencies."[67] Since 1948 the number of assistant secretaries has multipled, staff resources available to a secretary have been augmented, and new systems such as PPB have been installed to enhance a secretary's decision-making powers. However, department heads remain the weakest link in the chain of federal administration. Unless departmental management can be improved,

65. Quoted in the *Washington Post*, June 8, 1969, p. B1.

66. Hugh Heclo, "Political Executives and the Washington Bureaucracy," *Political Science Quarterly*, Vol. 92, Fall, 1977.

67. Memorandum to staff of Division of Administrative Management from Donald C. Stone, Assistant Director for Administrative Management, April 5, 1948.

reorganization cannot be counted on to yield more than marginal benefits.

If we are to do something meaningful about the organization and management of the executive branch, we must start first with department and agency heads. New approaches are needed—approaches based on what the political executives' functions really are—not on obsolete concepts of what they should be.

7

Cooperative Feudalism

Federal "professional" agencies and their state and local counterparts may have their differences, but they are as one when it comes to combating attempts by outsiders to encroach upon their fiefdoms. Outsiders include lay administrators and competing professions, but the most feared are elected executives charged with representing the broader public interests—the president of the United States, governors, and mayors—and those such as budget officers who assist political executives in a general staff capacity. This bias is clearly evident in replies by federal grant-in-aid administrators to a questionnaire prepared by the Senate Subcommittee on Intergovernmental Relations. The subcommittee found: "In the administration of these programs, counterparts tend and prefer to deal with counterparts. Chief executives and top management generalists are viewed by these program administrators as potential or actual enemies, subject to the fluctuating whims of the electorate."[1]

Hostility to political executives is shared and encouraged by

1. Senate Committee on Government Operations, Subcommittee on Intergovernmental Relations, "The Federal System as Seen by Federal Aid Officials," December 15, 1965, p. 55.

committees and subcommittees of the Congress and state legislatures which are as preoccupied as the administrators with protecting and promoting the purposes of the individual programs under their respective jurisdictions. The bias against politicians does not extend to legislators who often are eager and powerful allies in the fight against the common enemy.

The federal system as seen by federal and local program specialists and as it now in fact operates bears little resemblance to classical concepts of federalism which emphasize the independence of each of the levels of government and separation of powers. Traditional, or "layer-cake," theory assumes that the functions appropriate to each level can be defined with reasonable precision and should be kept distinct from and independent of each other. The problems of federalism are believed to relate mainly to the proper allocation of responsibilities. President Eisenhower's Commission on Intergovernmental Relations and the Joint Federal-State Action Committee organized by President Eisenhower and the Governors' Conference in 1957 took this approach. As stated by the commission, its task was "to determine, within the constitutional limits of National and State powers, and in the light of 165 years of practical experience, what division of responsibilities is best calculated to sustain a workable basis for intergovernmental relations in the future."[2]

"Layer-cake" theory is rejected by some students of the federal system, notably Morton Grodzins and Daniel J. Elazar, whose culinary tastes run to "marble cake."[3] The "marble-cake" school rejects separateness as the keystone of federalism. Separation of functions by levels of government is considered to be both impractical and undesirable when governments operate in the same territory, serve the same clienteles, and seek comparable goals. While the system involves both com-

2. The Commission on Intergovernmental Relations, A Report to the President, June 1955, p. 33.

3. Senate Committee on Government Operations, *op. cit.*, p. 95.

petition and cooperation, the latter is the most important. As far as it goes, this description of "cooperative federalism" comes much closer to reality than traditional theories. Yet it is seriously deficient in failing to recognize that separatism can and has developed within the system without clear-cut separation of functions by levels of government.

What we have in several important functional areas are largely self-governing professional guilds, or what the Advisory Commission on Intergovernmental Relations calls "vertical functional autocracies."[4] In other areas federal agencies have established their own independent local government systems. Former governor of North Carolina, Terry Sanford, was speaking of the "vertical functional autocracies" when he wrote:

> The lines of authority, the concerns and interests, the flow of money, and the direction of programs run straight down like a number of pickets stuck into the ground. There is, as in a picket fence, a connecting cross slat, but that does little to support anything. In this metaphor it stands for the governments. It holds the pickets in line; it does not bring them together. The picket-like programs are not connected at the bottom.[5]

A 1975 survey by the Advisory Commission on Intergovernmental Relations reveals that the picket fence is still in place, although it has ceased to be of the sturdy, solid wood variety. David B. Walker suggests that "bamboo fence" federalism now more "accurately captures the vertical functionalism, continuing professionalism, greater flexibility and realism" of contemporary administrators. While the emphasis continues to be on functionalism and program protectionism, the standpatism and indifference to broader intergovernmental issues

4. Advisory Commission on Intergovernmental Relations, Tenth Annual Report, January 31, 1969, p. 8.

5. Terry Sanford, *Storm Over the States,* McGraw-Hill Book Co., p. 80.

evident in the responses to the Senate Subcommittee on Intergovernmental Relations have become somewhat muted.[6]

The federal system is not a single system, but a loose grouping of relatively autonomous confederations of federal, state, and local professional agencies. Senator Edmund Muskie was one of the first to discern and describe accurately the true character of twentieth-century federalism. He classifies intergovernmental relations "as almost a fourth branch of government," but one which "has no direct electorate, operates from no set perspective, is under no special control, and moves in no particular direction. . . ."[7]

No one deliberately planned to create this fourth branch of government. In fostering the establishment of autonomous local units or in organizing special districts and independent paragovernments, the federal government was responding to existing patterns of state and local organization and, in some instances, endeavoring to compensate for some of its more obvious weaknesses. Fragmentation of authority, both horizontal and vertical, is the distinguishing feature of our local government systems. As in the Congress, "power is nowhere concentrated; it is rather deliberately and of set policy scattered amongst many small chiefs."

Power is diffused among 50 states and over 80,000 local governments including, in round numbers, 3,000 counties, 18,000 municipalities, 17,000 townships, 21,000 school districts, and 21,000 special districts.[8] Within one city there may be 5 or more "governments" (county, city, school district, sanitary district, fire district, water district, library district,

6. David B. Walker, "Federal Aid Administrators and the Federal System," *Intergovernmental Perspective,* Vol. 3, No. 4. Fall 1977.

7. Senate Committee on Government Operations, Subcommittee on Intergovernmental Relations, "The Federal System as Seen by State and Local Officials," 1963, p. 2.

8. Advisory Commission on Intergovernmental Relations, "Fiscal Balance in the American Federal System," Vol. 1, October 1967, p. 72.

etc.) levying taxes and exercising authority over the same citizens.

Executive power in most jurisdictions is also weak and fragmented. Many of the largest cities have vested effective administrative authority in "strong mayors," but "weak mayors" still constitute the vast majority. The Committee for Economic Development identified "lack of a chief executive officer" as "one of the most glaring deficiencies in the structure of most local governments."[9]

In many states the governor is chief executive in name only. It is said that "the American governorship was conceived in mistrust and born in a strait jacket, the creature of revolutionary assemblies."[10] A governor's powers with respect to the budget, planning, organization structure, executive appointments, and administration are in most states hedged about with restrictions.

Executive power may be shared with several independently elected department heads who owe no allegiance to the governor and who may be his political enemies. The number of independently elected department heads ranges from two (Maryland, Michigan, New Hampshire, New York, Virginia) to 10 (Mississippi), with an average of five. Alaska, Hawaii, New Jersey, and Pennsylvania are the only states which have no independently elected department heads.

It is by no means a coincidence that a governor's appointive powers are most often limited or nonexistest in selecting the heads of agencies with federal sponsors. His or her authority to appoint the head or heads of education is limited or nonexistent in 45 states, of agriculture in 24, of health in 19, of mental health in 19, of highways in 18, and of welfare in 17.[11] Not surprising are the findings of several studies which show that state agencies which are heavily dependent on federal

9. Committee for Economic Development, "Modernizing Local Government," July 1966, p. 49.

10. Sanford, *op. cit.*, p. 30.

11. Advisory Commission on Intergovernmental Relations, *op. cit.*, p. 222.

funds consider themselves to be less subject to supervision and control by the governor than nonaided departments.[12]

At the outset, there was no intention to create privileged sanctuaries or to thwart governors in the exercise of whatever legitimate powers they might possess. Safeguards were believed necessary to simplify administrative relationships between the federal government and the recipients of federal grants, to maintain accountability, and, above all, to assure that the national purposes of programs authorized by the Congress were not obscured or lost by dividing up administrative responsibility among the host of state agencies which could advance jurisdictional claims.

National objectives were a matter of little moment during the early years of the republic when federal assistance consisted mainly of land grants to the states. Congress specified the general purposes for which the proceeds from land sales could be used (generally education or internal improvements), but it imposed few other restrictions and made no provision for federal supervision. The Morrill Act of 1862 marked the beginning of a trend toward increased emphasis on national objectives with federal supervision and regulations to see that grants were used for the intended purposes. With the proliferation of grant-in-aid programs and the growing dependence on grants to promote national purposes, either by stimulating state action or through cooperative education, health, welfare, and employment security programs, the organizational and administrative disarray within most state governments no longer could be safely ignored.

The single-state-agency requirement was devised as one means for bringing some order out of administrative chaos. Provisions designating the state agency to administer or supervise federal grants and establishing direct relationships between the designated agency and its federal counterpart first appear in the 1916 Federal Highway Act. To be eligible for

12. Advisory Commission on Intergovernmental Relations, *op. cit.*, pp. 202, 213.

federal highway assistance, a state must have "a State highway department which shall have adequate powers and be suitably equipped and organized to discharge to the satisfaction of the Secretary the duties required by this title. Among other things, the organization shall include a secondary road unit." The secretary (now the secretary of transportation) is directed to enter into "formal project agreements" with state highway departments and to "certify to each of the departments the sums which he has apportioned." There is no requirement that the secretary seek a governor's advice and approval before concluding project agreements or even that he keep the governor informed.

The 1917 Smith-Hughes Act stipulates that to receive the benefits of federal appropriations for vocational education a state must designate or create as the administering agency a state board consisting of not less than three members, and having "all necessary powers" to cooperate with the federal program agency, or designate the state board of education for this purpose. Again no role is specified for the governor. Vocational education grants are treated as the exclusive concern of the federal government and its chosen state instrument.

Congress went beyond the requirement for a "sole local agency" in authorizing grants for vocational rehabilitation services and provided, in addition, that the vocational rehabilitation bureau, division, or other unit of a state vocational education agency designated under the Act "shall be subject only to the supervision and direction of such agency or its executive officer."

Currently applicable federal laws either name a specific state agency or call for designation of a "single state agency" or "sole agency" for such programs as school lunch, highways, maternal and child health, maternity and infant care, child welfare, community health, mental retardation, library services, urban planning, manpower development and training, water pollution control, national defense education, vocational education, vocational rehabilitation, civil defense, public assistance, hospital and medical facilities construction, and law enforcement assistance.

Without question these requirements have served to rationalize state administration within prescribed functional areas and have helped to improve the quality of state personnel by introducing professional standards and merit-system principles. As tangible evidences of "success," one can cite the state highway and welfare departments and vocational education boards which were established as the direct result of federal "stimulation." Integration within functional areas has been obtained, however, at the cost of professional inbreeding, organizational and administrative rigidity, further impairment of central executive authority, and loss of political responsibility.

Until very recently few worried about the adverse effects, although a survey group reported to the Commission on Intergovernmental Relations in 1955, based on its study of Michigan State government, that

> Federal grant programs have done nothing to strengthen the State government as a political entity. Rather, the divisive elements in the political situation have been emphasized by the close professional and functional relationships that have grown up in the grant fields between Federal and State program officials. In the Federal-State grant relationship the political leadership of the State often has been ignored to the detriment of sound statewide development.
>
> Professional association of administrators and private citizens has promoted further compartmentalization of interest and loyalty along program lines to the detriment of overall government unity.[13]

Strict construction of the single-state-agency provision has

13. Commission on Intergovernmental Relations, "The Fiscal and Administrative Impact of Federal Grants-in-Aid," June 1955, p. 38.

enabled state program administrators to evade central fiscal controls and to block attempts at administrative reform. Channeling of requests for vocational education and child welfare services grants through state budget bureaus was opposed because it "would undermine the 'single agency' requirement."[14] The Department of Health, Education, and Welfare vetoed a proposal by Oregon to establish a state agency in its own image. Objections were raised because (1) the head of the proposed Department of Social Services would be interposed between the governor and the administrators of federally assisted programs; (2) program administrators would be appointed outside the merit system; and (3) administrative authority would be subject to review beyond that of the respective divisions.[15] The Department of Health, Education, and Welfare also disapproved the Florida Department of Health and Rehabilitative Service's 1976 vocational rehabilitation plan because it violated the single-state-agency provision. HEW Secretary Joseph A. Califano denied the Florida governor's request for a waiver. Secretary Califano explained: "The decision is reached because of restrictions in the law and does not reflect my personal view that states should have more latitude than at present to organize and manage programs funded by the Federal government."[16]

Wilbur Cohen's sensitivity about allowing any modifications of the single-state-agency provision is understandable. For the professional guilds, these statutory provisions are the equivalent of corporate charters, the indispensable source of both power and legitimacy. Any questioning of the single-state-agency concept represents a challenge to their existence.

The consequences of organizational compartmentalization and functionalism both within the executive and legislative

14. Senate Committee on Government Operations, "The Federal System as Seen by Federal Aid Officials," *op. cit.*, p. 53.

15. *Ibid.*, p. 45.

16. National Academy of Public Administration, *Reorganization in Florida*, Washington, D.C., September 1977, p. 65.

branches of the federal and state governments are to be seen in the multiplication of narrow categorical programs. By restricting the purposes for which federal grants may be utilized, each legislative committee and subcommittee, and professional discipline and subdiscipline, seeks to reinforce its jurisdictional claims and to make certain that funds cannot be diverted to competing programs. Support of general health has become submerged in a multiplicity of separate grants for heart disease, cancer, venereal disease, mental retardation, maternal and child health, mental health, communicable disease, and so forth. The Partnership for Health Act in 1966 made some progress by consolidating and combining several categorical health grants, but progress was to be short-lived. The Congress soon backslid by enacting new categorical health programs for migrant workers, alcoholics, and drug addicts.

There has been considerable debate about the number of categorical grant programs. According to a count by the Advisory Commission on Intergovernmental Relations, there are approximately 442 categorical grants administered by 21 federal departments and agencies.[17] This number is considerably below previous estimates.

Regardless of legal impediments, strong and politically adroit governors are not without influence. Centrifugal forces are subject to some restraints, except in weak-governor, strong-legislature states. Single state agencies are established within the framework of the state government, in contrast to some federally sponsored organizations at the local level which are outside and independent of the established city and county governments. These special arrangements were deemed necessary because (1) few general units of local government have the jurisdictional authority, administrative capacity, and professional competence required for the effective performance of federally assisted programs; (2) many city halls and county

17. Advisory Commission on Intergovernmental Relations, *Categorical Grants: Their Role and Design*, 1977, p. 91.

courthouses have displayed a reluctance to tackle controversial social problems; and (3) in some communities local governments could not be depended upon to make available to blacks and other racial minorities the full benefits of federal programs. Professionals' distrust of politicians and potential political rivalry between members of the Congress and mayors and county executives were no doubt contributing factors.

The Department of Agriculture was the first federal agency to develop its own local government network. We have discussed in the previous chapter the role of the elected farmer committees and the soil conservation districts. The Forest Service has similar elected advisory boards. Grazing districts under the Department of Interior also have elected boards of grazing district advisers representing local stockmen.

According to the Advisory Commission on Intergovernmental Relations, "about a quarter of Federal programs affecting urban development induce or even require special districts for their administration."[18] Federally encouraged special districts include law enforcement districts, community action agencies, comprehensive area manpower programs, comprehensive health and area planning agencies, air quality regions, local development districts within the Appalachian area, and resource conservation development districts. Another approach is illustrated by the public housing program and, to a lesser extent, by urban renewal, where federal officials have demonstrated a preference for independent or semi-independent local authorities.

There was some grumbling about federal encroachment on local domains, but local officials hardly were in a position to argue in principle against a few more special districts and independent authorities. Development of federal "little governments" attracted no public attention or outright opposition until the poverty program. Mayors and county executives were

18. Advisory Commission on Intergovernmental Relations, "Fiscal Balance in the American Federal System," *op. cit.*, p. 259.

accustomed to being bypassed; but federally financed assaults against "the establishment" hit them in their political vitals where it hurt the most.

Ironically the community action agency initially was conceived of by the Bureau of the Budget as a unifying force to meld together the resources of the federal, state, and local governments and the private community in the war against poverty. There was no desire to fight city hall. The original Economic Opportunity Act gave the local community the option to designate either a "public or private nonprofit agency" to administer a community action program, provided that the program "was developed, conducted, and administered with the maximum feasible participation of the areas and members of the groups served." The public agency could be an extension of the mayor's office or under his control.

The Bureau of the Budget's vehicle for "institutional cooperation" was transformed by the Office of Economic Opportunity into an instrument to promote "institutional change." Some went so far as to interpret community action "as a mandate for Federal assistance in the effort to create political organizations for the poor."[19] Emphasis was shifted from coordination and collaboration with established federal, state, and local agencies to competition.

A public agency is not the instrument of choice for promoting institutional change. Few community action programs have been organized under public auspices. As of June 30, 1968, only 34 of 1,012 community action agencies were government instrumentalities.[20] The rest were private nonprofit corporations.

Some community action agencies have developed their own constituencies and sufficient political power to earn the respect, if not the enthusiastic support, of most elected local

19. Daniel P. Moynihan, *Maximum Feasible Misunderstanding,* The Free Press, 1969, p. 131.

20. Comptroller General of the United States, "Review of Economic Opportunity Programs," March 18, 1969, p. 54.

officials. A measure of accommodation has been achieved, as demonstrated by the fact that fewer than 2 percent of the communities exercised the option accorded local officials under 1968 amendments to the Economic Opportunity Act to convert private community action agencies to public agencies.[21]

The Model Cities Act also called for "citizen participation." City development agencies bore a striking resemblance to community action agencies, but the Department of Housing and Urban Development profited from OEO's experience. HUD stressed that problems would never be resolved if city hall and the city development agency got "tangled up in the rhetoric of total control." Citizen access to and influence on the decision-making processes was provided, but subject to the rights of responsible elected city officials to make final decisions and to supervise and control the use of public funds.[22] Though they had somewhat different objectives, the extent of overlap between city development agencies and community action agencies further complicated the problems of coordinating federal urban assistance programs.

"Citizen participation" is a very slippery term and means very different things to different people. If participation is measured by the number of people who vote for members of farmer committees and community action boards, it rests on a very narrow base. Many so-called "representatives of the poor" were elected by as little as 1 percent of the eligible voters. Citizen participation can be and has been used as a means for transferring power from officials who have at least some political responsibility to the community at large to self-perpetuating local cliques or the bureaucracy. It can operate in ways that provide nominal citizen participation but minimal citizen influence and maximum citizen frustration. Fifty-three percent of the funds appropriated for the community action program

21. *Ibid.*, p. 21.

22. Remarks of H. Ralph Taylor, Assistant Secretary for Model Cities and Governmental Relations, Department of Housing and Urban Development, before the Model Cities Midwest Regional Conference, September 6, 1968.

in 1968 were earmarked for "national programs" devised by the Office of Economic Opportunity in Washington, not by the local citizenry.

Former White House counselor and present U.S. senator Daniel P. Moynihan has observed that citizen participation is a "bureaucratic ideology." "The bureaucracy increasingly gets its way, and acquires a weapon against the elected officers of 'representative' government, but it is not clear that it gets its results. A process of cooptation, of diminished rather than enhanced energies, somehow seems to occur." Moynihan concludes:

> The Federal Government should constantly encourage and provide incentives for the reorganization of local government in response to the reality of metropolitan conditions. The objective of the Federal Government should be that local government be stronger and more effective, more visible, accessible, and meaningful to local inhabitants. To this end the Federal Government should discourage the creation of paragovernments designed to deal with special problems by evading or avoiding the jurisdiction of established local authorities, and should encourage effective decentralization.[23]

Some of the chosen federal instruments are not unlike parasitic growths living on the body of their federal hosts. Their appetite for power and appropriations can only be satisfied by what is fed into the host agency. Any reduction in appropriations, elimination or transfer of programs, or tightening of political controls is strongly resisted. To be separated from the host is to risk survival.

The antipolitical biases, conflicts, and pressures present within the intergovernmental system have been transmitted to the federal body politic. As the price for congressional approval of the reorganization plan creating the Department of

23. Daniel P. Moynihan, "Toward a National Urban Policy," speech delivered at Syracuse University, May 8, 1969.

Health, Education, and Welfare, President Eisenhower was compelled to provide assurances that "the Office of Education and the Public Health Service retain the professional and substantive responsibilities vested by law in those agencies or in their heads.[24] Statutory functions of the Public Health Service were transferred to the secretary in 1966, but the Office of Education continues to enjoy a quasi-autonomous status. Seeming irrationalities in the federal structure, as in the organization of manpower, poverty, occupational health and water pollution control programs, have their roots in jurisdictional disputes among vertical functional autocracies.

President Kennedy underestimated the influence of the vocational education guild when he proposed to break its monopoly over vocational training established by the Smith-Hughes Act. The administration manpower development and training bill sent to the Congress in 1961 provided for a direct federal operation administered by the secretary of labor and financed wholly from federal funds. State vocational education facilities were to be employed at the discretion of the secretary of labor by individual agreements negotiated through the Department of Health, Education, and Welfare, but principal emphasis was to be given to on-the-job training.

The American Vocational Association centered its attack on the sections of the administration bill which permitted manpower development and training programs to be conducted without reference to the states or to HEW. It wanted HEW to control the program, with money to be distributed to the states by formula grants. The compromise bill enacted by the Congress in 1962 split jurisdictional responsibility between Labor and HEW. Except for on-the-job training, the law provided for state administration and financing by funds apportioned to the states in accordance with "uniform standards" agreed upon by the secretaries of Labor and HEW.[25]

24. Message transmitting Reorganization Plan No. 1 of 1953, March 12, 1953.

25. For the legislative history of the Manpower Development and Training Act see James L. Sundquist, *Politics and Policy*. The Brookings Institution, 1968, pp. 85–91.

Within the Department of Labor, the United States Employment Service, which has an independent power base in the Interstate Conference of Employment Security agencies, the Bureau of Apprenticeship and Training supported by its allies in the AFL-CIO, and the Office of Manpower, Automation, and Training, all contested for control. Secretary Wirtz's announced plans to consolidate departmental manpower programs in a new Manpower Administration had to be withdrawn because of widespread state complaints that the proposed reorganization was both "surprising and detrimental."[26] The opposition was spearheaded by one of the most powerful guilds, the Interstate Conference of Employment Security Agencies. The daily work of the conference was carried out by an executive secretary on the Department of Labor payroll. Former Manpower Administrator and Assistant Secretary of Labor Stanley H. Ruttenberg complained: "Taking a stubborn stance of unremitting opposition to almost any suggestion for change, the Interstate Conference offers protective cover for those who would use the employment service to prevent change instead of making it a positive instrument of social reform."[27]

The Council of Chief State School Officers, the National Association of State School Boards, and the National Education Association had the necessary political muscle to secure passage of a Senate amendment transferring the popular Head Start program from the Office of Economic Opportunity to the Office of Education over protests by OEO and the secretary of HEW. Senator Clark condemned the amendment as a power play by the education lobby. He stated:

> Of course, the education lobby is for this transfer. Why would it not be? They would like to run the program just as they would like to run all the rest of the programs

26. *The New York Times,* November 28, 1968.

27. Stanley H. Ruttenberg and Jocelyn Gutchess, *The Federal-State Employment Service: A Critique,* The Johns Hopkins Press, 1970.

> which are not under their jurisdiction now, whether they are education programs, or not. . . .[28]

The Senate amendment did not stand up in the House of Representatives, and language was substituted directing the president to make a special study of whether responsibility for administering the Head Start program should be left with OEO or transferred to another agency. President Nixon determined that Head Start should be delegated to HEW, but with the important proviso that the program be lodged directly under the secretary, not in the Office of Education.[29] The education guild had won something of a Pyrrhic victory.

So long as a guild can maintain its support within the Congress, it has little to fear from executive reorganization proposals. When it loses congressional confidence, it is in serious trouble. Successive measures to reorganize federal water pollution programs were designed deliberately to wrest power from the Public Health Service and the state health departments. Members of Congress were fed up with what they considered to be "foot-dragging" by the health agencies. Congressman John Blatnik complained that all he could get from the Public Health Service were bland assurances that "Everything is fine. The States are doing a good job. The municipalities are doing a good job. We are getting along well with them." Meanwhile "year by year pollution was getting worse and worse."[30] Blatnik sympathized with the problems faced by HEW Secretary Gardner and told him:

> We are dealing with the Public Health Service. They did not care who was the Secretary of HEW. In fact, their attitude was an open, brazen one: "These Secretaries upstairs come and go. We are going to tell you."[31]

28. *Congressional Record,* July 17, 1968, p. S8811.
29. *Weekly Compilation of Presidential Documents,* February 24, 1969.
30. House Committee on Government Operations, hearings on Reorganization Plan No. 2 of 1966 (Water Pollution Control), March 30 and May 4, 1966, p. 42.
31. *Ibid.,* p. 10.

Congress enacted legislation to transfer water pollution control functions from the Public Health Service to a new Water Pollution Control Administration in the Department of Health, Education, and Welfare, but this reorganization did not wholly sever the ties with the Public Health Service. Complete separation was achieved by Reorganization Plan No. 2 of 1966 which transferred the program to the Department of the Interior, except for certain limited health functions retained by the secretary of HEW. Four years later the program was transferred to a new independent Environmental Protection Agency.

Federal reorganization proposals may attract criticism by local agencies even when guild interests are not directly involved. New organization fashions developed within the federal government tend to set the style for state and local governments. State environmental reorganizations, for example, have tended to follow the federal model.[32] Intergroup relations officials took exception to the reorganization plan transferring the Community Relations Service to the Department of Justice, principally because of the precedent it might create for their own communities.[33] Only one of the thirty-two state intergroup relations agencies was located in the attorney general's office. Although the Federal Department of Justice has important functions in fields other than law enforcement, community relations officials were concerned that identification of the federal program with an agency that had a law-enforcement "image" would weaken their case for keeping community relations separate from law enforcement.

Governors and mayors are now only beginning to appreciate the political implications of federal organization structure and

32. The Council of State Governments, *Integration and Coordination of State Environmental Programs,* Lexington, Kentucky, 1975, p. 25.

33. See the statement of Frederick B. Routh, Executive Director, National Association of Intergroup Relations Officials, before the House Committee on Government Operations, hearings on Reorganization Plan No. 1 of 1966, March 18, 1966.

administrative arrangements. Some of the reports for the 1955 Commission on Intergovernmental Relations showed that federal aid programs could have a significant impact on the balance of power within a state, but the commission did not think the problem was worth mentioning in its final report. As late as 1962, the Council of State Governments reported that federal grants had a minor influence on state governmental structure and organization, a view not shared by the Governors' Conference which in 1961 deplored "the tendency of Federal agencies to dictate the organizational form and structure through which States carry out Federally supported programs."[34] Almost 47 percent of the state and local officials who responded to a 1962 questionnaire circulated by the Senate Committee on Intergovernmental Relations answered "no" to the question: "Has the kind of State and local government required by Federal grant-in-aid statute or administrative ruling hampered the flexibility of State and local organization structure?"[35] Few governors and mayors would answer "no" today.

Governors have endeavored to strengthen their power position by establishing an office in Washington wholly dedicated to their interests. Until this office was organized, many governors had to rely for intelligence about federal policies and operations on information filtered through communications channels controlled by the guilds. Fourteen states and several cities and counties have established liaison offices in Washington, but most of these offices do not act as the "eyes and ears" of the governors and mayors. Their activities are concentrated principally on obtaining federal grants and contracts and "casework."[36]

34. Senate Committee on Government Operations, "The Federal System as Seen by Federal Aid Officials," *op. cit.*, pp. 40, 41.

35. Senate Committee on Government Operations, Subcommittee on Intergovernmental Relations, "The Federal System as Seen by State and Local Officials," 1963, pp. 42, 43.

36. Peter J. Jones, "Cooperative Federalism and the Role of the State and City Washington Representatives," 1969 (unpublished thesis, University of Virginia).

In contrast to governors and mayors, the guilds are supported by strong power bases within the federal establishment and have developed a close rapport with functionally oriented congressional committees. They have the capacity to block or delay reform measures which they suspect contain hidden traps. As a result, progress in obtaining needed reforms has been painfully slow.

Decentralization is viewed as a subterfuge to strengthen the power of local politicians. The National Education Association was able to bring sufficient pressure to bear through the Appropriations Committees to compel the Office of Education to rescind its plans for decentralized administration of Titles I, II, and III of the Elementary and Secondary Education Act and Titles III and V of the National Defense Education Act. The Office of Education had been urged to decentralize its operations by the White House and the secretary of HEW. The NEA and other school organizations argued that establishment of Office of Education regional offices would conflict with the policy that all elementary and secondary educational programs should be channeled through the state departments of education.

Highway interests were nearly successful in their attempt to cut off funds for the administration of Section 204 of the Model Cities Act requiring coordinated review and comment at the metropolitan level on federal grant-in-aid applications submitted by individual local agencies and political subdivisions. The intent was merely to "subject highway planners," among others, "to other points of view and to some more persuasion,"[37] but for the highway guild this raised the possibility that metropolitan agencies could mobilize public support against freeways and overturn plans promoted by the state highway departments and Bureau of Public Roads. Section 204 also drew fire from critics who believed that any strength-

37. Senate Committee on Government Operations, hearings on S.561, Intergovernmental Cooperation Act of 1965, March and April 1965, p. 218.

ening of metropolitan agencies was part of a plot to impose white suburban control on the black inner cities.[38]

Guilds are politically powerful, but not invincible. Recent measures to strengthen the relative power of the generalists within the system at least provide the opportunity over the long run to produce significant change.

Passage of the Intergovernmental Cooperation Act was held up for three years, but it was finally enacted in 1968. In addition to authorizing waiver of the single-state-agency provision, the act provides that (1) governors and state legislatures shall be informed of federal grants to state agencies; (2) federal aid, to the extent possible, shall be consistent with and further the objectives of state, regional, and local comprehensive planning; and (3) loans and grants should be made to units of general local government rather than to special purpose units.

In a brief but historic statement on November 11, 1966, President Johnson directed federal department heads "to take steps to afford representatives of the chief executives of state and local government the opportunity to advise and consult in the development and execution of programs which directly affect the conduct of state and local affairs." President Johnson emphasized:

> If Federal assistance programs to State and local governments are to achieve their goals, more is needed than money alone. Effective organization, management and administration are required at each level of government. These programs must be carried out jointly; therefore, they should be worked out and planned in a cooperative spirit with those chief officials of State, county and local governments who are answerable to their citizens.

The professional bureaucracy was inclined to dismiss the presidential statement as a pious expression of good intentions.

38. Frances Fox Piven and Richard A. Cloward, "Black Control of Cities," *The New Republic,* September 30, 1967 and October 7, 1967.

Most reported that existing consultative arrangements constituted full compliance and nothing more had to be done. Some believed sincerely that their fellow guildsmen were the "chief officials . . . answerable to their citizens."

Presidential directives are not self-executing. A workable system had to be designed to afford chief executives of state and local governments a reasonable opportunity to comment on significant proposed federal rules, regulations, standards, and guidelines applicable to federal assistance programs. Bureau of the Budget Circular No. 85, June 28, 1967, established the procedures and incorporated consultation in an action-forcing process. But it did something more. The Bureau of the Budget set policies which, if observed faithfully, and this was a very big "if," could inaugurate a new era in federal-state-local relationships and help to contain the power of the guilds. The circular directed that agencies would be guided by the following policies in developing regulations for administering programs of assistance of state and local governments:

> A. The central coordinating role of heads of State and local governments, including their role of initiating and developing State and local programs, will be supported and strengthened.
>
> B. Federal regulations should not encumber the heads of State and local governments in providing effective organizational and administrative arrangements and in developing planning, budgetary, and fiscal procedures responsive to needs.

In spite of initial resistance by federal, state, and local program administrators, the Advisory Commission on Intergovernmental Relations reported that by the end of 1968 "the clearance procedure had mustered some solid support, and showed some promise of achieving its intended purpose."[39] This promise has not been realized. A 1973 ACIR evaluation

39. Advisory Commission on Intergovernmental Relations, "Tenth Annual Report," *op. cit.*, pp. 8–9.

concluded that the failure was due not to basic deficiencies in the A-85 process but "in the half-hearted commitment which the participants—all the participants, give to it." State and local representatives complained that they did not have time to prepare and submit their comments and that many proposals of vital interest to state and local governments bypassed the review process. Federal agencies objected because the review process caused undue delays, and state and local representatives either responded late or did not respond at all. Apparently neither the public interest groups representing the states and local governments nor the federal agencies were willing to allocate the necessary staff time and resources to make the system work effectively.

Circular A-85 was rescinded in 1978 when President Carter issued an executive order calling on executive agencies to adopt procedures to improve existing and future regulations. In a memorandum explaining the rescission, President Carter emphasized that "nothing in this memorandum shall be construed as in any way diminishing the affirmative obligation of the executive departments and agencies to actively seek out, encourage, and facilitate the submission of state and local comments in the development of Federal regulations."

Procedures such as "annual arrangements," "planned variations," and "chief executive review and comment" were instituted in the early 1970's to give local elected officials enhanced authority in the negotiation and coordination of categorical grants. These achieved only limited success because of organizational fragmentation and the autonomous status of many local agencies.[40]

Block grants have the potential for containing the power of the guilds and eliminating some of the complexities and rigidities of the present system of categorical grants. Block grants occupy a middle position between categorical aids and

40. *Advisory Commission on Intergovernmental Relations, Improving Federal Grants Management,* 1977, p. 234–40.

general revenue sharing and permit greater local discretion, within broad functional areas, in the use of federal funds. Major block grants include the Partnership for Health, Safe Streets, Comprehensive Employment and Training, and Community Development acts. Here again the full potential has not been realized because of the tendency of the Congress to recategorize block grants.[41]

Reorganization by region or area is perhaps the most commonly prescribed antidote to functional parochialism. When a geographic area is used as the basis of organization, the influence of the functional specialist is reduced. President Nixon's emphasis on regionalization reflected his desire to curb bureaucratic power and to break the lines of communication between the federal specialists and their state and local counterparts.

President Nixon's aim was to vest significant decision-making power with respect to federal grants in ten federal regional councils chaired by presidential appointees and subject to direction by the Office of Management and Budget. The Departments of Health, Education, and Welfare, Housing and Urban Development, Transportation, Agriculture, and Justice (Law Enforcement Assistance Administration), the Community Services Administration, and the Environmental Protection Agency were represented on the councils either by regional directors or by secretarial representatives.[42] Department and agency representatives are generalist political appointees "who have the responsibility for intersecting the very strong functionalist-specialist lines that have been developed in past years."[43] In its Washington office, OMB has a repre-

41. Advisory Commission on Intergovernmental Relations, *Summary and Concluding Observations,* 1978, p. 9–12.

42. Membership of the Regional Councils has been expanded to include representatives of the Departments of Energy, Commerce, and Interior and the Small Business Administration.

43. Leigh E. Grosenick, editor, *The Administration of the New Federalism: Objectives and Issues,* American Society for Public Administration, 1973, p. 52.

sentative for each region who attends council meetings and provides guidance to the chairman and his staff.

The attempt to superimpose a system of regional administration on an executive branch structure organized by function and purpose is calculated further to weaken the Cabinet secretaries and to sow discord within the executive establishment. One secretary objected to the interposition of the OMB and the regional councils between him and his regional directors. As reported by William H. Kolberg, his protest to the White House "had little effect. The change was intentionally made to alter the power situation in the field."[44]

Regionalization may enhance the president's relative power position, but it has the opposite effect on state and local political executives. If a regional council were able, in fact, to control the flow of federal funds into a region, then the council chairman inevitably would become the dominant political force within the region, superior to the governors and mayors. Federal influence over local decisions would be increased, not decreased.

David B. Walker attributes the present feeble functioning of the federal system to the "fractured concept of public responsibility spawned by . . . intrusive intergovernmentalization." Cooperative feudalism coupled with newer developments such as the concept of state and local governments as federal "agents," the loading of grants with conditions, and undiscriminating requirements for citizen participation have "twisted much of the real meaning out of traditional concepts of administrative and elected official responsibility. When combined with the older linkages between and among specialized sectors of the bureaucracies on all planes of government, a multifaceted notion of official responsibility emerges with several fractured dimensions."[45]

44. *Ibid.*, p. 54.
45. David B. Walker, "The State of American Federalism—1977," *Publius*, Vol. 8, No. 1, Winter 1978.

What the Advisory Committee on Intergovernmental Relations terms the "federalism of balkanized bureaucracies, segmented legislative committees and fragmented program administration" has lost its capacity to respond to the most urgent needs of our society.[46] We condemn governors and mayors for their failure to prescribe cures for urban blight, substandard housing, and crime; but in too many cases we deny them the means to take remedial action. As a result many executives feel constrained to substitute symbolic actions or public relations for performance. The paralysis caused by the diffusion of power and responsibility within the system has contributed to loss of confidence in our governmental institutions.

46. Advisory Commission on Intergovernmental Relations, "Tenth Annual Report," *Op. cit.*, p. 10.

8

Coordination: The Search for the Philosopher's Stone

In ancient times alchemists believed implicitly in the existence of a philosopher's stone which would provide the key to the universe and, in effect, solve all of the problems of mankind. The quest for coordination is in many respects the twentieth-century equivalent of the medieval search for the philosopher's stone. If only we can find the right formula for coordination, we can reconcile the irreconcilable, harmonize competing and wholly divergent interests, overcome irrationalities in our government structures, and make hard policy choices to which no one will dissent.

When interagency committees such as the Economic Opportunity Council fail as coordinators, the fault is sought in the formula, not in deeper underlying causes. The council's inability to perform its statutory duties as coordinator of the federal government's antipoverty efforts was attributed to the fact that the law (1) placed coordinating responsibility on a body of peers who could not be expected voluntarily to relinquish decision-making control over planning for or operation of programs, and (2) designated the director of the Office of Economic Opportunity, then a non-Cabinet-level official, as chairman with coordinative authority over officials of greater status. The formula was changed to provide that the council have an independent chairman and staff, but with no better results. The original council at least met a few times; the restructured council was never convened at all. Again, revision of the formula was prescribed as the remedy. The comptroller general proposed that the council's functions be transferred to an Office of Community Resources in the Executive Office of the President which would provide staff support for President Nixon's interdepartmental Urban Affairs Council.[1]

Whether we are dealing with poverty, science, telecommunications, or international and national security programs, the search for a coordinating formula seems to follow almost a set pattern: (1) establishment of an interagency committee chaired by an agency head and with no staff or contributed staff; (2) designation of a "neutral" chairman and provision for independent staff; and (3) transfer of coordinating functions to the White House or Executive Office of the President, establishment of a special presidential assistant, and reconstitution of the interagency committee as a presidential advisory council.

Our efforts to discover effective means for coordinating international and national security programs have taken us the complete cycle.

PHASE ONE

1944 State-War-Navy Coordinating Committee created by agreement of respective secretaries (Air Force added in 1947).

1947 National Security Council established.

1949 State-War-Navy-Air Coordinating Committee abolished and functions assumed by National Security Council staff. NSC staff nominated by agencies represented on the council.

1. Comptroller General of the United States, "Review of Economic Opportunity Programs," March 18, 1969, pp. 163–65.

PHASE TWO

1950 NSC staff group reconstituted and designated as "senior staff."

1953 NSC "senior staff" formalized as Planning Board. Operations Coordinating Board, chaired by undersecretary of state, created with responsibility for coordinating implementation of national security policies.

1953 Special assistant to the president for National Security Affairs established and designated as chairman of the Planning Board.

1957 OCB incorporated in NSC structure. Provision made for presidential appointment of chairman and vice-chairman.

PHASE THREE

1961 Senate Subcommittee on National Policy Machinery criticizes "over-institutionalization" of NSC system, and over-reliance on the Planning Board and OCB. It recommends that OCB be abolished and that "responsibility for implementation of policies cutting across departmental lines . . . be assigned to a particular department or a particular action officer."

1961 President Kennedy reduces NSC staff, downgrades NSC role, and abolishes OCB. Responsibility for coordinating policy and operations assigned to the secretary of state.

PHASE FOUR

1966 National Security Action Memorandum 341 ostensibly "provides the authority and machinery for the effective leadership of the country's foreign affairs by the Department of State." NSAM 341 established a two-tiered structure of interagency committees: (1) Interdepartmental regional groups chaired by the assistant secretary of state for each regional bureau; (2) a senior interdepartmental group chaired by the undersecretary of state. Theoretically, the chairman of each group was empowered to decide all matters within the purview of the group, subject to appeal to next higher authority.

The Nixon administration changed the names of the committees to interdepartmental groups and the undersecretaries Committee and restricted the latter to "operational matters." Both committees reported to an NSC review group chaired by Henry Kissinger. The NSC committee structure was again reorganized by President Carter with the stated purpose of placing "more responsibility in the departments and agencies while insuring that the NSC, with my assistant for National Security Affairs, continues to integrate and facilitate foreign and defense policy decisions."[2] The number of NSC staff committees was reduced from seven to two, the Policy Review Committee and Special Coordination Committee. The latter chaired by the assistant for National Security Affairs and the former by the secretary of state.

Defective machinery may contribute to the difficulties of coordinating multi-faceted federal programs which cut across traditional agency jurisdictions, but it is seldom, if ever, at the root of the problem. If coordination is construed as the power to make decisions, as it is in NSAM 341, the chairmen of the senior interdepartmental group and interdepartmental regional groups were called upon to exercise authorities which the president himself may not possess. Executive orders customarily confer broad powers "to facilitate and coordinate" federal programs and direct each department and agency to "cooperate" with the official designated as coordinator. However, buried in the boiler plate at the end of the order there is usually a section reading: "Nothing in this order shall be construed as subjecting any function vested by law in, or assigned

2. Presidential Directive/NSC-2, January 20, 1977.

pursuant to law to, any Federal department or agency or head thereof to the authority of any other agency or officer or as abrogating or restricting any such function in any manner."[3]

Neither the president nor a coordinator appointed by him can perform the functions vested by law in the heads of departments and agencies. Where conflicts result from clashes in statutory missions or differences in legislative mandates, they cannot be reconciled through the magic of coordination. Too often organic disease is mistakenly diagnosed as a simple case of inadequate coordination.

If agencies are to work together harmoniously, they must share at least some community of interests about basic goals. Without such a community of interests and compatible objectives, problems cannot be resolved by coordination. Senator Frank Moss ascribed the conflict between the National Park Service and the Army Corps of Engineers over the Florida Everglades to "uncoordinated activities." Park Service officials complained that the Engineers drained the Everglades National Park almost dry in their efforts to halt wet-lands flooding and reclaim glade country for agriculture. The Engineers argued that wet lands were "for the birds" and flood control for the people.[4] Coordinating devices may reveal or even exacerbate the conflict, but they cannot produce agreement among the agencies when a choice must be made as to whether a single piece of land should be drained for flood control and reclaimed for agriculture, or maintained as wet lands to preserve unique and valuable forms of aquatic life.

Coordination is rarely neutral. To the extent that it results in mutual agreement or a decision on some policy, course of action, or inaction, inevitably it advances some interests at the expense of others or more than others. Coordination contains no more magic than the philosopher's stone. It does contain,

3. See, for example, Section 4 of Executive Order No. 11452, January 23, 1969, establishing the Council for Urban Affairs.

4. Senate Committee on Government Operations, hearings on S.886 to redesignate the Department of the Interior as a Department of Natural Resources, October 17, 1967, p. 16.

however, a good deal of the substance with which alchemists were concerned—the proper placement and relationship of the elements to achieve a given result.

Coordinators are seldom judged objectively or evaluated by realistic standards. Coordination may influence people, but it makes few friends. The tendency is to consider that coordination most effective which operates to one's own advantage. Few coordinating systems have worked as successfully as OMB's procedures for clearing proposed legislation and reports on legislation and advising agencies as to the relationship of legislative proposals to "the Administration's program," but the legislative clearance process is by no means universally admired. By doing its job well, OMB has gained few friends among members of Congress and interest groups whose pet bills have been held "not in accord with the Administration's program."

The term "coordination" is used in laws and executive orders as if it had a precise, commonly understood meaning. Yet there is probably no word in our administrative terminology which raises more difficult problems of definition. For James D. Mooney, coordination is no less than "the determining principle of organization, the form which contains all other principles, the beginning and the end of all organized effort."[5] Coordination also is defined as concerted action, animated by a common purpose, responding to recognized signals and utilizing practiced skills. Coordination describes both a process—the act of coordinating—and a goal: the bringing together of diverse elements into a harmonious relationship in support of common objectives. The power to coordinate in and of itself confers no additional legal authority, but merely provides a license to seek harmonious action by whatever means may be available under existing authorities.

In current usage, coordination has come to be identified

5. James D. Mooney, "The Principles of Organization," in *Papers on the Science of Administration,* edited by Luther Gulick and L. Urwick, Institute of Public Administration, 1937, p. 93.

primarily with the formal processes by which we attempt to adjudicate disagreements among agencies. Mooney would regard the proliferation of coordinating mechanisms, such as interagency committees, as prima facie evidence of "lack of coordinated effort" resulting from inexact definitions of jobs and functions.[6] Coordinating machinery becomes necessary only when coordination cannot be achieved by sound organization, good management, and informal cooperation among agencies engaged in related and mutually supporting activities.

Formal coordinating processes are time consuming and the results are generally inconclusive. True coordination sometimes may be obtained only by going outside the formal processes.

By overemphasizing coordinating machinery, we have created the false impression that most federal activities are uncoordinated. This is by no means the case. Without informal or so-called "lateral" coordination, which takes place at almost every stage in the development and execution of national programs and at every level within the federal structure, the government probably would grind to a halt. Skilled bureaucrats develop their own informational networks. Managers who are motivated by a desire to get something done find ways and means of bridging the jurisdictional gaps. Informal coordination is greatly facilitated when people share the same goals, operate from a common set of legal authorities and informational assumptions, agree on standards, have compatible professional outlooks, and can help each other. Where these conditions exist, there is no need for the intervention of third parties to secure harmonious action.

Coordination does not necessarily require imposition of authority from the top. State and local governments have the crucial role in the process of administering and coordinating federal assistance programs. The functions of establishing state, regional, or local goals, developing comprehensive plans, and determining priorities among grant proposals in terms of

6. *Ibid.*

these goals and financial restraints is a local responsibility. Effective performance of these functions by state and local governments can reduce or eliminate need for coordinating arrangements at the federal level.

Complete reliance on voluntary cooperation is not feasible, however, except in Utopia. The goals of our pluralistic society, as reflected in federal programs, are frequently contradictory. No matter how the government is organized, it is impossible to define jobs and design programs in such a way as to eliminate all overlaps and potential conflicts among agencies. Even where the will to cooperate is present, good intentions may be thwarted by the size of the federal establishment, the growing complexity and compartmentalized character of federal programs, differences among professional groups, and the absence of a clear sense of direction and coherence of policy either in the White House or in the Congress. We cannot produce harmony by synthetic substitutes where the essential ingredients are lacking within the governmental system. The much maligned interagency committees are the result, not the cause, of our inability to agree on coherent national objectives and to find a workable solution to our organizational dilemma.

Interagency committees are the crabgrass in the garden of government institutions. Nobody wants them, but everyone has them. Committees seem to thrive on scorn and ridicule, and multiply so rapidly that attempts to weed them out appear futile. For every committee uprooted by Presidents Kennedy and Johnson's much publicized "committee-killing" exercises, another has been born to take its place.

In 1965 President Johnson launched a campaign to kill obsolete and unnecessary committees, whether established by the president or by the Congress. The agencies came up with an impressive total of 5 out of the 785 then existing committees that they were willing to offer up for sacrifice. The Bureau of the Budget estimated in January 1970 that the number of interagency committees had increased to about 850.

Interagency committees as a general institutional class have no admirers and few defenders. Former Secretary of Defense Robert Lovett ascribed the proliferation of interagency committees to the "foul-up factor," or the tendency of every agency with even the most peripheral interest to insist on getting into the act. According to Lovett, committees have now so blanketed the whole executive branch as to give it "an embalmed atmosphere."[7] From his observation, committees are composed of "some rather lonely, melancholy men who have been assigned a responsibility but haven't the authority to make decisions at their levels, and so they tend to seek their own kind. They thereupon coagulate into a sort of glutinous mass, and suddenly come out as a committee."[8] Lovett concluded that "two heads are not always better than one, particularly when they are growing on the same body."[9]

Nelson Rockefeller, W. Averell Harriman, and Lyndon B. Johnson were no less critical. Rockefeller contended that interagency committees "reduce the level of Government action to the least bold or imaginative—to the lowest common denominator among many varying positions. In such circumstances, policy may be determined not for the sake of its rightness—but the sake of agreement."[10] Harriman condemned committees as organs of "bureaucratic espionage" employed by agencies to obtain information about the plans of other departments which could be used to "obstruct programs which did not meet with their own departmental bureaucratic objectives."[11] In a memorandum to the heads of departments and agencies, President Johnson cautioned that "improper use of committees can waste time, delay action, and result in undesirable compromise."[12]

7. Senate Committee on Government Operations, Subcommittee on National Policy Machinery, "Organizing for National Security," hearing, Vol. 1, p. 15.
8. *Ibid.*, p. 30.
9. *Ibid.*, p. 17.
10. *Ibid.*, p. 945.
11. *Ibid.*, p. 635.
12. Lyndon B. Johnson, Memorandum for Heads of Departments and Agencies, February 25, 1965.

Like most things in nature, interagency committees do fulfill a purpose, although this may be at times poorly defined or understood. The harshest critics have been unable as yet to devise satisfactory substitutes. Those who condemn interagency committees as a class are not in the least inhibited when it comes to safeguarding "their committees" or in proposing new ones when it suits their purposes, even though they may feel obliged to resort to such high-sounding titles as "council" as a form of disguise. It depends on whose ox is being gored.

Of the 199 committees in existence in November 1967 which in one way or another involved the president, 123 were created by presidential executive order, 69 by laws enacted by the Congress, and 7 by agency action. Presidents may be unenthusiastic about interagency committees in general, but they object most to those created by the Congress. As we have indicated in Chapter 2, interagency committees are effectively utilized by the Congress as a means for circumscribing and limiting the president's powers. Bureau of the Budget Circular No. A-63, March 2, 1964, admonished agencies that "Committees should be established, insofar as possible, by means which permit maximum flexibility in determining the membership, functions, and duration of the group. Therefore, agencies should not propose the establishment of committees by legislation unless there is a clear need to do so." This language was echoed in President Johnson's message transmitting Reorganization Plan No. 4 of 1965 in which he argued that statutory provisions "are rarely sufficiently flexible to permit the membership or role of the committees to be accommodated to changing circumstances or to permit their termination when they have outlived their usefulness." The plan abolished nine statutory committees, but the Board of Foreign Service and the National Advisory Council on International Monetary and Financial Problems were quickly re-established by executive action.

The Congress also professes a distaste for interagency committees, but its fire is directed mainly against those created by the president or department heads. Senator Edmund Muskie was highly critical of the twenty odd interagency committees with responsibility for coordinating federal grant-in-aid programs, but his solution was a bill to establish another interagency committee to be called the National Intergovernmental Affairs Council with a strong executive secretary directly responsible to the president.[13]

Use of interagency committees as a legal subterfuge to get around the provisions of a 1909 law (31 U.S.C. 673) prohibiting the use of federal funds to finance commissions, councils, boards, and similar bodies not created or authorized by the Congress has contributed to congressional hostility. The one exception to the law is a statute (31 U.S.C. 691) permitting agencies to use their funds to pay the expenses of "interagency groups engaged in authorized activities of common interest." These restrictions are not applicable to the president's emergency and special projects funds, which are subject, however, to the Russell rider establishing one-year limitation for commissions financed from these funds.

Interagency committees have been created by the president solely for the purpose of making it possible legally to divert agency appropriations to pay the costs of controversial bodies such as the Consumer Advisory Council and various study commissions. Congress called a halt to this in 1968 by including language in appropriation acts prohibiting the use of funds appropriated to agencies to finance interagency groups "which do not have prior congressional approval of such method of financial support."[14]

Contributory financing is an irritant, but the Congress has more basic concerns about committees which are wholly creatures of the executive. Interagency committees may be employed to alter subtly the balance of power among executive

13. Senate Committee on Government Operations, Subcommittee on Intergovernmental Relations, hearings on "Creative Federalism," Part I, "The Federal Level," p. 5.

14. Public Law 90–479, Section 510.

agencies and, consequently, the balance of power among congressional committees with program jurisdiction. If the president were to establish a committee chaired by the OMB director or the chairman of the Council of Economic Advisers to coordinate water resources programs, it would bring an immediate and violent response from the Interior Committees.

Congressional mistrust of presidential committees was evidenced by the Federal Aviation Act of 1958 which provided that the FAA Administrator "shall not submit his decisions for the approval of, nor be bound by the decisions or recommendations of, any committee, board or other organization created by Executive order."

Interagency committees cannot be discussed rationally without distinguishing among the distinct types of committees and the varied purposes which they serve. These differences relate primarily to method of establishment, duration, chairman, membership, staff, financing, and functions.

Statutory committees financed by separate appropriations and employing their own staff are nothing more or less than an independent agency headed by an interagency board. The president may be authorized to designate the chairman, or the law may designate a Cabinet officer or agency head as chairman. The president may be given some discretion in selecting committee members, or membership may be determined by statute.

Difficulties occur when the law endows these agencies with something more than advisory functions. Budget Bureau Circular No. A-63 observed that "committees should be used for such functions as advising, investigating, making reports, exchanging views, etc." As a matter of executive branch policy, the circular instructed agencies that "responsibility for performance of operating or executive functions, such as making determinations or administering programs should not be assigned to committees." This admonition is repeated in the Federal Advisory Committee Act of 1972 which declares that "committees should be advisory only, and that all matters under their consideration should be determined, in accordance with law, by the official, agency, or officer involved."

The bureau's directive was intended to head off the establishment of interagency committees on the model of the National Advisory Council on International Monetary and Financial Problems and comparable bodies. NAC's statutory authorities included such broad and far-reaching powers as (1) "coordination by consultation or otherwise" of the United States representatives in international financial institutions and all federal agencies engaged in international monetary and financial transactions; (2) approval on behalf of the United States of the Articles of Agreement of various international institutions; (3) issuance of binding instructions to United States representatives to the World Bank and similar institutions. Consonant with its status as an independent agency, the NAC was directed to submit special reports to both the president and the Congress.

Most of the powers of the NAC were exercised, not by the Council as a whole, but by the Treasury and the NAC staff. During the regime of George Humphrey as secretary of the treasury, the council itself seldom met. The staff concentrated its attention on reviewing individual loan applications and day-to-day agency operations. The council's role as a "coordinator" and policy adviser to the president, except to the extent this function was performed in scrutinizing loan applications, ceased to be its major focus. The net effort of these statutory provisions and the NAC mode of operations were severely to restrict the president's discretion in his choice of advisers on international monetary and financial policy and in organizing, coordinating, and administering executive branch activities.

By far the largest number of interagency committees deal with highly technical problems and provide a convenient vehicle for exchanging information and bringing the technical people together on a regular basis to discuss problems of mutual concern. These include the Ship Structure Committee, Committee on Exports, Committee on Atmospheric Water Resources, and Range Weed Research Group. Other than providing a source of fun for columnists on dull days—the Interdepartmental Screw Thread Committee is always worth a chuckle—technical committees present few problems except in controversial areas such as pesticides where there are deep divergencies in agency objectives and policies which cannot be resolved by technicians. There are many professional "communities" in the federal government which cut across jurisdictional lines, and the committees in part serve as a forum and meeting place for the "law enforcement," "intelligence," foreign affairs," "scientific," and "educational" communities, among others.

Controversy centers principally around a relatively limited number of interagency committees that have become, in the words of the Jackson Subcommittee, "the gray and bloodless ground of bureaucratic warfare—a warfare of position not of decisive battles."[15] The battle for position is never-ending and grows more intense as agencies seek to gain control or at least exercise influence over the growing number of new and important programs which cut across established jurisdictional lines. Sometimes there is a stalemate evidenced by co-chairmen or rotating chairmanships. Occasionally, the stalemate is resolved by making the vice president or some other "neutral" the chairman.

Members of these committees act as instructed delegates of their agencies. They judge their effectiveness by how many points they win for their side. With this emphasis on gamesmanship, agency staff assigned to the committee become highly expert in identifying and escalating interagency differences, even when the issues are insignificant or nonexistent. Staff of the

15. Senate Committee on Government Operations, Subcommittee on National Policy Machinery, *op. cit.*, Vol. 3, p. 50.

NSC Planning Board, before the board was abolished by President Kennedy, were among the leading exponents of this art.

Whatever their other drawbacks, interagency committees can be useful in setting the metes and bounds of agency jurisdictions and areas of legitimate interest. Without them, or a reasonable substitute, we would have no criteria for discriminating among the many federal agencies asserting jurisdictional claims in such areas as education, water resources, science, poverty, economic and trade policy, and manpower. Agencies vie for membership on committees established by the Congress or the president, not necessarily because they expect the committee to play a decisive role, but to establish their right to request information and to be consulted about matters which concern them. Otherwise their colleagues could charge them with "meddling." The fact that the committee may never meet, or, if it does, only third- and fourth-echelon officials attend, becomes a matter of relatively little importance.

Chairmanship of a committee establishes primacy within a given program area but confers no authority, other than that which the chairman already possesses by law. Membership in an exclusive club such as the National Security Council carries with it a certain amount of prestige but, in and of itself, little influence.

Membership can provide greater access to the president when the president meets frequently with a committee and looks upon it as a part of his council. The informal committee dubbed the "Troika," composed of the secretary of the treasury, the budget director, and the chairman of the Council of Economic Advisers, exercised a dominant influence over financial and economic policy during the Kennedy and Johnson administrations. The committee was called the "Quadriad" when it included the chairman of the Federal Reserve Board.

Much of the criticism of interagency committees is directed at the wrong target. Committees can perform effectively when they are assigned appropriate tasks which are within their competence. The Alaska Reconstruction Commission was successful because each of the committee members had the statutory authority and motivation to do things which were necessary to assist Alaska's recovery from the disastrous Good Friday earthquake. The committee was not called upon to revise basic government policies, except for a few modifications which it recommended to meet the special circumstances in Alaska, but to obtain agreement among the agencies on the work that needed to be done and to see that it was carried out on a phased time schedule.

On the other hand, the federal executive boards proved totally ineffective in dealing with critical urban problems because they were given a job which they were inherently incapable of accomplishing and which was wholly alien to the purpose for which they were organized. President Kennedy established federal executive boards in ten of the largest cities in 1961. The number was, by the end of 1969, increased to twenty-five. Board membership was limited to the principal federal civilian and military officials who happened to be located within the designated geographic area. Unless the agencies most concerned with critical urban problems—the Departments of Housing and Urban Development, Health, Education, and Welfare, and Labor, and the Office of Economic Opportunity—had offices in a city, they were not represented on the federal executive board. When they were represented, it might be by someone from a specialized bureau, such as the Food and Drug Administration, who was not competent to discuss departmental programs.

The objectives in creating the boards were reasonably modest and attainable: improvement of communications between Washington and the field and among federal officials in the field; encouragement of cooperation among federal agencies in areas where cooperation might be to their mutual advantage; support of community activities such as blood donor drives and community chest campaigns. In each of these areas, members of the boards had the authority to act. As long as the boards confined their activities to such programs as equipment sharing, joint training, and improved public services, they were able to make a valuable contribution.

The boards failed when they were directed in 1965 to identify unmet urban needs and to devise and carry out interagency and intergovernmental efforts to help solve critical urban problems. A 1969 Bureau of the Budget-Civil Service Commission evaluation identifies three principal reasons for this failure, all of which should have been anticipated before the assignment was made: (1) interagency committees have no decision-making authority and cannot resolve fundamental conflicts about agency priorities; (2) collaborative efforts among members of the boards could not be effective because of the weaknesses in the boards' composition and the disparity among the boards' members in the powers delegated to them by their respective agencies; and (3) members of the boards with full-time jobs elsewhere could not be expected to devote the necessary time to activities which were extraneous to their official duties.[16]

The federal executive boards' manifest failure as coordinators did not deter efforts to assign comparable functions to a somewhat differently constituted group of interagency committees, the 10 federal regional councils. It should have come as no surprise that the councils also proved incapable of reconciling "conflicting policies and practices among their member agencies."[17]

The deficiencies associated with interagency committees can be avoided or minimized if (1) missions are tailored to their capabilities; (2) membership is kept as small as possible; (3) institutionalization of staff and procedures is held to a minimum; and (4) the end product is advice to someone who

16. Bureau of the Budget and U.S. Civil Service Commission, Memorandum for the President, "Evaluation of Federal Executive Boards," July 22, 1969.
17. Advisory Commission on Intergovernmental Relations, *Improving Federal Grants Management,* 1977, pp. 181–87.

has authority to decide and who wants the advice. Committees perform poorly when compelled to act as collective decision-makers, either as program administrators or as policy coordinators.

Standing interagency committees with responsibility to coordinate *in general* are to be distinguished from *ad hoc* interagency groups organized by the president or agency heads to study and report on *specific problems,* such as delays in the processing of federal grants, management of automatic data processing equipment, and contracting for research and development. These committees operate with a high degree of informality and are staffed by agency personnel with the requisite professional skills rather than by professional coordinators. The committees go out of business once their assigned task is accomplished. Problem-oriented working committees have been extremely useful.

President Johnson's executive orders directing the secretaries of housing and urban development and agriculture to act as "conveners" represented an attempt to institutionalize the problem-oriented approach to coordination.[18] The secretary of HUD had proposed an interdepartmental council as a means for carrying out his statutory responsibility "to exercise leadership at the direction of the President in coordinating Federal activities affecting housing and urban development." As an alternative to a standing committee, the Bureau of the Budget suggested that the secretary be given responsibility by executive order to convene, or authorize his representatives to convene, meetings at appropriate times and places of the heads, or representatives designated by them, of such federal departments and agencies with programs affecting urban areas as he deemed necessary to seek solutions to identified or anticipated urban development problems. Comparable responsibility with respect to rural development was to be given to the secretary of agriculture.

18. Executive Order No. 11297, August 11, 1966; Executive Order No. 11307, September 30, 1966.

Budget Director Charles L. Schultze argued that "coordination is best done when it is done with respect to specific identifiable problems on a case-by-case basis."[19] The executive orders conferred no authority on the secretaries but it held them accountable for seeing to it that the right people were brought together at the right time to solve specific problems. Matters requiring a decision were to be referred promptly to the person with the authority to act, up to and including the president.

The very simplicity of the convener concept guaranteed that it would be almost universally misunderstood. Senator Muskie was convinced that the convener order did nothing more than establish another interagency committee.[20] Others contended that the orders merely confirmed powers which every secretary already possessed. Secretary Robert Weaver, on the other hand, thought the convener authority was so significant that he was unwilling to delegate it to any of his subordinates, although the Bureau of the Budget had contemplated that the key role would be assigned to HUD regional administrators so that problems could be tackled immediately at the point of origin. For all these reasons, the convener approach had only a minimal impact and, despite some minor success, proved only slightly more effective than the traditional coordinating formulas.

A variant of the convener approach is to be found in Bureau of the Budget circulars designating "lead" agencies for coordinating meteorological programs and federal activities in the acquisition of water data. For example, the Department of the Interior is made responsible "for exercising leadership in achieving effective coordination of national network and specialized water data acquisition activities" and is directed to "prepare and keep current a federal plan, and the status of its

19. Senate Committee on Government Operations, Subcommittee on Intergovernmental Relations, hearing on "Creative Federalism," Part 1, "The Federal Level," November 1966, p. 399.
20. *Ibid.*, p. 116.

implementation, for the efficient utilization of network and related water data acquisition activities."[21] These arrangements have raised few of the questions associated with the convener orders, mainly because the issues tend to be more technical than political.

Problems are created when multiple lead agencies share responsibility for coordinating the implementation of similar and overlapping policies. Five lead agencies are concerned with enforcing fair employment practices in the administration of federal grants. Functions are assigned according to type of discrimination such as discrimination against the handicapped or under construction contracts.[22]

Interagency committees, conveners, and lead agencies are basically organized ways of promoting voluntary cooperation. Many believe that they are fatally flawed because there is no provision for a central directive authority. The Area Redevelopment Act of 1961 attempted to overcome this deficiency by centralizing authority and funding in a small coordinating agency—the Area Redevelopment Administration—and requiring decentralized operations through delegate agencies. The ARA was thought of as the "prime contractor" for federal depressed-area assistance, with the delegate agencies performing in the role of subcontractors.[23] The administration's primary focus was expected to be on the development and approval of overall economic development plans for each depressed area and coordination of proposed projects with the approved plans. Much the same concept is incorporated, in major or minor degree, in the foreign assistance, civil defense, and poverty programs.

The delegate agency approach appears to have considerable

21. Bureau of the Budget Circular No. A-67, "Coordination of Federal Activities in the Acquisition of Certain Water Data," August 28, 1964.

22. Advisory Commission on Intergovernmental Relations, *Categorical Grants: Their Role and Design,* 1977, pp. 262–63.

23. Sar A. Levitan, *Federal Aid to Depressed Areas,* The Johns Hopkins Press, 1964, p. 42.

promise and offers an opportunity to move toward "systems managers" for designated program areas. So far this promise has not been realized, however, because of the inability to resolve the novel problems of relationships among federal agencies which are introduced by the delegation process. These relate to selection and direction of personnel, communications, and final project approval.

ARA was unable to exercise effective control over the selection of personnel to administer delegated programs. Where responsibility for ARA programs was merely added to an employee's normal duties, first priority inevitably was given to the work for his own agency. A study by Sar Levitan indicated that "communications between the ARA and its cooperating agencies were so poor that in some cases field offices were issued conflicting instructions from their parent agencies. Suspicions and resentments were widespread among officials both in Washington and field."[24] Delegate agencies were inordinately slow in processing applications for ARA financial assistance, but it was the ARA officials who were blamed for the delays. Convinced that the system was inherently defective, the ARA urged in 1963 that it be modified drastically or abandoned.

If left to its own devices, ARA in time probably could have established a mutually acceptable and workable *modus vivendi* with delegate agencies. The insuperable obstacle was the pressures from the White House and the Congress. These pressures meant that ARA could not divorce itself wholly from decisions on individual applications. Political realities compelled ARA to divert its major efforts from overall economic development plans to projects of interest to the White House and influential members of Congress. Consequently, ARA tended to duplicate the reviews conducted by delegate agencies, thus contributing to the excessive delays in processing applications. Some believe that the delegate agency system was never given a fair test in ARA.

24. *Ibid.*, p. 45.

Evaluations of Office of Economic Opportunity experience with delegate agencies are conflicting. OEO contended that it "was the first agency at the Federal level to develop, set up and live by a system of interagency delegation agreements."[25] Delegate agencies included Labor (Neighborhood Youth Corps), Agriculture (rural loan program), Health, Education, and Welfare (work experience and adult basic education), and Small Business Administration (economic loans). While the system had not "worked perfectly," in OEO's judgment "a significant start" had been made.

The comptroller general did not share OEO's optimism and recommended that the Congress permanently transfer those programs which were administered under delegation from OEO or recommended for delegation by the president. In five instances—work study, lending and loan guarantees, adult basic education, upward bound, and work experience—the Congress had directed transfer of the programs to delegate agencies. The comptroller general held that OEO had "not been in an effective position to exercise oversight and direction for programs which have been delegated to other agencies."[26] He asserted that the appearance of central direction and coordination had been obtained at the expense of further dividing responsibility for closely related programs and blunting OEO's innovative capacity by weighing it down with administrative burdens.

Much the same line of reasoning is to be found in President Nixon's 1969 message outlining a proposed reorganization of the Office of Economic Opportunity.[27] To maintain strict accountability for the way in which work was performed, President Nixon recommended that functions should be assigned to specific agencies wherever possible, thus avoiding the blurring

25. Comptroller General, *op. cit.,* p. 22.

26. *Ibid.,* p. 168.

27. *Weekly Compilation of Presidential Documents,* August 18, 1969, pp. 1132–36.

of lines of responsibility resulting from OEO delegations. The reorganized OEO's mission would be concerned principally with innovating new domestic programs. When an experiment proved successful, the program would be transferred "to other agencies or other levels of government or even the private sector if that seems desirable." OEO would retain, however, certain proven programs which were national in scope, particularly in those cases where OEO's "special identification with the problems of the poor" made this desirable.[28]

The Congress has been willing to experiment with almost every conceivable type of coordinating formula, but it has drawn the line at proposals for "super coordinators" or "super Cabinet" officers. Except in wartime, the Congress objects to changes which transfer power from the heads of the established agencies to "czars" who are answerable only to the president.

For this reason, John Gardner's proposal for a home-front executive officer or executive vice president attracted little serious attention outside the press.[29] Gardner told *The New York Times* that the federal government "cannot go on much longer with its present organization" of overlapping and conflicting agencies on domestic problems, and so the president should appoint an "executive officer" to mobilize and coordinate talent and resources in various departments for the home front. The president cannot do the job because he is "too busy" and "he doesn't really like to get in and deal with fights" between Cabinet members. The Budget Bureau and White House staff have only "partial and limited coordinating functions" and "have proven wholly inadequate to the task of coordination."

Gardner's plan was by no means new. In 1955 Herbert Hoover suggested creating two appointive vice presidents, one responsible for foreign and the other for domestic affairs.

28. President Nixon recommended in his 1975 Budget Message that OEO be abolished.

29. *The New York Times,* July 18, 1968.

President Eisenhower recommended the establishment of a "first secretary" of the government who would function, in effect, as prime minister with respect to national security and international affairs. From time to time it has been suggested seriously that the vice president be made "coordinator-in-chief," although it is doubtful that any president would be willing to delegate this kind of power to a person whom he did not appoint and cannot remove. Paul David has observed: "The functions, duties and prerogatives of the Vice President, as a member of the Executive Branch are not likely to be expanded except with the formal or informal concurrence of the President; but once such functions, duties and prerogatives are in place, withdrawal through action by the President becomes more difficult than their initial establishment."[30]

As we have seen, President Nixon's "experiment" with the equivalent of assistant presidents for domestic affairs, foreign affairs, economic affairs, and executive management and with counsellors for Human Resources, Natural Resources, and Community Development was short-lived. In unveiling the plan in January 1973, President Nixon stated that its purpose was "to integrate and unify policies and operations throughout the executive branch of the Government" and "to bring about better operational coordination and more unified policy development."[31] On May 10, 1973, Press Secretary Ronald L. Ziegler announced that the president "intended to have more direct lines of communication with members of the Cabinet." Consequently, "the Counsellor role, as originally announced and conceived would be moved aside at this time."[32]

The problems of the modern presidency clearly cannot be resolved by converting the White House into a corporate headquarters with several appointed subexecutives authorized to

30. Paul T. David, "The Vice-Presidency: Its Institutional Evolution and Contemporary Status," *The Journal of Politics,* November 1967.

31. White House Press Release, January 5, 1973.

32. *Weekly Compilation of Presidential Documents,* May 11, 1973, pp. 662–63.

speak for the corporation. Within the executive branch the president alone has the constitutional duty to exercise leadership in establishing national goals and priorities. The setting of these goals and priorities in terms that can be understood and communicated in actionable form to the operating agencies is the first prerequisite for coordination.

Under existing law the president can delegate coordinating responsibilities to officers appointed by and with the advice and consent of the Senate and agency heads (White House staff are excluded), but he cannot delegate those powers necessary to carry out the responsibility.[33] The president's political powers as our one nationally elected official other than the vice president, and as the leader of his political party, and his constitutional powers to approve legislation and to hire and fire the heads of executive agencies are nondelegable. An assistant president or "super-Cabinet" officer without political influence or statutory powers would have nothing going for him but the majesty of his title, unless he were accepted as the president's alter ego. It is doubtful that our constitutional system can accommodate both an elected president and appointed presidential alter egos without impairing the unity of executive power.

If statutory functions were transferred from the departments to a counsellor or "super-Cabinet" officer, or if the performance of functions were made subject to his control, he would cease to be a coordinator and become a superdepartment head. Arguments can be made for superdepartments, but no one contends that superdepartments will improve the coordination of programs that cut across superdepartmental jurisdictions.

The Jackson Subcommittee was of the view that "super Cabinet" officers would not ease the president's problems but "would make his burdens heavier." The committee concluded:

33. McCormack Act, 3 U.S.C. 302.

> Reforms, to be effective, must be made in terms of the real requirements and possibilities of the American governmental system.
>
> That system provides no alternative to relying upon the President as the judge and arbiter of the forward course of policy for his administration. It provides no good alternatives to reliance upon the great departments for the conduct of executive operations and for the initiation of most policy proposals relating to those operations.[34]

Our governmental system has nothing comparable to the ministers without portfolio who perform coordinating functions in many countries with a parliamentary form of government. In Great Britain, for example, ministers without portfolio have been used to coordinate research and development programs and the formulation of coordinated government information policies. Under Chancellors Adenauer and Erhard, a minister without portfolio was responsible for coordinating various matters among members of the German Cabinet who belonged to the chancellor's party and for acting as a liaison with the Cabinet members and leadership of the opposition party.

An American equivalent of a minister without portfolio would increase the options now available to the president. Without such an office, presidents occasionally have utilized Cabinet officers to perform special tasks unrelated to their official duties. A minister without portfolio would be more acceptable to the Congress than a White House coordinator, if he were appointed by the president, by and with the advice and consent of the Senate. He would not be barred by tradition from testifying before congressional committees. Furthermore, as a matter of law, the president could delegate functions to such an officer—something he cannot do to White House staff. As in the case of White House staff, however, a minister's potential effectiveness would be limited by the absence of a

34. Senate Committee on Government Operations, Subcommittee on National Policy Machinery, *op. cit.*, Vol. 3, pp. 21–22.

constituency and statutory control over federal funds and programs. Nonetheless, a minister without portfolio under some circumstances might afford a desirable alternative to existing coordinating arrangements or the further multiplication of White House staff.

Congress's ambivalence toward coordination is reflected in its discontent with the Bureau of the Budget, an organization which Senator Ribicoff described "as the most mysterious part of the entire Federal Government."[35] Many congressmen saw no contradiction in demanding at one and the same time that executive branch coordination be strengthened, but that the Budget Bureau's powers to coordinate be curtailed. We suspect that some proposals for new coordinating formulas stemmed more from a desire to cut the Budget Bureau down to size and thereby to undermine the president's authority than to improve coordination.

The Bureau of the Budget admittedly had its institutional biases. Its style was negative and critical, rather than positive and creative. But this reflected the fact that its assigned role was essentially negative. The development of new programs and advocacy of increased spending were viewed as inconsistent with the bureau's basic mission. This "negativism" inevitably caused conflicts with activists on the White House staff mainly concerned with promoting the president's political interests.[36]

Whatever the Bureau of the Budget's limitations may have been, it has yet to be demonstrated that its work can be done better by the Office of Management and Budget, Domestic Policy Staff, or White House counsellors with specific program responsibilities. The latter tend to be special pleaders. The

35. Senate Committee on Government Operations, Subcommittee on Executive Reorganization, "Modernizing the Federal Government," January–May 1968, p. 42.

36. Allen Schick, "The Budget Bureau That Was: Thoughts on the Rise, Decline and Future of a Presidential Agency," *Law and Contemporary Problems*, Vol. 25 Summer 1970. Hugh Heclo, "OMB and the Presidency: The Problems of 'Neutral' Competence," *The Public Interest*, Vol. 38, Winter 1975. Larry Berman, "OMB and the Hazards of Presidential Staff work," *Public Administration Review*, Vol. 38, No. 6, November–December 1978.

important distinction between agencies in the Executive Office of the President, such as the Bureau of the Budget, serving the presidency as an institution, and those serving the president in a personal, political capacity has been lost. President Nixon acknowledged "a tendency to enlarge the White House staff—that is, the President's personal staff as distinct from the institutional structure. This has blurred the distinction between personal staff and management institutions."[37] The director of OMB and the executive director of the Domestic Policy Staff are housed in the White House and function in a dual capacity as assistants to the president. OMB and the Domestic Policy Staff are regarded not as professional agencies but as extensions of the White House apparatus. As now organized and staffed, it is doubtful that OMB and the Domestic Policy Staff can duplicate completely the Bureau of the Budget's institutional memory, professionalism, knowledge of the government as a whole, general perspective, critical outlook, and dedication to the interests of the presidency as an institution.

By holding out the promise of a perfect coordinating formula, we have provided a plausible excuse for not facing up to the hard political choices that now confront us. Layers of coordinating machinery can conceal but not cure the defects and contradictions in our governmental system.

If we want coordination, we must first be able to identify and agree on our national goals and priorities and to design programs to accomplish them. Our present mechanisms for national planning and goals-setting work very imperfectly and are in a highly rudimentary stage of development. Solution of the urgent problems confronting America in the 1980's demands something more than skills in political tactics and public relations. We no longer can afford indiscriminately to fritter away our human and material resources on poorly conceived and often contradictory programs whose major purpose is to pacify competing and conflicting group interests.

37. House Doc. No. 91–275, Message of the President transmitting Reorganization Plan No. 2 of 1970.

[illegible] programs [illegible] of the [illegible] the [illegible] Congress [illegible] planning [illegible] the Executive [illegible] the [illegible] [illegible] planning [illegible] and the [illegible] government [illegible] situation.

In seeking out the [illegible] agencies coordinating [illegible] planning [illegible] and [illegible] our governmental system.

If we are to [illegible] we must first be able to identify [illegible] and to design programs to accomplish them. The principal mechanism for national planning and [illegible] development [illegible] and [illegible] relations [illegible] no longer [illegible] programs whose major purpose [illegible].

37. Message of the President transmitting Reorganization Plan No. 2 of 1970.

II

The Politics of Institutional Type

9

Administrative Agencies

The interplay of competing and often contradictory political, economic, social, and regional forces within our constitutional system and pluralistic society has produced a smorgasbord of institutional types. There is something to suit almost every taste, no matter how exotic. Choices from among this rich assortment are seldom determined by strict application of established organizational "principles." Choices are influenced by a complex of tangible and intangible factors reflecting divergent views about the proper sphere of government activity, politics, institutional folklore, program importance and status, visibility, political and administrative autonomy, and, most important, who should exercise control. The theoretical arguments frequently have little relevance to the real issues. The president, the Congress, the bureaucracy, and the constituencies each judge institutional types from a somewhat different perspective and favor those arrangements which they believe will best serve their interests.

The constitution itself provides few guides for institutional development. Numerous proposals in the Constitutional Convention of 1787 to spell out the details of executive branch structure were rejected. The intent of the Constitution-makers can only be inferred from the provisions vesting executive power in the president, including the power to appoint, by and with the advice and consent of the Senate, all officers of the United States, whose appointments are not otherwise provided for in the Constitution, and authorizing the president to "require the opinion in writing, of the principal officer in each of the executive departments, upon any subject relating to the duties of their respective offices." Under the Constitution the Congress may by law vest the appointment of inferior officers, as they think proper, in the courts of law, or in the heads of departments.

The references to the "principal officer in each of the executive departments" and the "heads of departments" are significant. There appears to have been a clear intention that the departments of administration be headed by a single officer. George Washington was expressing a view widely held at the time when he stated: "Wherever, and whenever one person is found adequate to the discharge of a duty by close application thereto it is worse executed by two persons, and scarcely done at all if three or more are employed therein. . . ."[1] Federalists generally joined with Washington and Hamilton in considering multi-headed administrative agencies to be weak and irresponsible.

In the successive enactments of the Congress establishing executive agencies, there was no departure from the principle of single-headed administration. Some argued that the Treasury Department ought to be administered by a board of commissioners because "the duties of the office of financier were too arduous and too important to be entrusted to one man," but the proposal was rejected.[2]

Although the Constitution is almost wholly silent on the subject of executive branch organization, there seems to be little doubt that the framers intended that all executive functions be grouped under a limited number of single-headed

1. Quoted in Leonard White, *The Federalists,* The Macmillan Co., 1948, p. 91.
2. Lloyd M. Short, *The Development of National Administrative Organization in the United States,* The Johns Hopkins Press, 1923, p. 92.

executive departments. James Monroe, as secretary of state, reflected the prevailing concept of executive branch organization when he said:

> I have always thought that every institution, of whatever nature soever it might be, ought to be comprised within some one of the Departments of Government, the chief of which only should be responsible to the Chief Executive Magistrate of the Nation. The establishment of inferior independent departments, the heads of which are not, and ought not to be members of the administration, appears to me to be liable to many serious objections. . .. I will mention only, first that the concerns of such inferior departments cannot be investigated and discussed with the same advantage in the meetings and deliberations of the administration, as they might be if the person charged with them was present. The second is that, to remedy this inconvenience, the President would, necessarily, become the head of that department himself. . . .[3]

Until 1913, it was most unusual for agencies to be created outside of the principal departments. There were a considerable number of commissions established from time to time to perform special tasks, but these were always of a temporary nature. The one notable exception is the 1846 Act providing for the incorporation of the Smithsonian Institution, but the Smithsonian was funded initially by the Smithson bequest and, consequently, was looked upon as a quasi-public institution rather than as a government agency. The first major departures from the accepted pattern of organization came with the establishment of the Civil Service Commission in 1883 and the Interstate Commerce Commission in 1887. In the case of the ICC the Congress did not break completely with tradition. The secretary of the interior was given authority to approve the number and compensation of all commission personnel, except the secretary to the commission. A link between the ICC and the executive department was maintained by requir-

3. *Ibid.*, footnote, pp. 417–18.

ing that the commission's annual reports be submitted to the secretary. Independent status was not accorded to the ICC until 1889, when the Congress granted the secretary of the interior's request to be relieved of his supervisory responsibilities.

Hubert Humphrey described our constitutional system as "a Government of pressures, outside pressures, working on inside people."[4] Outside pressures began to mold and shape executive branch structure as early as the 1860's. The United States Agricultural Society sought the establishment of a Department of Agriculture to place "agriculture upon a plane of equality with the other executive departments."[5] The National Association of School Superintendents lobbied for a Department of Education, and the Knights of Labor for a Department of Labor. In response to these constituency pressures, the Congress created three departments of less than Cabinet rank headed by commissioners: Agriculture (1862), Education (1867), and Labor (1888). The Department of Agriculture was given Cabinet rank in 1889 and the Department of Labor was made a constituent of the Department of Commerce and Labor in 1903. The Department of Commerce and Labor was divided into two separate executive departments in 1913.

Restraints on the organization of agencies independent of the executive departments began to crumble with the establishment of the Federal Reserve Board and Board of Mediation and Conciliation in 1913 and practically disappeared during World War I. World War I also witnessed the first significant use of the corporate form of organization. Except for the War Finance Corporation, which was created by the Congress, World War I corporations such as the Shipping Board, Food Administration, and War Trade Board were chartered under

4. Senate Committee on Government Operations, hearings on S.1571 to establish a Department of Consumers, June 23 and 24, 1960, p. 34.
5. Short, *op. cit.*, p. 383.

the general incorporation laws either of the states or of the District of Columbia. Federal control was maintained over the corporations mainly through the power to appoint directors and such supervision as might be exercised by the Cabinet officer who organized the corporation. The corporate form of organization did not achieve legitimacy until the 1940's, although it was widely employed during the depression of the 1930's when such alphabet agencies as the RFC, HOLC, TVA, CCC, FDIC, USHA, and RACC achieved considerable notoriety.[6] Many believed that only war or depression could justify resort to the corporate device.

By 1937 the President's Committee on Administrative Management was able to identify over a hundred separately organized establishments and agencies presumably reporting to the president. President Franklin Roosevelt endorsed the committee's recommendation that the country return to first principles and organize the government's activities within twelve major executive departments. Roosevelt contended that this reorganization was necessary to "bring many little bureaucracies under broad coordinated democratic authority."[7]

We have made some progress since 1937 in reducing the number of independent agencies, but the 1978–79 Government Manual shows that there are still at least fifty-five agencies organized outside the twelve executive departments. If there were added to the fifty-five mixed-ownership government corporations, government-sponsored enterprises, private corporations organized and financed by the government to furnish contractual services to federal agencies, and intergovernmental bodies, the decrease in the number of independent agencies since 1937 would be even smaller.

6. Reconstruction Finance Corporation, Home Owners Loan Corporation, Tennessee Valley Authority, Commodity Credit Corporation, Federal Deposit Insurance Corporation, United States Housing Authority, Regional Agricultural Credit Corporation.

7. Franklin D. Roosevelt, Message to the Congress on Administrative Reorganization, January 12, 1937.

The number and variety of institutional arrangements presently utilized by the federal government almost defy classification. Each major grouping contains important subcategories, and significant differences may be identified within any of the subcategories. The following classification makes no claim to scientific exactness; it is intended merely to identify significant organizational types. The word "independent" means only independent of an executive department, and does not imply independence from the president or the executive branch. In popular usage the word has come to have the latter meaning, particularly when applied to the independent regulatory commissions. The listings under each of the headings are not necessarily complete.

EXECUTIVE DEPARTMENTS

State, Treasury, Defense, Justice, Interior, Agriculture, Commerce, Labor, Health and Human Services, and Housing and Urban Development, Transportation, Energy, Education.

EXECUTIVE OFFICE OF THE PRESIDENT

White House Office, Council of Economic Advisers, Council on Environmental Quality, Council on Wage and Price Stability, Domestic Policy Staff, National Security Council, Office of Science and Technology Policy, Office of Administration, Office of Management and Budget, Special Representative for Trade Negotiations.

INDEPENDENT AGENCIES

Single-headed: ACTION, Arms Control and Disarmament Ageny, Central Intelligence Agency, Canal Zone Government, Community Services Administration, Federal Emergency Management Agency, Federal Mediation and Conciliation Service, General Services Administration, International Communications Agency, National Credit Union Administration, Selective Service System, Office of Personnel Management, Veterans Administration.

Multi-headed: American Battle Monuments Commission, National Capital Planning Commission, Board for

International Broadcasting, International Trade Commission, Postal Rates Commission, Federal Election Commission, Merit System Protection Board, Commission on Civil Rights, Equal Employment Opportunity Commission, Federal Coal Mine Safety Board of Review, Farm Credit Administration, National Mediation Board, Railroad Retirement Board, Renegotiation Board, National Transportation Safety Board.

FOUNDATIONS

National Science Foundation, National Foundation on Arts and Humanities.

INSTITUTIONS AND INSTITUTES

Smithsonian Institution.

HEW: National Institutes of Health, National Cancer Institute, National Heart Institute, National Institute of Allergy and Infectious Diseases, National Institute of Arthritis and Metabolic Diseases, National Institute of Dental Research, National Institute of Neurological Diseases and Blindness, National Institute of General Medical Sciences, National Institute of Child Health and Human Development, National Eye Institute, National Institute on Aging.

Commerce: Institutes for Environmental Research, Institute for Basic Standards, Institute for Materials Research, Institute for Applied Technology.

State: Foreign Service Institute.

Justice: National Institute for Law Enforcement and Criminal Justice.

CLAIMS COMMISSIONS

Foreign Claims Settlement Commission, Indian Claims Commission.

REGULATORY COMMISSIONS

Civil Aeronautics Board, Federal Communications Commission, Federal Home Loan Bank Board, Federal Maritime Commission, Federal Reserve Board, Federal Trade Commission, Interstate Commerce Commission, National

Labor Relations Board, Securities and Exchange Commission, Consumer Product Safety Commission, Commodity Futures Trading Commission, Nuclear Regulatory Commission, Federal Energy Regulatory Commission.

CONFERENCES

Administrative Conference of the United States.

GOVERNMENT CORPORATIONS

Wholly-owned Corporations Under Executive Department

Single-headed: St. Lawrence Seaway Development Corporation, Government National Mortgage Association.

Multi-headed: Commodity Credit Corporation, Federal Crop Insurance Corporation, Federal Financing Bank, Federal Prison Industries, Inc., Federal Savings and Loan Insurance Corporation, Panama Canal Company, Community Development Corporation, federal Home Loan Corporation, Pension Benefit Guaranty Corporation, Neighborhood Reinvestment Corporation, Pennsylvania Avenue Development Corporation.

Wholly-owned Independent Corporations

Multi-headed: Federal Deposit Insurance Corporation,[8] Export-Import Bank of Washington, Tennessee Valley Authority, Inter-American Foundation, Overseas Private Investment Corporation.

Mixed-ownership Government Corporations

Multi-headed: Central Bank for Cooperatives, Regional Banks for Cooperatives (12), Federal Intermediate Credit Banks (12), Rural Telephone Bank, U.S. Railway Association.

INTERAGENCY BOARDS, COUNCILS, AND COMMITTEES

Statutory: Federal Records Council, Water Resources Council, Consumer Advisory Council, etc.

Executive Order: Federal Interagency Committee on Edu-

8. Classified as mixed-ownership in Government Corporation Control Act, but, in fact, wholly-owned since retirement of capital stock in 1948.

cation, National Advisory Council on International Monetary and Financial Policies, Federal Regional Councils, etc.

STATUTORY ADVISORY BODIES (*majority private citizens*)

Advisory Board of St. Lawrence Seaway Development Corporation, National Historical Publications Commission, Advisory Councils to each of the HEW Institutes, Advisory Council on Vocational Education, National Advisory Council on Extension and Continuing Education, etc.

JOINT EXECUTIVE-CONGRESSIONAL COMMISSIONS

Advisory Commission on Low Income Housing, Agricultural Trade Development Advisory Committee, National Forest Reservation Commission, Migratory Bird Conservation Commission.

INTERGOVERNMENTAL ORGANIZATIONS

National: Advisory Commission on Intergovernmental Relations.

Regional: Appalachian Regional Commission, Delaware River Basin Commission, Ozarks Regional Commission, Upper Great Lakes Regional Commission, New England Regional Commission, Coastal Plains Regional Commission, Four Corners Regional Commission, Region No. 6 Commission, Pacific Northwest River Basins Commission, Great Lakes River Basin Commission, Souris-Red-Rainy River Basins Commission, New England River Basin Commission.

TWILIGHT ZONE

Federal Reserve Banks, Federal Land Banks, Federal Home Loan Banks, Federal National Mortgage Association, National Home Ownership Foundation, National Housing Partnership, Corporation for Public Broadcasting, National Parks Foundation, National Railroad Passenger Corporation, Securities Investor Protection Corporation, Student Loan Marketing Association, U.S. Railway Association, Legal Services Corporation.

PRIVATE INSTITUTIONS ORGANIZED AND FINANCED BY THE FEDERAL GOVERNMENT TO PROVIDE CONTRACTUAL SERVICES

Independent Nonprofit Corporations: Aerospace Corporation, Institute for Defense Analyses, Logistics Management Institute, Institute for Urban Studies, Rand Corporation, Research Analysis Corporation, Youthwork, Public/Private Ventures, etc.

University-Affiliated Research Centers: Applied Physics Laboratory, Human Relations Research Organization, Brookhaven Laboratory, MITRE, Lincoln Laboratory, Los Alamos National Laboratory, etc.

Research Center Operated by Private Industry: Oak Ridge National Laboratory.

There are no general federal laws defining the form of organization, powers, and immunities of the various institutional types. Each possesses only those power enumerated in its enabling act, or in the case of organizations created by executive action, set forth by executive order in a contract. Whatever special attributes may have been acquired by the various organizational classes are entirely a product of precedent, as reflected in successive enactments by the Congress, judicial interpretations, and public, agency, and congressional attitudes. For some of the organizations, public attitudes tend to be based more on folklore than on fact.

Few of these institutional types emerged full-blown in their present form. There is very little evidence of conscious thought and planning in the development of new institutions. The approach generally has been highly pragmatic and eclectic. The process has been more derivative than creative. The Interstate Commerce Commission was established in the image of the regulatory organizations then existing in a number of states. The search for an agency with sufficient operating and financial flexibility to conduct the business enterprises undertaken in World War I was solved by borrowing the corporate form of organization from private enterprise. As we have indicated previously, most of the World War I corporations were chartered under the general incorporation laws of states or the District of Columbia. These laws often prescribed forms of organization and financing not particularly well adapted to a public body, and subterfuges sometimes were required to provide *pro forma* compliance. Until the Panama Railroad Company was reincorporated under federal charter in 1948, it was necessary to issue each director one share of stock to comply with the provisions of the corporation's New York charter. The foundation represents the culmination of efforts by scientists to duplicate within the federal government an organization structure devised for institutions of higher learning. The "captive" corporation was born of improvisations by the Office of Scientific Research and Development in World War II to meet its unique requirements. The Defense Department and the National Institutes of Health inherited certain contractual arrangements when the OSRD was liquidated after the war. The Judicial Conference provided the model for the Administrative Conference of the United States. Inherited factors have been considerable significance in influencing relationships within the executive branch, internal organization, mode of operations, method of financing, and public and congressional responses.

Some institutional types are more acceptable than others because they have been borrowed from and are identified in the public mind with nongovernment institutions. This has proved to be of critical importance when the federal government has entered into new and controversial areas of activity. Harold Laski has noted that "most Americans have a sense of deep discomfort when they are asked to support the positive state. . . . They tend to feel that what is done by a government institution is bound to be less well done than if it were undertaken by individuals, whether alone or in the form of private corporations."[9] If a service cannot be performed by private enterprise, then obviously the next best thing is an organization which appears to be insulated against "politics"

9. Harold J. Laski, *The American Democracy,* Viking Press, 1948, p. 167.

and which looks as nearly as possible like a private institution. This feeling is evident in the argument raised by the chairman of the Federal Deposit Insurance Corporation against legislation proposed in 1960 to subject the corporation to budget control. Chairman Wolcott contended that "an agency having responsibility for protection of the Nation's money supply should be independent while remaining in the framework of Government. It must be part of the Government in order to escape private pressures; yet, within the Government it must be free of political pressures."[10] The Neighborhood Reinvestment Corporation is described in its enabling act as a "nonbureaucratic approach," an approach which Congressman Stewart B. McKinney argued, freed the corporation from things which make government programs "almost incomprehensible to the average, ordinary citizen."[11] Public distrust of government is somewhat alleviated when programs are administered by corporations or foundations and these agencies are organized in such a way that they are of but not in the government. The same distrust underlies arguments for the use of nonprofit intermediaries and reprivatization.

Analysis of statutory provisions reveals that the Congress has followed a reasonably consistent pattern with respect to the organization structure, powers, and immunities of each of the major institutional types. Critical differences among the types are to be found in the provisions of law relating to composition of the directing authority (single- or multi-headed); qualifications for appointment; procedures for the appointment and removal of principal officers; method of financing; budget and audit controls; personnel regulations; and advisory councils and committees. These provisions determine the degree of organizational and operating autonomy and in large measure control an agency's relationship to the president, the Congress, and its clientele.

10. Committee on Government Operations, Hearings on H.R. 12092 to make the FDIC subject to budget review, June 21, 1960, p. 34.

11. *Congressional Record,* July 21, 1978, p. H7136.

The one official guide to the relative status and protocol ranking of executive agencies is to be found in the Executive Schedule Pay Rates. Agencies are by no means equal in terms of their prestige within the executive establishment or standing in the Congress and the community. The significance of their heads being included in Level II rather than in Level III goes beyond the mere $2,600 difference in salary. The infighting can be bitter when amendments to the Executive Schedule are being considered, and some congressional favorites, such as the director of the Federal Bureau of Investigation, have been rewarded with higher rankings than their position would seem to warrant.

The following pecking order is established by the Executive Schedule:

Level I: Executive departments.

Level II: Major agencies of the executive office of the President, such as the Office of Management and Budget; major independent agencies, such as the National Aeronautics and Space Administration, Central Intelligence Agency, Veterans Administration, International Communications Agency; Federal Reserve; Military departments.

Level III: Independent agencies, such as the General Services Administration, Small Business Administration; major regulatory agencies, such as the Interstate Commerce Commission and Federal Communication Commission; government corporations, such as the Federal Deposit Insurance Corporation, Export-Import Bank, Tennessee Valley Authority; foundations; major administrations or bureaus within executive departments, such as the Federal Bureau of Investigation, Comptroller of the Currency, and Highway Administration.

Level IV: Independent agencies, such as the Selective Service System, Equal Employment Opportunity Commission, National Transportation Safety Board, St. Lawrence Seaway Development Corporation; bureau heads within executive departments, such as Director, Community Relations Service, and Director of Public Roads.

Level V: Minor agencies, such as Renegotiation Board, Foreign Claims Settlement Commission; heads and deputy heads of principal constituent units within executive departments and agencies.

Next to the top pay levels, heavy sedans are the most eagerly sought-after status symbols. Under OMB regulations, heavy sedans are reserved for heads of executive departments, the Ambassador to the United Nations, and Chiefs of Class I diplomatic missions. All others must ride in medium or light sedans.

Executive Departments. The executive departments' position at the apex of the organizational hierarchy remains unchallenged, although the principal assistants to the president now rank above Cabinet officers in public prestige and influence. Major independent agencies such as the Veterans Administration and the General Services Administration may employ more people and spend more money than some of the executive departments, but both the White House and the Congress make subtle distinctions between the heads of these agencies and Cabinet secretaries. While there is no statutory basis for the distinctions, other than the Executive Schedule Pay Rates, those who have served in both capacities can testify that they are real and important.

No exact criteria have ever been prescribed for establishing executive departments. The Congress generally has applied certain pragmatic tests relating to permanence, size, scope, complexity, and, above all, national significance of the programs to be administered by the department. According to the Bureau of the Budget, "departmental status is reserved for those agencies which (1) administer a wide range of programs directed toward a common purpose of national importance; and (2) are concerned with policies and programs requiring frequent and positive Presidential direction and representation at the highest levels of the Government."[12]

12. Statement of David E. Bell, Director of the Bureau of the Budget, on S. 1633 to establish a Department of Urban Affairs and Housing, June 21, 1961.

Executive departments do symbolize basic national commitments and values, and for this reason the Congress has responded slowly to demands for new departments. Creation of a new department is always regarded as an historic occasion. The reorganization establishing the Department of Defense in 1949 marked the first change in the top executive branch structure since 1913, although this represented more of a merger of the previously existing War and Navy departments than the birth of a new department. The first genuinely new executive department was Health, Education, and Welfare established in 1953. This was followed by the Department of Housing and Urban Development in 1965, the Department of Transportation in 1966, and the Department of Energy in 1977.

Each of the executive departments created since the Civil War, except Energy, Commerce, and Transportation, was required to serve an apprenticeship as a non-Cabinet department or agency before being elevated to executive department status. Proposals to convert the Federal Security Agency, the predecessor of HEW, and the Housing and Home Finance Agency, the predecessor of HUD, to executive departments were flatly turned down by the Congress on more than one occasion before they were adopted. The first bill to establish a Department of Transportation was introduced in the Congress in 1890.[13] Seventy-six years were to go by before the department became a reality.

Except for such aberrations as the Tenure of Office Act, the Congress has observed faithfully the organizational precepts laid down by the framers of the Constitution in creating executive departments. Congress has not felt bound by these precepts in dealing with agencies below the executive department level.

Each executive department has a single head. No restrictions are placed on the president's authority to appoint or remove

13. S. 4106 introduced by Congressman John J. Ingalls (Kansas) in the 51st Congress, 1st Session.

department heads. The statutes differ in specifying presidential authority to direct and supervise a Cabinet officer. The secretary of defense is "subject to direction by the President" and the secretary of state "shall conduct the business of the Department in such manner as the President shall direct." Other acts are silent on the subject of presidential direction. Regardless of the statutory language, Congress recognizes that the heads of executive departments are the "President's men."

Except for a few prerogatives, such as the right to request a formal opinion of the attorney general, there is little that a Cabinet officer can do as a matter of law, that cannot also be done by an independent agency head. Budget Bureau witnesses were hard pressed to explain the legal differences between a Housing and Home Finance Agency and a Department of Housing and Urban Development. The differences have their roots in custom and tradition and cannot be discovered in law books.

The Cabinet itself is a creature of custom and tradition without a constitutional or statutory basis. The Cabinet has always functioned at the pleasure of the president and in the manner of his choosing. Whatever the role assigned to the Cabinet as a collective entity, and this has varied greatly from one president to another, membership in the Cabinet is of tremendous importance as a symbol of status and rank. Appointment as head of an executive department always has been assumed to confer Cabinet membership without further presidential designation. Of the original Cabinet, all except the attorney general were department heads. The attorney general was included as the government's legal advisor. The Department of Justice became an executive department in 1870.

Others may be invited by the president to attend Cabinet meetings or accorded Cabinet rank. These have included the vice president, the speaker of the House of Representatives, the ambassador to the United Nations, the chairman of the Atomic Energy Commission, the director of OMB, as well as from time to time various special assistants to the president. There are shades of difference between those who are invited to attend Cabinet meetings and those who are present because of the office they hold. Under Eisenhower, only the vice president and the heads of executive departments had a high-backed chair, with their name on an engraved plaque, at the Cabinet table.

Invitees are reluctant to volunteer opinions unless the president specifically calls upon them. In 1956 the Housing and Home Finance administrator was invited to discuss a subject of vital concern to his agency. But he was seated in the back row against the wall, and President Eisenhower appeared to be wholly unaware of his presence.

Changes in attitude resulting from elevation to departmental status are translated into easier access to the White House staff and the chairmen of congressional committees, an improved bargaining position in dealing with other federal agencies and organized constituencies, and better coverage by the communications media. Rufus Miles, assistant secretary for administration of the Department of Health, Education, and Welfare, observed from his experience in both HEW and the Federal Security Agency that there was a "very rapid change in public attitude which came about from the elevation of the status of the then Federal Security Agency to a departmental status. The amount of increased attention that was given to the total organization and its problems was very marked."[14]

The gradations which exist within the executive hierarchy also may be found among the executive departments. Executive departments are by no means equal in power, prestige, or closeness to the president. The presidential inner circle is generally composed of Cabinet members without strong constituency ties, the secretaries of state, defense, and treasury, and the attorney general, to whom the president looks for

14. Senate Committee on Government Operations, hearings on "Modernizing the Federal Government," January–May 1968, p. 115.

expert advice, rather than for political support. President Nixon formalized the "inner Cabinet" by his designation of the secretaries of state and treasury and the director of OMB as assistants to the president, and the secretaries of agriculture, HEW, and HUD as presidential counsellors. As we have seen, departments differ significantly in personality and outlook, administrative habits, and relationships to the president, the Congress, and the outside community.

Executive Office of the President. Relatively youthful upstarts in the Executive Office of the President have stolen some of the glamour from the Cabinet secretaries. Such level II luminaries as the director of OMB and the chairman of the Council of Economic Advisers wield more power and receive a greater press coverage than the heads of most executive departments. In arguing for Senate confirmation of the director of OMB, the House Committee on Government Operations emphasized "the reality" that the director "with his vast power and importance, holds an office of superior rank."[15] As these executive office institutions have approached middle age, their "passion for anonymity" has waned noticeably. But, contrary to popular belief, there is no special magic associated with location in the Executive Office of the President. Heads of executive departments are vested with a certain status by reason of the office they hold. This is not true of those in the Executive Office. The directors of some executive office units would like to give the impression that they are the powers behind the throne, but they are often so far behind the throne as to be almost invisible.

Classical concepts of organization have not been observed as rigorously by the Congress in establishing the constituent elements of the Executive Office of the President as they have been in the case of executive departments. When the Executive Office of the President was created in 1939, it contained one multi-headed unit, the National Resources Planning Board.

15. House Report No. 93–109.

Today the Executive Office includes two agencies headed by interagency committees: Council on Wage and Price Stability, and National Security Council. The Council of Economic Advisers and the Council on Environmental Quality are also collegiate bodies, but Reorganization Plan No. 9 of 1953 transferred to the CEA chairman the function of reporting to the president with respect to the Council's work.

The Budget and Accounting Act of 1921 recognized that the relationship between a president and his budget director necessarily must be one of intimacy and trust. Consequently, the president was given the power to appoint the director and assistant director without Senate confirmation. Congressman Good pointed out during the floor debate on the act that "these offices would be so peculiarly the President's staff, the President's force, the President, without being questioned with his regard to his appointment, should appoint the men whom he could trust to do his will in the preparation of the budget. . . ."[16] This special status was revoked in 1974, a casualty of Watergate and resentment against President Nixon's use of impoundment to curtail or discontinue programs authorized by the Congress. Except for White House staff, the heads of the principal executive office agencies are now all subject to Senate confirmation. The Congress has refrained from establishing terms of office, or, except for members of the Council of Economic Advisers and the Council on Environmental Quality, specifying qualifications for appointment.

Congress has been unwilling to give the president a free hand with respect to the organization of the Executive Office of the President. Most department heads now have authority to organize and reorganize their agencies without formal congressional approval, but the president lacks comparable power. President Eisenhower recommended in his 1961 Budget Message that the President be authorized to reorganize the Execu-

16. Bureau of the Budget, Staff Orientation Manual, April, 1958, p. 7.

tive Office so as to "insure that future Presidents will possess the latitude to design the working structure of the Presidential Office as they deem necessary for the effective conduct of their duties under the Constitution and the laws." A bill was introduced for this purpose, but no further action was taken, partly due to a conspicuous absence of enthusiasm on the part of some of the more important people in the Bureau of the Budget who wanted to preserve the bureau's unique position as *primus inter pares.*

The present structure of the Executive Office of the President does not reflect the Committee on Administrative Management's intention that no institutional resources be provided within the office other than those which the president found essential to advise and assist him in carrying out functions which he could not delegate. As the number of agencies and personnel in the Executive Office of the President has increased, their usefulness as general staff to the president has decreased. The number of employees in the Executive Office of the President grew from 1,255 in 1956 to 1,796 in 1976.[17] Congressional pressure to provide visibility and enhanced status for favored programs diverted the Executive Office of the President from its exclusive concern with *presidential* business by establishing within it the Office of Economic Opportunity, the National Council on Marine Resources and Engineering Development, and the Council on Environmental Quality. The president was similarly motivated in recommending the establishment of the Special Action Office for Drug Abuse. As a consequence, recent presidents have tended to look to the White House office, not to the institutional agencies within the Executive Office of the President, for necessary staff support.

President Nixon called for "a sharp reduction in the overall size of the Executive Office of the President and a reorientation

17. House Committee on Post Office and Civil Service, Committee Print No. 95–17, 95th Congress, 2nd session, "Presidential Staffing—A Brief Overview."

of that office back to its original mission as a staff for top-level policy formation and monitoring of policy execution in broad functional areas. The Executive Office of the President should no longer be encumbered with the task of managing or administering programs which can be run more effectively by the departments and agencies."[18] Reorganization Plan No. 1 of 1973 streamlined the Executive Office by abolishing the Office of Emergency Preparedness, the Office of Science and Technology, and the National Aeronautics and Space Council.

While concern was expressed that abolition of OST signified "a downgrading of our science apparatus," the House Committee on Government Operations interposed no objection to the reorganization. The committee concluded: "As a practical proposition, the President cannot be compelled to utilize a policy making and advisory apparatus in the Executive Office against his own preferences. Furthermore, the President should have considerable latitude in determining the composition of the Executive Office."[19] There were those who suspected that abolition of the Office of Science and Technology was motivated more by a desire to punish the scientific community for its opposition to the Vietnam war than by zeal for streamlining the Executive Office.[20] Scientists were unhappy with their eviction from the Executive Office and succeeded in persuading President Ford and the Congress to authorize re-establishment of the office in 1976 as the Office of Science and Technology Policy.

The Executive Office of the President was again reorganized by President Carter "based on the premise that the EOP exists to serve the President and should be structured to meet his needs."[21] Reorganization Plan No. 1 of 1977 either discontinued or transferred the functions of the Offices of Drug

18. House Document No. 93–43.
19. House Report No. 93–106, p. 18.
20. *The New York Times,* October 6, 1973.
21. House Document No. 95–185, July 15, 1977.

Abuse Policy and Telecommunications Policy and the International Economic Policy, Federal Property, Energy Resources, Economic Opportunity, and Domestic Councils. The Domestic Council was redesignated the Domestic Policy staff. The plan established an Office of Administration to provide centralized administrative services for components of the EOP.

The implications of executive office organization for the effective functioning of our constitutional system and the distribution of power among the three co-equal branches of government are as yet insufficiently recognized. Given the present involvement of White House staff in functions formerly performed by career personnel within the Executive Office, the exodus of senior staff upon the inauguration of a new president could threaten the continuity of government. The president ought to have the capability to adapt the Executive Office to his perceived needs, but he should not be permitted in the process to ignore the needs of future presidents, the Congress, and the people.

Independent Agencies. Columnist David Lawrence was reflecting a common misconception when he wrote: "Basically the RFC is supposed to be an 'independent agency' and not part of the executive department or the White House, but a creature of Congress, *as are all other independent Boards and Agencies*" (italics supplied.)[22] The Constitution makes no provision for a fourth branch of government, independent of the president, or for limitations on the president's exercise of executive powers. Whether or not the president can exercise his powers effectively is another matter. Some of the independent agencies have been so structured as to blunt the president's powers and provide *de facto* independence.

Independent agencies come in all shapes, sizes, and forms. Both the Small Business Administration and the Federal Aviation Agency, prior to its incorporation in the Department of Transportation, were spun off from the Department of Com-

22. *Washington Star,* February 27, 1951.

merce in an effort to escape an unsympathetic operating environment. The Maritime unions would also like to divorce the Maritime Administration from the Department of Commerce. None of the independent agencies at present is an embryo executive department comparable to the Housing and Home Finance Agency. As we have indicated, the General Services Administration and the Veterans Administration do exceed in size, measured in personnel and budget, smaller executive departments. Some, such as the Veterans Administration and the General Services Administration, are expressly subject to presidential direction or regulations, while others, such as the Farm Credit Administration, are almost outside the government altogether.

So far as independent agencies are concerned, the Congress does not believe that the injunctions against multi-headed agencies and limitations on the president's powers of appointment and removal apply. Several have been given all the trappings of a regulatory commission, including multi-member boards selected on a bipartisan basis with fixed, overlapping terms of office. Qualifications for appointment may be spelled out in detail, as for the Small Business Administrator and members of the Farm Credit Board.

The Central Intelligence Agency, the International Communications Agency, the National Aeronautics and Space Administration, the U.S. Postal Service, and the Veterans Administration Department of Medicine and Surgery are excepted, either in whole or in part, from Civil Service regulations. ICA, CIA, TVA, Postal Service, and VA have their own personnel systems. Special personnel systems also exist within executive departments, notably the Foreign Service, Public Health Service, and ESSA Corps.

These restrictions and exemptions in and of themselves weaken, but do not eliminate presidential power. For those who demand sovereignty, not merely autonomy, within the federal structure, the priceless ingredient is financial self-sufficiency. The Farm Credit Administration and U.S. Postal Service are the classic illustrations.

During the 1952 campaign, General Eisenhower was persuaded by the farm organizations to include in an Omaha speech a pledge "to remove the Federal domination now imposed on the farm credit system. . . . A Federal Farm Credit Board, elected by farmer members, should be established to form credit policies, select executive officers, and to see that sound credit operations will not be endangered by partisan political influence."[23] Farmer ownership and control of the credit institutions somehow became translated into farm organization control of the federal agency responsible for regulating the credit institutions.

When advised that election of members of the Federal Farm Credit Board would be unconstitutional, the farm organizations agreed reluctantly to accept a compromise bill providing for a thirteen-member, part-time board consisting of one member designated by the secretary of agriculture and twelve members appointed by the president, by and with the consent of the Senate, after considering nominations submitted by the national farm loan associations, the production credit associations, and the cooperatives who are stockholders of or subscribers to the guaranty fund of the bank for cooperatives. The Board, in turn, appoints the governor of the Farm Credit Administration, subject to the president's approval. The governor had been a presidential appointee. To assure that any ties with the president were severed, the law makes it the governor's duty to comply with all board orders and directions.

For all practical purposes, the farm organizations have accomplished their objectives. In practice, the nomination of directors has become the equivalent of election. President Eisenhower held up the appointment of directors for several months in 1957 when confronted by a direct challenge to his authority, but ultimately went along with the nominations. The gover-

23. Speech at Omaha, Nebraska, September 18, 1952.

nor and the board openly lobbied against the president's proposal to subject the farm credit institutions to budget control. The president could not use his budget powers to bring the Farm Credit Administration into line because, except for appropriations to finance the Cooperative Research and Service Division, all FCA funds are obtained from assessments against the supervised institutions. Without this self-financing provision, open defiance of the president would have been far more hazardous.

The U.S. Postal Service is the most independent of the independent agencies and is practically a law unto itself. The Postal Service is defined by law as "an independent establishment of the executive branch of the United States," but in all other respects it is endowed with the powers and characteristics of a wholly-owned government corporation. The service is headed by an eleven-member part-time board of governors, appointed by the president with Senate confirmation. Governors serve for nine-year overlapping terms. The service's chief executive officer, the postmaster general, is appointed by and serves at the pleasure of the board.

The U.S. Postal Service is not subject to the Government Corporation Control Act or the controls normally applied to wholly-owned government corporations. The Postal Service Act (Public Law 91–375) includes language comparable to that in Sec. 102 of the Government Corporation Control Act requiring annual submission of a business-type budget to the Office of Management and Budget, but does not authorize OMB to amend or modify the budget. There is no requirement that the budget be transmitted to the Congress. As it is now written the act creates the impression of control where in fact none exists. Indeed, elsewhere the Postal Service Act provides specifically that "no Federal law dealing with public or Federal contracts, property, works, employees budgets or funds . . . shall apply to the exercise of the powers of the Postal Service."

The Postal Service is intended to be self-financing, except for reimbursement of any "public service costs" incurred in providing "a maximum degree of effective and regular postal service nationwide." The service is authorized to borrow money and to issue and sell such obligations as it determines necessary in amounts not to exceed $10 billion outstanding at any one time. Avoidance of the "annual battle between the Post Office Department and the Bureau of the Budget, which notoriously results in limitations upon funds available to be appropriated" was cited by the Senate Post Office and Civil Service Committee as "the basic purpose in authorizing the sale of bonds by the Postal Service and exempting it from budget control."[24]

When he proposed that the Post Office Department be reorganized as an autonomous and independent non-cabinet Postal Service, President Nixon contended that an efficient postal service could not be obtained without insulating the Postal Service "from direct control by the President, the Bureau of the Budget and the Congress" and "partisan political pressure."[25] This argument reflects distrust of our governmental institutions and loss of faith in the democratic process.

Congress is beginning to have second thoughts about the degree of autonomy granted to the U.S. Postal Service. Congressman Morris K. Udall, an original proponent of postal reform, complained that the legislation passed by a vote of 370 to 70 or so, but "I cannot find a single member who voted for it or who will admit voting for it. . . . I am constantly referred to as one of the fathers. I have been thinking of denying paternity."[26] The House of Representatives passed a bill in 1978 to abolish the board of governors and transfer its functions to a presidentially appointed postmaster general. The bill died in the Senate.

24. Senate Report 91–912, p. 9.

25. House Document No. 91–313.

26. Hearings before a Subcommittee of the House Committee on Governmental Operations on Reorganization Plan No. 2 of 1978, June 13, 1978, p. 107.

Institutions, Foundations, and Institutes. It seems somehow fitting that the Smithsonian Institution should have an organization charter worthy of display with other museum pieces. The Smithsonian Institution remains *sui generis,* and does so for reasons which shall become evident. Purists would find it difficult to reconcile the organizational arrangements established for the Smithsonian with the constitutional doctrine of separation of powers. Appointing authority is vested in the speaker of the House of Representatives and the president of the Senate, seemingly in direct violation of Article II, Section 2 of the Constitution.

Smithsonian has an "establishment" composed of the president, the vice president, the chief justice, and the heads of executive departments, but with no known functions, other than as the institution's "incorporators." The business of the institution is conducted by a Board of Regents consisting of the vice president, the chief justice, three members of the Senate appointed by the president of the Senate, three members of the House of Representatives appointed by the speaker, and six other persons appointed by joint resolution of the Senate and the House. Presumably the president could veto the joint resolution, but this is the extent of his powers over appointments to the Board of Regents. The Institution's principal executive officer, the secretary, is selected by the board.

Congress has appropriated to the institution the annual interest on the $541,379.63 Smithson bequest, but this income constitutes an infinitesimal part of the institution's budget. In 1973 salaries and expenses alone exceeded $50 million. Private financing has had a symbolic value, and certain personnel restrictions have been avoided by paying the secretary and his chief assistants from private funds.

Except for its extra-constitutional organization structure, the Smithsonian is now treated in all respects as an executive agency subject to general laws and presidential directives with respect to budget, audit, property and supply management,

Civil Service, legislative clearance, and the like. The institution is highly dependent on the cooperation and good will of the president and federal agencies, and its secretary has been most discreet in asserting his prerogatives as the agent of an independent establishment.

While problems of relationships within the executive branch have been minimal, Smithsonian's anomalous organization structure has at times prevented the most effective utilization of the institution's resources. Smithsonian would provide a more scholarly environment for the National Archives than the General Services Administration. Smithsonian also was a logical candidate to house the National Foundation on Arts and Humanities. But under present circumstances, these organizational options are not available without sacrificing the president's powers.

Foundations and institutes have become the preferred form of organization for institutions making grants to local governments, universities, nonprofit organizations, and individuals for research in the natural and social sciences, or artistic endeavors. The unique characteristic of these organizations is an elaborate superstructure of advisory arrangements designed to give representatives of grantee groups maximum influence over the allocation of funds. In Chapter 1 we described the structure of the National Science Foundation. The National Foundation on the Arts and Humanities creates the appearance of a single organization, although, in fact, it consists of two independent entities—the National Endowment for the Arts and the National Endowment for the Humanities. Each endowment is headed by a chairman appointed by the president, subject to Senate confirmation, for a four-year term. The chairmen, however, cannot approve or disapprove grant applications without first obtaining the recommendations of a council. The National Council on the Arts is composed of the secretary of the Smithsonian Institution and twenty-four members appointed by the president for six-year terms. In making appointments, the president is requested to give consideration to the recommendations of leading national organizations in each branch of the arts. The National Council on the Humanities has twenty-six members, also appointed for six-year terms. Recommendations for appointments are to be submitted by the leading national organizations concerned with the humanities.

A National Advisory Council is attached to each of the Institutes under the National Institutes of Health. The councils consist of twelve members, appointed for four-year terms by the surgeon general, with the approval of the secretary of health, education, and welfare. Members must be leaders in fundamental sciences, medical sciences, and public affairs, and six must be specialists in the field covered by the institute. No grants may be made without council approval.

The title "institute" has been used for agencies engaged in research and training, but this has had no significance, except to provide a name with a better academic standing.

Regulatory and Claims Commissions, Administrative Conference. The independent regulatory commissions and claims commissions have evolved into what the President's Committee on Administrative Management termed "a headless 'fourth branch' of the Government." From what were intended originally to be somewhat differently structured executive agencies, these commissions have been transformed into "arms of the Congress" by constituency pressures, custom, and Supreme Court decisions.

When the Interstate Commerce Commission was established in 1887, the Congress did not believe it was violating sacred writ by giving the secretary of the interior powers over the commission's personnel. In 1902 there was strong sentiment in the Congress for transferring the ICC to the new Department of Commerce and Labor.[27] No conflict was seen in designating the secretary of the treasury as chairman of the Federal Reserve Board in 1913. The secretaries of agriculture,

27. Short, *op. cit.*, p. 422.

interior, and war constituted the Federal Power Commission when it was established in 1920. By deliberate congressional choice, regulatory functions under the Packers and Stockyards Act of 1921 were assigned to the secretary of agriculture rather than to the Federal Trade Commission. Concepts drawing sharp distinctions between regulatory and executive functions are of relatively recent origin, and to some extent, are an historical accident.

Marver Bernstein has defined "independence," as applied to the regulatory commissions, as relating to one or more of the following conditions: "location outside an executive department; some measure of independence from supervision by the president or a cabinet secretary; immunity from the president's discretionary power to remove members of independent commissions from office."[28] The last condition listed by Bernstein has been of key importance.

The ICC has been the model for the regulatory commissions. The number of commission members varies from three on the Home Loan Bank Board to eleven on the ICC. All, except the National Labor Relations Board, are bipartisan and members serve for fixed, overlapping terms of office. At one time it was common for commissions to elect their own chairmen, but all commission chairmen are now designated by the president.

The ICC Act authorizes the president to remove any commissioner "for inefficiency, neglect of duty, or malfeasance in office." Similar language is found in almost all of the statutes creating regulatory commissions, although it has been omitted for some performing exclusively judicial functions. There is indisputable evidence, however, that the language which the Supreme Court has construed to be a limitation on the president's powers was intended by the Congress to be just the opposite. The Tenure of Office Act of 1867 was still in effect when Congress enacted the ICC Act. By including a provision

28. Marver H. Bernstein, *Regulating Business by Independent Commission,* Princeton University Press, 1955, p. 130.

authorizing the president to remove commissioners, even though only for specified causes, the Congress conferred upon the president considerably more latitude than he had with respect to other executive officers appointed with the consent of the Senate.

The Supreme Court decisions in the case of *Humphrey's Executor* v. *United States* [295 U.S. 602 (1935)] and *Wiener* v. *United States* [357 U.S. 349 (1958)] have provided the legal foundation for the theory of commission independence. In the Humphrey case, the Court drew a distinction between an agency performing quasi-legislative and quasi-judicial functions, such as the Federal Trade Commission, and an agency primarily concerned with administrative or executive duties. Justice Sutherland held that the Federal Trade Commission "to the extent that it exercises any executive function, as distinguished from executive power in the constitutional sense, it does so in the discharge of its quasi-judicial and quasi-legislative powers, or as an agency of the legislative or judicial branches of government." It was the Court's unanimous view that the president could remove an FTC Commissioner for the causes enumerated in the statute and for no other reasons. The Court went beyond the Humphrey case when it ruled in the Wiener case that President Eisenhower could not remove a member of a claims commission, even though the Congress had not specifically limited the president's removal powers.

Regardless of the Supreme Court decisions, until 1973 the regulatory commissions in some areas enjoyed less independence than some executive agencies. The president was able through OMB review of budgets, legislation and data questionnaires, and Department of Justice control of litigation significantly to influence commission policies, administration, and operations. The Congress in 1973 overrode White House objections and amended the Alaska pipeline bill (1) to authorize the Federal Trade Commission to represent itself in civil court proceedings and (2) to transfer authority for review of independent regulatory commission data requests under the Federal Reporting Services Act from OMB to the General Accounting Office.

The current congressional emphasis on independence is reflected in the exclusion of regulatory commissions from the president's reorganization authority. Until 1977 such a limitation was not contained in the Reorganization Statute. To protect further the independence of regulatory programs the Senate Committe on Governmental Affairs has recommended: (1) Independent regulatory commissions should conduct and control their own substantive litigation, except for litigation taking place in the Supreme Court; (2) Independent regulatory commissions should transmit any budget request to the Congress at the same time such messages are submitted to the Office of Management and Budget, as now provided for the Commodity Futures Trading Commission, Consumer Product Safety Commission, and the Interstate Commerce Commission; (3) Legislative communications from an independent commission to the Congress should not be subject to prior clearance by the Office of Management and Budget; and (4) Top staff officials at the independent regulatory commissions should be selected wholly on the basis of merit, and the selection decision by the agency should not be subject to clearance by officials outside the agency.

To increase political accountability, the Senate committee proposed that the heads of other executive departments be accorded powers comparable to those now vested in the secretary of energy. The secretary of energy is authorized to intervene in proceedings before the Federal Energy Regulatory Commission that have a significant policy impact and to initiate proposed rulemaking.[29]

Presidents are willing to concede a degree of independence, but not total independence, to the regulatory commissions.

29. Senate Document No. 95–91, 95th Congress, 2nd Session, December 1977, p. XIII.

President Kennedy stressed the continuing responsibilities of the president with respect to the operations of these agencies in his message on "Regulatory Agencies of Our Government."[30] He asserted that "the President's responsibilities require him to know and evaluate how efficiently these agencies dispatch their business, including any lack of prompt decision of the thousands of cases which they are called upon to decide, any failure to evolve policy in areas where they have been charged by the Congress to do so, or any other difficulties that militate against the performance of their statutory duties."

President Kennedy did agree that intervention in individual cases would be improper, unless the executive departments appeared formally as an intervenor in a particular proceeding. Indirect means may be employed, however, to convey the president's views to the commission on an individual case. President Eisenhower sent a letter to the chairman of the Senate Foreign Relations Committee urging that "the United States should promptly take whatever action might be necessary to clear the way for commencement of the project [St. Lawrence Seaway]," and forwarded a copy of his letter to the chairman of the Federal Power Commission.[31] The project could not proceed until the commission approved a pending New York–Ontario power application. The Commission got the message and acted favorably.

Evidence has yet to be produced which demonstrates that an autonomous commission most effectively assures protection of the public interest. On the contrary, the evidence would indicate that "independence" makes the commissions more susceptible to industry influence and congressional intervention. Roger Noll concludes that "independence serves primarily to insulate the agency from the general public."[32]

Many researchers have isolated and confirmed the regulatory

30. Message to the Congress, April 13, 1961.

31. *Congressional Record,* April 25, 1953, p. 40009.

32. Roger G. Noll, *Reforming Regulation: An Evaluation of the Ash Council Proposals,* The Brookings Institution, 1971, p. 35.

commission syndrome. The symptoms of this geriatric malady are disorientation and growing inability to distinguish between the public interest and the interests of those subject to regulation. Noll brands the agencies "as a form of legal cartel for regulated firms."[33]

Similar problems arise from a commission's intimate involvement with the legal profession and the practitioners appearing before it. The fact that lawyers have dominated the commissions can be seen in the case-by-case approach to regulation, emphasis on adversary proceedings, and complex judicialized processes and procedures. It can be seen also in the structure of the organization created to simplify, speed up, and insure fairness in regulatory processes—the Administrative Conference of the United States.

The Bureau of the Budget favored a conference limited in membership to responsible federal officials—the chairmen of the major regulatory commissions and the heads of the agencies performing regulatory functions. Although the bureau could and did argue that it was conforming strictly to the Judicial Conference model in excluding the practicing bar from voting membership, its views did not prevail. As constituted by law, the Administrative Conference more nearly resembles the House of Delegates of the American Bar Association than it does either the Judicial Conference or an executive branch agency. The conference's chief executive officer is a chairman appointed by the president, with the consent of the Senate, for a five-year term. A ten-member council appointed by the president for three-year terms is responsible for approving the agenda, budget, and appointments made by the chairman of conference members from outside the government. Not more than half the council members may be employees of federal regulatory agencies or executive departments.

Plenary powers are vested in an Assembly consisting of not more than 91 or less than 75 members. At least one third of the

33. *Ibid.*, p. 38.

Assembly members are to be selected to give broad representation of the views of the practicing bar, scholars in the field of administrative law or government, or others specially informed by knowledge and experience with respect to federal administrative procedure. Appointments of nonlawyers so far represent little more than tokenism. The Assembly conducts its business with all the formality and elaborate procedures of a legislative body. There are committee reports, resolutions, debates, and roll-call votes. Among federal agencies, the Administrative Conference is unique.

Government Corporations. Institutional types are seldom loved or hated for themselves alone. Partisan heat may be aroused by the substance of a program or the personality of the administrator, but rarely by the institutional type. The one notable exception is the government corporation. While emotions are not as strong as they once were, there are still those who regard the corporate device as good or evil, regardless of how it is used or the purpose which it serves.

No responsible person or organization has ever demanded that all departments, bureaus, boards, or commissions be abolished. But the Congress from time to time is flooded with mail demanding that all government corporations be abolished, and bills have been introduced with this objective. At the other extreme are a number of businessmen and scholars who attribute almost mystic qualities to the corporation and find in it a panacea for most of the ills which beset the government.

The government corporation has become a symbol, and symbols stir strong, and often ambivalent, emotions. At one and the same time the corporation represents the evils of government in business, and the virtues of business efficiency and organization in government. The latter view was embraced by the President's Commission on Postal Organization, chaired by Frederick R. Kappel, retired chairman of the board of directors of American Telephone and Telegraph Company, which advocated conversion of the Post Office from an executive department to a government corporation as a means of solving the postal "crisis" and assuring that the postal service would be run as a "business."[34] Differences of opinion about the value and uses of government corporations are not necessarily a reflection of differences in economic and political ideologies.

Preconceptions have so colored most discussions of government corporations that folklore is often mistaken for fact. Among the most commonly accepted myths are: (1) incorporation by itself gives a government corporation certain basic authorities not possessed by other government agencies; (2) a government corporation is not a part of the executive branch but an agency of the Congress; (3) a government corporation is by definition autonomous; and (4) a board of directors is an indispensable attribute of a government corporation. None of these is true.

States have enacted general incorporation laws, but the federal government has not. The distinguishing attributes of a United States government corporation are not inherent in the corporate form but stem solely from specific grants of power that have been customarily included in corporate charters enacted by the Congress. The Government Corporation Control Act is, as its name implies, a control act and confers no authority on a corporation.

The government corporation is essentially an empirical response to problems posed by increasing reliance on government-created business enterprises and business-type operations to accomplish public purposes. The United States acquired the Panama Railroad Company when it purchased the assets of the French Canal Company in 1904, but it was not until World War I that the United States government became a business entrepreneur on a large scale and established the first wholly-owned government corporations.

To accomplish its wartime objectives, the government found

34. President's Commission on Postal Organization, *Towards Postal Excellence*, a report to the President, June 1968.

it necessary to construct and operate a merchant fleet, to build, rent, and sell houses, to buy and sell sugar and grain, to lend money, and to engage in other commercial enterprises. All these activities had certain unique characteristics which clearly set them apart from what up to then had been construed to be "normal" and acceptable Government functions: (1) the government was dealing with the public as a businessman rather than a sovereign; (2) users, rather than the general taxpayer, were expected to bear a major share of the cost for goods and services; (3) expenditures necessarily fluctuated with consumer demand and could not be predicted accurately or realistically financed by annual appropriations; (4) additional expenditures to meet increased demand did not necessarily in the long run increase the net outlay from the Treasury; and (5) operations were being conducted within areas in which there were well-established commercial trade practices. Experience demonstrated that enterprises with such characteristics could not be managed effectively under an administrative and financial system designed to control totally different types of government activities.

The keystone of financial control was then, and to a large extent still is, the requirement that Congress provide funds through annual appropriation acts. For this reason, most agencies are not permitted to retain and utilize incidental revenues or to carry over unexpended balances at the end of the fiscal year. Governmental accounting and auditing had the limited purposes of preventing the over-obligation of appropriated funds and unlawful expenditures. Furthermore, the Congress was unwilling to permit administrative discretion in those areas of most vital concern to a business—procurement, contracts, sales of goods and property, and personnel. While administrators often found that the myriad of regulatory and prohibitory statutes was a serious inconvenience, loss of flexibility was considered to be but a small sacrifice to place on the altar of public honesty and accountability. But it became evident that any attempt to operate a business enterprise within such a framework would entail not mere inconvenience, but certain failure.

The first solution was to charter government corporations under the general incorporation laws of the states and the District of Columbia. While this device provided necessary flexibility, it created new and equally difficult problems. Considerable doubt existed concerning the propriety of subjecting a federal instrumentality to the provisions of state law. Furthermore, most existing controls to assure public accountability were abandoned without providing satisfactory substitutes. Sporadic attempts were made by the Congress and the comptroller general to apply traditional budget and audit controls to government corporations, but the results were such as to discourage further efforts along these lines.

The Government Corporation Control Act of 1945 represents the first official recognition by the Congress of the need for a new type of government institution tailored to the requirements of business programs and for new types of controls over such institutions which would assure accountability without impairing essential flexibility. The Congress expressly recognized that "the corporate form loses much of its peculiar value without reasonable autonomy and flexibility in its day-to-day decisions and operations. The budget and financial controls imposed upon Government corporations should not deprive them of this freedom and flexibility in carrying out auhorized programs. . . ."[35]

The Government Corporation Control Act prohibited the creation of government corporations except by or pursuant to an act of Congress and required that all corporations chartered by the states or the District of Columbia be reincorporated by act of Congress or liquidated by June 30, 1948. The Control Act did not significantly alter or impair the distinguishing

35. Senate Report No. 694, 79th Congress.

characteristics and special powers which had been acquired by government corporations.

There is no reference to the Government Corporation Control Act in statutes enacted during 1970 to establish a Federal Home Loan Mortgage Corporation and a Community Development Corporation. Whether the omission reflected a conscious attempt to escape ceilings on net corporate outlays (not a requirement of the Control Act), as was the case when the Congress placed programs of the Export-Import Bank, Rural Telephone Bank, and Rural Electrification Administration outside the budget, or merely sloppy legislative drafting is difficult to determine.

As a body corporate, a government corporation has a separate legal personality distinct from that of the United States. A corporation, therefore, does not enjoy the traditional immunity of the United States from being sued without its consent. A corporation can also be authorized to borrow money in its own name without directly pledging the credit of the United States, although the financial community recognizes that the government would be most unlikely to refuse to make good in the event of default. The principal advantage is that such unguaranteed corporate obligations are not included under the public debt ceiling.

A corporation is usually given power "to determine the character and the necessity for its expenditures, and the manner in which they shall be incurred, allowed and paid." A corporation is thus exempted from most of the regulatory and prohibitory statutes applicable to the expenditure of public funds, except those specifically applicable to government corporations. Although subject to audit, their expenditures cannot be "disallowed" by the General Accounting Office, which is limited to reporting questionable transactions to the Congress. Some in the General Accounting Office have never become fully reconciled to the loss of disallowance authority and this has been reflected from time to time in hostility to the conversion of such agencies as the Washington Airports and the Alaska Railroad to corporations.

A very great part of the difference between a corporation and an agency arises from the method of financing its operations. A corporation's funds are generally derived from such sources as capital appropriations, which are not subject to fiscal year limitations, revenues, and borrowings from the Treasury or public. With a few exceptions, such as the Federal Crop Insurance Corporation (administrative expenses) and the TVA (nonrevenue programs), corporations are rarely dependent on annual appropriations for their funds.

The principle is now generally accepted by the Congress and the public that a government corporation should endeavor to operate, so far as practicable, on a self-sustaining basis and recover through user charges all costs of its operations, including interest, depreciation, and the cost of services furnished by other government agencies. Some fall short of this goal, notably the Commodity Credit Corporation's price support program which incurs substantial annual losses, but, for most, a break-even operation remains the ultimate objective. Attempts to recover the costs of noncorporate programs from user charges have met with considerable resistance on the grounds that these are no different from traditional government services properly chargeable, in whole or in part, to the general taxpayer.

Mixed-ownership government corporations are not subject to any form of budget control, although within recent years the budgets of the Federal Intermediate Credit Banks and the Banks for Cooperatives have been included in the Budget Appendix. The budgets of the Federal Land Banks and the Federal Home Loan Banks, which have retired the government-owned capital stock, are published in a Budget "annex." Stronger measures advocated by President Eisenhower in his 1961 Budget Message to apply the budget provisions of the

Control Act to mixed-ownership corporations were rejected by the Congress.

Wholly-owned government corporations are generally required by law to present "business-type" budgets which the Corporation Control Act provides shall be plans of operations "with due allowance for flexibility." Unlike an agency, which requests specific appropriations, a corporation seeks congressional approval of its budget program as a whole. Congress is authorized to limit the use of corporate funds for any purpose, but it has seldom chosen to do so, except for administrative expenses. In essence, the business-type budget provides for a qualitative rather than a quantitative review of proposed corporate expenditures.

The comptroller general is directed by the Control Act to make an annual audit of all government corporations "in accordance with principles and procedures applicable to commercial corporate transactions." The comptroller general may make a "comprehensive audit" of noncorporate government enterprises. A comprehensive audit in many respects resembles a commercial audit, but it may include also an examination of the legality of individual items of expenditure.

Employees of government corporations are considered to be employees of the United States[36] subject to the general laws and regulations applicable to government employees. Exceptions have been granted when a need has been established for special flexibility in hiring and dismissing employees and establishing wage scales, as in the case of the Panama Canal Company, Tennessee Valley Authority, Banks for Cooperatives, and Federal Intermediate Credit Banks. Other exceptions are the U.S. Railway Association and the Neighborhood Reinvestment Corporation whose officers and employees "shall not be considered to be officers and employees of the United States."

A board of directors was once considered to be the hallmark

36. Sidney D. Goldberg and Harold Seidman, *The Government Corporation: Elements of a Model Charter,* Public Administration Service, 1953, pp. 23–29.

of a government corporation, due largely to the fact that state incorporation laws generally require the establishment of boards of directors elected by the stockholders. Boards of directors persist in many varieties and forms, even though the need for and usefulness of most boards are highly debatable. David Lilienthal began to entertain serious reservations about the usefulness of the Tennessee Valley Authority Board when he served as its chairman. He wrote in his diary that "the board has come to mean me."[37] The Congress replaced the board of directors of the Reconstruction Finance Corporation with a single administrator because the board arrangement had resulted in "diffusion of responsibility." It was noted that existence of a five-man board of directors had made it possible "for individual members to avoid, obscure, or dilute their responsibilities by passing the buck from one to another."[38] Existing corporations or quasi-corporations with single heads are the St. Lawrence Seaway Development Corporation, Federal Housing Administration, and the Government National Mortgage Association.

The Tennessee Valley Authority, Export-Import Bank, and Federal Deposit Insurance Corporation have full-time boards of directors. The Home Loan Bank Board also serves as the board of directors of the Federal Savings and Loan Insurance Corporation and the Federal Home Loan Mortgage Corporation. The Community Development Corporation, Federal Crop Insurance Corporation, Federal Prison Industries, and Panama Canal Company have part-time boards composed of both public officials and private individuals. The Commodity Credit Corporation, Pension Benefit Guaranty Corporation, Neighborhood Reinvestment Corporation, and Federal Financing Bank have "in-house" boards made up exclusively of federal officials. The Banks for Cooperatives, Federal Inter-

37. David E. Lilienthal, *The Journals of David E. Lilienthal: The TVA Years, 1939–1945*, Vol. 1, Harper & Row, 1964, pp. 280–81.
38. Senate Report No. 76, 82nd Congress.

mediate Credit Banks, and Rural Telephone Bank are managed by part-time boards consisting of directors appointed by the government and directors elected by borrower associations.

The procedures permitted under the Budget and Accounting Procedures Act of 1950, together with the increased use of revolving funds, have considerably narrowed the differences between agencies and corporations. There is nothing to prevent the Congress from conferring on a noncorporate agency some or all of the powers normally granted to a government corporation, except separate corporate status, but the burden of proof shifts to those arguing for special treatment.

The secretary of housing and urban development, in effect, has been constituted as a "corporation sole" for the purpose of administering the college housing, urban renewal, and other public enterprise funds. These funds have not been organized as corporations, but, nonetheless, the secretary in carrying out his duties under the laws creating the funds may sue and be sued, borrow money, and exercise comparable powers and is subject to the budget and audit provisions of the Government Corporation Control Act applicable to wholly-owned government corporations. This approach was developed initially to shore up the position of a weak Housing and Home Finance administrator by vesting powers in him rather than in one of the highly autonomous agency constituents subject only to his "coordination." Other agencies, such as the Alaska Railroad, have acquired gradually through the years some but not all of the attributes of a government corporation.

Government corporations are organized to achieve a public purpose authorized by law. So far as purpose is concerned, a wholly-owned government corporation cannot be distinguished from any other government agency.[39] This view was vigorously stated by the United States Supreme Court in the

39. Harold Seidman, "The Theory of the Autonomous Government Corporation: A Critical Appraisal," *Public Administration Review,* Vol. 12, No. 2, 1952.

case of *Cherry Cotton Mills* v. *U.S.* [327 U.S. 536 (1945)] when it held that the fact "that the Congress chose to call it a corporation [Reconstruction Finance Corporation] does not alter its characteristics so as to make it something other than what it actually is, an agency selected by the government to accomplish purely governmental purposes." The functions of a corporation are the same as those of any administrative agency; the differences between the two are to be found in the *methods* employed to perform the functions and in the techniques utilized by the president and the Congress to fulfill their constitutional responsibilities.

Not since Mr. Arthur E. Morgan, the first chairman of the Tennessee Valley Authority, has a director of a wholly-owned corporation attempted to challenge the president's overriding authority. Mr. Morgan insisted that he was solely responsible to the Congress, not the president, and refused to answer questions asked by President Franklin D. Roosevelt.[40] When President Roosevelt removed Mr. Morgan for "contumacy," his action was sustained by the courts.[41]

As a general rule, the president looks to the heads of executive departments and agencies for immediate direction and supervision of government corporations. Corporations are generally made subject to supervision by the department head responsible for the functional area in which the corporation is operating. Only three wholly-owned corporations, the Tennessee Valley Authority, Export-Import Bank, and Federal Deposit Insurance Corporation,[42] report directly to the president. In some instances, independence has been the equivalent of "isolation" from those with ultimate authority for making na-

40. Senate Document 155, 75th Congress, 3rd Session, p. 105.

41. *Morgan vs. Tennessee Valley Authority,* 115 F 2d. 900, certiorari denied, 312 U.S. 701.

42. The Federal Deposit Insurance Corporation is classified in the Government Corporation Control Act as a "mixed-ownership" corporation, but the stock held by the Federal Reserve Banks has been retired. FDIC is presently a "no-stock" corporation as are most wholly-owned government corporations.

tional policy. As a regional agency without a national constituency, the Tennessee Valley Authority is especially vulnerable if it does not have strong presidential backing, since no Cabinet officer is responsible for defending its interests and some have looked upon it as a competitor. Not until the Congress authorized the TVA to maket its own revenue bonds was the authority able to obtain funds necessary to finance major expansion of its power-producing facilities.

Mixed-ownership corporations present a distinct class of supervisory problems. These corporations have at times demanded all of the privileges of a public agency without being willing to accept the responsibilities. Mixed-ownership corporations have been successful in maintaining at least a degree of independence from both the president and the Congress, particularly those which are self-financing and have a majority of directors nominated or elected by private stockholders. For this reason the Eisenhower administration decided in 1956 to oppose the establishment of additional mixed-ownership corporations, even though the second Hoover Commission had endorsed the principle of "mutualization."[43]

The very fact that government corporations are "different" causes them to be viewed with some suspicion by the General Accounting Office and the Appropriations Committees. Bureaucracies, whether in the legislative or executive branches, have an innate distaste for institutions which do not fit neatly into the existing system and upset established routines. Nonetheless, the legitimacy of the government corporation as a member of the federal institutional family is no longer open to question. The corporation gained full respectability when President Truman laid down criteria for the use of government corporations in his 1948 Budget Message.[44] President

43. Commission on Organization of the Executive Branch of the Government, "Lending, Guaranteeing and Insurance Activities," a report to the Congress, March 1955, pp. 11–13.

44. House Document 19, 80th Congress, pp. M57–M62.

Truman stated:

> Experience indicates that the corporate form of organization is peculiarly adapted to the Administration of governmental programs which are predominantly of a commercial character—those which are revenue producing, are at least potentially self-sustaining, and involve a large number of business-type transactions with the public. In their business operations such programs require greater flexibility than the customary type of appropriation budget ordinarily permits. As a rule the usefulness of a corporation lies in its ability to deal with the public in the manner employed by prvate enterprise for similar work.

10

Advisory and Intergovernmental Bodies: Twilight Zone

Advisory Bodies. Alexander Hamilton in Federalist Paper No. 70 argued that the unity of executive power could be destroyed "either by vesting the power in two or more magistrates of equal dignity and authority, or by vesting it ostensibly in one man, subject in whole or in part to the control and cooperation of others, in the capacity of counselors to him."[1] No executive can disregard with impunity "advice" by his counselors, particularly when they represent powerful elements in the community and their advice is not offered privately. Advice becomes limiting when an executive's discretion in the choice of his advisers is restricted by law or executive order and advisory bodies assume an independent status.

As with interagency committees, a distinction needs to be maintained between *ad hoc*, task-oriented advisory groups and continuing advisory bodies with a right to review, question, and be consulted about program policies and execution. It is the latter category that is of concern to us here.

For several so-called advisory bodies the title "advisory" is

1. Clinton Rossiter, editor, *The Federalist Papers,* The New American Library, Inc., 1961, p. 424.

a misnomer. Advice ceases to be advice when a grant cannot be made without first obtaining the approval or recommendations of an advisory council. In the previous chapter, we cited the powers vested in advisory councils to the National Foundation on Arts and Humanities and the various institutes under the National Institutes of Health. Other advisory committees have coveted such authorities and some have succeeded in obtaining them without express statutory sanction.

Congress customarily has established fixed, overlapping terms of office for committee members. Qualifications for committee membership normally are couched in quite broad language. For example, the twelve public members of the Advisory Committee on Vocational Education are to be persons "familiar with the vocational education needs of management and labor (in equal numbers), persons familiar with the administration of state and local vocational educational programs, other persons with special knowledge, experience or qualifications with respect to vocational education, and persons representative of the general public." Statutory provisions, such as those authorizing the Council of the American Historical Association to appoint two members of the National Historical Publications Commission or permitting designated organizations or groups to nominate or recommend committee members, are the exception.

While the statutes may appear to allow considerable executive latitude in selecting "advisers," the president or other appointing officer seldom is in a position to ignore suggestions from the constituencies which they represent. Self-designated elites in some professional groups have monopolized appointments to advisory committees. The House Committee on Government Operations noted with concern that a majority of the advisers to the National Institutes of Health were drawn from the relatively small number of institutions which receive the bulk of NIH grant funds.[2] Few nonmembers of the National

2. House Committee on Government Operations, "The Administration of Research Grants in the Public Health Service," House Report No. 800, 90th Congress, 1st Session, P. 61.

Academy of Sciences were named to serve on the prestigious and influential President's Science Advisory Committee.[3] It is doubtful that the president would appoint labor advisers without first clearing the appointments with the leadership of the AFL-CIO. If members of advisory committees are supposed to reflect the views of broad sectional, professional, economic, or social interests, obviously they must have a standing with and be acceptable to the organizations which represent those interests.

Advisory committees are by no means essential to assure that affected individuals or groups have a voice with respect to federal programs or policies. Consultation is considered to be a prerequisite for democratic administration. Indeed, Section 4 of the Administrative Procedures Act requires, with some exceptions, public notice of proposed agency rule-making and an opportunity for interested persons to express their views before a final decision is taken. In some instances, advisory committees merely formalize and legitimatize consultative arrangements established by custom and practice.

David Truman correctly points out that for groups with effective access to the president, department heads, and congressional committees, "the advisory committee and similar devices of consultation may be more a handicap than an advantage."[4] It is no accident that the veterans organizations have made no efforts to institutionalize their role as advisers to the Veterans Administration. Whatever the intentions of the government or interest group, formalization of consultative arrangements is likely to result in mutual "co-optation"—to borrow a word from the social psychologists. Each may find his freedom of action significantly reduced. The outside organization may be identified with government policies which are unpopular among some elements of its constituency, but which for one reason or another it is unable or unwilling to oppose publicly. An organization quickly loses influence when

3. Daniel S. Greenberg, *The Politics of Pure Science,* The New American Library, Inc., 1967, p. 15.
4. David B. Truman, *The Governmental Process,* Alfred A. Knopf, 1964, p. 461.

it becomes known that its advice on major issues has been rejected. Consequently, it must be highly selective in choosing the issues on which it is willing to risk a public rebuke. Furthermore, once arrangements are formalized, privileged access may be jeopardized by the admission into the club of others with competing or contrary interests.

What the government basically wants from advisory committees is not "expert" advice, although occasionally this is a factor, but support. Advisory boards may be utilized to lend respectability to new or controversial programs such as poverty and foreign assistance. It is hoped that board members will act as program missionaries and assist in mobilizing support for the program both in their home communities and in the Congress. Many have been extremely effective in this role, although their zeal does not always reflect selfless dedication to the public interest. The House Committee on Government Operations observed that "when some of the same individuals who have served on advisory councils for many years receive substantial NIH grants, and also testify before the Congress in support of the Agency's appropriations, the appearance of favoritism is unavoidable."[5] Testimony by these expert witnesses, coupled with skillful behind-the-scenes lobbying, certainly played a part in persuading the Appropriations Committees to recommend more money for NIH programs than requested in the president's budget.

Missionary ardor can boomerang and be turned against the president or department head. Zealots are predisposed to be willing accomplices of agency dissidents in covert and overt campaigns not only to overcome budgetary limits but also to thwart proposed policies and reorganizations which are not to their liking. Advisers are not subject to the restraints applicable to public employees and cannot be disciplined for insubordination. The Advisory Council to the National Institute of Mental Health worked closely with the institute director in

5. House Committee on Government Operations, *op. cit.*, p. 62.

organizing opposition to a 1960 proposal to reorganize the Public Health Service. The plan called for transfer of important elements of the NIMH to a new Division of Mental Health. The surgeon general was reluctant to alienate the council by going forward with the plan and it was abandoned.[6]

Attempts to use advisory bodies as "window-dressing" also can boomerang. President Kennedy created a Consumer Advisory Council under the aegis of the Council of Economic Advisers as what he hoped would be an innocuous alternative to a White House Office of Consumer Counsel promised during the campaign. Unfortunately, council activists took the executive order rhetoric seriously and were very aggressive in pressing demands for an elaborate program and budgetary resources. Wearied from his efforts to control this fractious group, a CEA staff man wrote a plaintive memorandum titled "Who left this bastard on our doorstep?" recommending that the Council of Economic Advisers be relieved of its onerous responsibilities. No agency was willing to volunteer for the assignment, so the council was reorganized and given independent status.

Individuals are attracted to service on advisory groups for a variety of reasons—honor, prestige, influence, curiosity, and opportunity for public service. The last is by no means the least important. Many people do accept a moral obligation to serve their country, but would prefer to do so in a way that does not compel them to give up their private interests.

Individuals may be motivated by dedication to the public interest, but this is seldom true of organizations concerned with promoting the economic interests of their members. Like the government, these organizations may try to utilize advisory groups for their own benefit. This poses a threat when advisory committees are allowed to develop into an invisible government responsible neither to the president, the Congress, nor

6. "The Reorganization of the Public Health Service," Edith T. Carper, in Federick C. Mosher, editor, *Governmental Reorganization: Cases and Commentary,* The Bobbs-Merrill Co., Inc., 1967.

the people. The danger is very real when public officials confuse advice with direction.

Secretary of Commerce Sinclair Weeks was criticized severely by the Anti-Trust Subcommittee of the House Judiciary Committee in 1956 for creating advisory arrangements which "effected a virtual abdication of administrative responsibility on the part of Government officials in that their actions in many instances are but the automatic approval of decisions already made outside the Government in business and industry. The Secretary of Commerce, in BDSA, has created an organization which in the name of the Government has been used to advance throughout the Government the cause of private interests. Failing to control its activities, he has allowed an agency of the Government to become an instrument for inside influence and advancement of special interests." The committee concluded: "In such circumstances the Government agency becomes a spokesman for private interests, and because it speaks in the guise of presumably disinterested Government, it is all the more disarming."[7]

The situation that existed in the Department of Commerce in the mid-1950's was unique only because Secretary Weeks apparently saw nothing wrong with this kind of an incestuous relationship between a government department and its advisory committees. Other departments had similar arrangements but were more discreet in talking about them.

With the proliferation of advisory bodies (as many as 1,439 by the OMB's own count in December 1972) and the growing dependence of diverse groups on the federal government for economic health and survival, the potential for conflicts of interest inherent in advisory arrangements no longer could be ignored. In February 1962 President Kennedy issued a memorandum on "Preventing Conflicts of Interest on the Part of Advisers and Consultants to the Government" and promul-

7. House Committee on Judiciary, Anti-Trust Subcommittee, "Interim Report on WOC's and Advisory Groups," August 24, 1956, pp. 90 and 99.

gated Executive Order No. 11007 prescribing regulations for the formation and use of advisory committees.

President Kennedy instructed agency heads to "oversee the activities of such consultants to insure that the public interest is protected from improper conduct and that consultants will not, through ignorance or inadvertance, embarrass the Government or themselves in their activities." The memorandum called attention to the conflict-of-interest statutes, defined ethical standards of conduct, and required advisers to disclose their financial interests. The conflict-of-interest laws were found to be unduly restrictive when applied to temporary and intermittent employees, and the Congress liberalized the restrictions in 1963. Public Law 87–849 established a category of persons designated "special Government employees" and exempted them from some but not all of the restrictions imposed on the private activities of full-time employees. A special employee is defined as an individual appointed or employed to serve, with or without compensation, for not more than 130 days during any period of 365 consecutive days.

Executive Order No. 11007 directed that "no committee shall be utilized for functions not solely advisory, and determinations of actions to be taken with respect to matters upon which an advisory committee advises or recommends shall be made solely by officers or employees of the Government." The order sets forth the following rules: (1) meetings shall not be held without government approval; (2) the government should formulate or approve the agenda; (3) all meetings must be conducted in the presence of a full-time government employee who may adjourn the meeting when he considers adjournment to be in the public interest; (4) minutes must be kept of each meeting, and, for Industry Advisory Committees, a verbatim transcript; and (5) unless otherwise provided by law, committees shall terminate not later than two years from the date of formation, except when the department head makes a finding that continuance is in the public interest. The Business Advisory Council severed its ties with the Department of Commerce rather than comply with these rules.

The force and effect of the Kennedy executive order were somewhat weakened by the necessity to exclude committees "for which Congress by statute has specified the purpose, composition and conduct." Such important committees as the advisory councils of the National Institutes of Health are not subject to the order.

Congress judged the guidelines established by Executive Order No. 11007 to be inadequate because (1) no provision is made for executive oversight of the formation, management, and use of advisory committees; (2) funding of advisory bodies is not covered; (3) most requirements can be waived by the agency head, if he declares it to be in the public interest; and (4) balanced representation of varying social and economic interests is not required.[8]

The Federal Advisory Committee Act of 1972 (Public Law 92–463) declares that "new advisory committees should be established only when they are determined to be essential and their number should be kept to the minimum necessary." Committee meetings shall be open to the public and "fairly balanced in terms of points of view represented and the functions to be performed." The act directs that a Committee Management Secretariat be established within the Office of Management and Budget with responsibility for reviewing committee performance, recommending the abolition of unnecessary or obsolete committees, and prescribing administrative guidelines and management controls.[9]

Joint Congressional-Executive Agencies. The Supreme Court's ruling in *Springer* v. *Philippine Islands* [277 U.S. 189 (1928)] that it is unconstitutional for legislators to serve on executive bodies has been violated both in spirit and in prac-

8. House Report No. 91–1731.

9. Office of Management and Budget regulations are set forth in Circular No. A–63 Revised.

tice. Joint executive-legislative study commissions have been common since the first Hoover Commission. Six were established between 1953 and 1957. More recent examples are the Public Land Law Review Commission (1964) and the Advisory Commission on Low Income Housing created in 1968. Membership on these commissions generally is weighted in favor of the congressional representatives. Congressional appointees outnumbered executive appointees on the Hoover Commission two to one. Furthermore, executive and legislative representatives do not serve in comparable capacities. Members appointed by the president, particularly from the executive branch, are construed to be administration spokesmen and can make commitments on the president's behalf. Congressional members obviously cannot commit the Congress and speak only for themselves. Any compromises are likely to be entirely one-sided.

While congressional membership on *ad hoc* study commissions can be defended as not constituting an overt violation of the separation-of-powers doctrine, congressional membership on permanent executive bodies does raise serious constitutional questions. Six of the fifteen members of the Smithsonian Institution's governing body, the Board of Regents, come from the Senate and House (three each). The Migratory Bird Conservation Commission consists of the secretary of the interior as chairman, the secretary of agriculture, two members of the House of Representatives selected by the speaker, and two senators selected by the president of the Senate. The commission has various administrative duties, including approval of land purchases or rentals and the fixing of prices at which bird sanctuaries may be purchased or rented. Three senators and three congressmen are members of the Advisory Commission on Intergovernmental Relations. Two senators and two congressmen constitute a majority of the seven-member National Forest Reservation Commission which passes upon lands recommended by the secretary of agriculture for acquisition as national forests by purchases or exchange. In administering the Agricultural Trade Development and Assistance Act, the president must obtain the advice of a committee consisting of the secretary of agriculture, the AID administrator, the director of Management and Budget, and chairmen and ranking minority members of the Agriculture Committees. The committee is required "to review from time to time the status and usage of foreign currencies . . . and shall make recommendations to the President as to ways and means of assuring to the United States (1) the maximum benefit from the use of such currencies . . . and (2) the maximum return from sales."

Intergovernmental Organizations. Our Constitution-makers anticipated that the several states might be confronted by problems which cut across state boundaries and would have to devise suitable arrangements to facilitate interstate cooperation in dealing with them. Article I Section 10 of the Constitution permits states, with the consent of the Congress, to enter into compacts and agreements with each other, although the authority is stated negatively. There is no evidence that the Constitution drafters envisaged circumstances which would warrant comparable agreements or compacts between the federal government and one or more sovereign states.

Until recently the constitutional, legal, financial, and organizational obstacles to the development of workable intergovernmental institutions were considered to be nearly insuperable. When the Tennessee Valley Authority was created, it was assumed generally that there was no feasible alternative to a strictly federal approach to regional development. But the TVA proved not to be the answer. Moves to duplicate the successful TVA experiment in the Columbia and Missouri river basins failed to generate enthusiasm either in the regions or within the federal establishment. The TVA seems destined to be the first and the last wholly federal regional development agency.

Halting steps were taken in the 1950's to provide for state participation in river basin planning. States were invited to propose individuals for appointment to the Arkansas-White-Red and New England–New York River Basin Committees chaired by the Army Corps of Engineers. In 1958, the Congress established a United States Study Commission for the Southeast River Basins and a similar study commission for Texas. These commissions consisted of federal and state representatives, with an unaffiliated chairman appointed by the president. There was no departure, however, from the concept that these commissions were federal agencies, and to conform with constitutional provisions it was believed necessary to give the state representatives federal appointments.

The same pattern was adopted when the Advisory Commission on Intergovernmental Relations was created in 1959. Panels of names are submitted by the Governors' Conference, Council of State Governments, American Municipal Association and United States Conference of Mayors, and the National Association of County Officials, but appointments to the Commission are made by the president. The president has some leeway since a panel must include two names for each vacancy. For example, the president selects four governors from a panel of eight proposed by the Governors' Conference.

Except for the somewhat unusual procedures for selecting commissioners, there appears to have been no congressional intention to create anything other than a permanent bipartisan federal commission. Commission employees are by law "federal employees" and, until 1966, the ACIR was not authorized to receive funds from state and local governments or nonprofit organizations. In accepting appointments to the commission, governors, mayors, and other local officials are placed in the anomalous position of being federal officials for some purposes. This has been a source of embarrassment, since local officials may be debarred by local law from accepting an appointment to a federal position, or if they are permitted to serve, they may be prohibited from accepting compensation or reimbursement for their expenses.

If linkages were to be forged among the sovereign but increasingly interdependent partners in the federal system, the organizational dilemma had to be resolved. The 1961 Governors' Conference urged federal-state collaboration to devise "a more comprehensive approach to joint Federal-State planning, and to closer Federal-State coordination in the development of plans and programs."[10] The emphasis was on *joint* federal-state planning within an appropriate institutional framework.

The proposed Water Resources Planning Act of 1961 became a target for those demanding a new approach. States objected strongly to presidential appointment of the states' representatives on the river basin commissions because this would make them mere instruments of the federal government. The bill was not enacted.

Different but no less vexing constitutional doubts had to be satisfied before the Congress approved the Delaware River Compact in 1961. The Delaware River Basin Advisory Committee—consisting of representatives of the governors of Delaware, Pennsylvania, New Jersey, and New York and the mayors of New York and Philadelphia—developed a legislative proposal for creation by interstate-federal compact of a unified water resource agency for the Delaware River Basin. Inclusion of the federal government as a party to an interstate compact was without precedent. Even though the plan called for the federal government to become a signatory, a federal representative was not invited to participate in negotiating the compact.

Apart from the general question of whether a federal-state compact was permissible under the Constitution or desirable as a matter of public policy, specific objections were registered against provisions which had the effect of limiting federal power in such critical areas as control of navigable waters,

10. Resolution adopted by the Governors' Conference, June 28, 1961.

interstate and foreign commerce, and project authorizations. The Congress approved the compact with reservations protecting federal powers in these areas, authorizing the president to modify any provision of the comprehensive plan adopted by the Delaware River Basin Commission insofar as it affects the powers and functions of federal agencies, and preserving the president's freedom to act in national emergencies.

While fears that a federal-state compact would make it possible for the signatory states to exert undue political pressure on federal agencies have not materialized, many remain uneasy about the compact approach. The Delaware River Commission's accomplishments to date are modest. Potential controversy was avoided when the Commission accepted as its own the comprehensive plan for the Delaware River Basin developed by the Army Corps of Engineers.

The troublesome issue of federal appointment of state members of joint bodies again was raised in 1962 by the governor of Alaska's request for establishment of a Federal-State Development Planning Commission for Alaska. This time the Bureau of the Budget proposed to bypass the constitutional issue by having the President create a Federal Development Planning Commission for Alaska and the governor a state planning commission, and then marrying the two commissions by a memorandum of understanding signed by the president and the governor. The action documents were drafted by a team representing the Bureau of the Budget and the governor.

Executive Order No. 1150, April 2, 1964, notes that "the Governor of Alaska has declared his intention to establish a State Commission for reconstruction and development planning" and directs the Federal Commission created by the order to work with its state counterpart in developing coordinated plans and preparing recommendations for the president and the governor with respect to both short-range and long-range development programs. President Johnson did not sign the memorandum of understanding, but both parties accepted the memorandum as the agreed-upon terms of reference for the commissions.

Enactment of the Water Resources Planning Act, the Appalachian Regional Development Act, and the Public Works and Economic Development Act in 1965 marks a watershed in federal-state cooperation. The Water Resources Planning Act made significant changes in intergovernmental relations and the machinery for coordination among federal agencies. River basin commissions authorized under the act are composed of a chairman appointed by the president, and representatives of interested federal agencies and the participating states, designated by federal agency heads and governors respectively. The commissions are to prepare joint, coordinated, and comprehensive plans for federal, state, interstate, local, and private development of water and related land resources and to recommend priorities for action.

Disputes about veto authority, the number of federal agencies to be represented on a commission, and voting procedures were resolved by providing that in the work of a commission "every reasonable endeavor shall be made to arrive at a consensus of all members on all issues." If a consensus cannot be obtained, then each member is to be afforded an opportunity to present and report his individual views. This approach was feasible since a commission's functions are exclusively advisory.

The Appalachian Regional Development Act was even more explicit in spelling out the terms of the new partnership between the states and the federal government. Federal membership of the Appalachian Regional Commission is limited to the "Federal co-chairman" appointed by the president. Each participating state in the Appalachian region is also entitled to one member, who shall be the governor or his designee. Decisions by the Commission require the affirmative vote of the federal co-chairman and of a majority of state members. The federal government agreed to pay administrative expenses for the first two years, but after that each state is to pay its pro rata share of the costs, as determined by the commission. No one employed by the commission "shall be deemed a Federal employee for any purpose."

The regional commissions authorized under the Public Works and Economic Development Act are almost exact duplicates of the Appalachian Regional Commission.

While the Appalachian Regional Commission is generally judged to be a "political success," it is regarded by some critics as "simply an unnecessary complication, a useless additional level of government."[11] The Advisory Commission on Intergovernmental Relations found that the commission "has not functioned as an overall coordinator and planner of Federal assistance to the region it serves. It lacks authority over the programs of other departments, and it has had little success in influencing their efforts."[12] The commission has been somewhat more effective in coordinating and targeting activities for which it has received direct funding and in fostering a "spirit of regionalism" among the members. The ARC and the River Basin Commissions have been accorded higher marks than the regional commissions established under Title V of the Public Works and Economic Development Act.

Twilight Zone. Once institutional types are assimilated into the family of government institutions, they lose much of their charm for those who prefer public services to be packaged in the trappings of private enterprise. Many advocates of the government corporation have now shifted their affections to what they describe as a "COMSAT-type corporation," although it is by no means certain what they mean by the term. COMSAT was used as the model for the National Housing Partnerships authorized by the Housing and Urban Development Act of 1968.

11. Advisory Commission in Intergovernmental Relations, *Improving Federal Grants Management,* 1977, p. 44.

12. *Ibid.* For an evaluation of regional organizations see Martha Derthick and Gary Bombardier, *Between State and Nation,* The Brookings Institution, 1974.

Confusion about the status of the Communications Satellite Corporation is understandable. It is not a covert government corporation, and the Congress, after prolonged and often bitter debate, rejected proposals for government ownership and operation of the communications satellite system. The Communications Satellite Act of 1962, however, does raise questions about the private character of the venture by providing for presidential appointment, with Senate confirmation, of the corporation's incorporators and three members of the board of directors.

Senator Javits was not alone in expressing the view that "the U.S. Government will sit in on management through three of fifteen directors."[13] Javits conceived of the presidential directors as the defenders of the public interest. But there is nothing in the legislative history to support this interpretation of the directors' role. Indeed, all the evidence runs to the contrary.

Under the Communications Satellite Act up to 50 percent of the corporation's stock may be held by communications common carriers. If half the stock were to be held by the carriers and half by the general public, obviously there would be a need for a "neutral" director or directors to resolve potential deadlocks. The Kennedy administration intended that the presidential directors perform this function. There was some concern that if the president named only one director, it would be difficult to avoid the implication that he was a government spokesman. It was suggested, therefore, that the president be authorized to designate three directors.

Attorney General Robert Kennedy emphasized that "neither the incorporators nor the Presidentially appointed directors are to be classified as officers of the United States." His opinion was backed by Senator Kefauver who stated that the three

13. Lloyd D. Musolf, editor, *Communications Satellites in Political Orbit*, Chandler Publishing Company, 1968, p. 143.

directors would owe a fiduciary obligation to the corporation but not to the government.[14]

Of all the means available to exert government influence and safeguard the public interest, presidential appointment of directors is probably the least effective and may have undesirable side-effects. According to Herman Schwartz, "their presence may reinforce the belief that the Government assures the profitability the Corporation" and "may dampen the zeal of the regulatory agencies."[15] As Senator Edmund Muskie stated with respect to the Securities Investor Protection Corporation:

> What I am fearful of is with industry representatives and public representatives on the board, that a request or application for a Treasury backup, use of the Treasury line of credit, could be interpreted as a public decision whereas actually the corporation is a private corporation, and it is a private request. . . . It seems to me the public membership on the private corporation, although it is a minority in fact, would be leaned upon as a crutch by the SEC and the Secretary of the Treasury for use of the Treasury backup.[16]

Presidentially appointed directors are committed to and must support board decisions, even when they vote against them.

Early experiments with mixed boards demonstrated that the arrangement had serious drawbacks. The government was represented on the board of the second Bank of the United States, established in 1816, by five directors. President Jackson complained in a message to the Congress on December 1, 1834, of "exclusion of the public directors from a knowledge of its most important proceedings."[17] The two government directors of the Union Pacific Railroad were treated as spies and antag-

14. *Ibid.*, pp. 136, 137.
15. *Ibid.*
16. Senate Committee on Bank and Currency, Subcommittee on Securities, hearings on S.2348, S.3978, 91st Congress, 2nd sess., p. 248.
17. Lloyd D. Musolf, *Mixed Enterprise*, Lexington Books, 1972, p. 55.

onists and in 1887 recommended that the appointment of public directors be discontinued.[18] Protection of the public interest can be better assured from the outside than from within a corporation.

COMSAT's status may be somewhat ambiguous, but it is crystal clear compared to several organizations which float suspended in a twilight zone between the public and private sectors. Among the oldest are the twelve Federal Reserve Banks. The capital stock of the Reserve Banks is held by the banks which are members of the Federal Reserve System. The board of directors of each bank is composed of six directors elected by the stockholders, three of whom must be engaged actively in agriculture, industry, or commerce, and three public directors appointed by the board of governors of the Federal Reserve System. Bank presidents are appointed for five-year terms by the board of directors, subject to approval by the board of governors. Among other functions, the banks have been given the privilege of issuing currency and act as depositories and fiscal agents of the United States. Although privately owned and controlled, the banks are public institutions performing public functions. This fact is recognized by the requirement that net earnings be paid into the United States Treasury and that, in the event of liquidation, any surplus remaining after payment of all debts, dividends, and the par value of capital stock shall become the property of the United States government.

The board of governors has resisted successfully periodic attempts by a few members of the Congress to apply budget and audit control to Federal Reserve operations. Any move along these lines, no matter how modest, is construed to be an attack on the system's integrity and independence. Chairman William Martin, for example, warned that ". . . budgetary control of our operations, of our budget, is fundamental in our concept of the independent status of the System. If you want

18. *Ibid.*

to nationalize the System, why the surest way to do it is through control of the budget."[19]

In his 1969 Economic Report, President Johnson proposed that (1) the term of the chairman of the Federal Reserve Board be appropriately geared to that of the president to assure "harmonious policy coordination"; (2) Congress review procedures for selecting Reserve bank presidents "to determine whether these positions should be subject to the same appointive process that applies to other posts with similar important responsibilities for national policy."

Institutions such as the Federal Land banks and Federal Home Loan banks have been allowed to drift into the twilight zone without surrendering important privileges which they possessed as government instrumentalities, including access, either directly or indirectly, to the federal Treasury. Retirement of government-owned stock has meant, however, a relaxation of government controls and exemption from the comptroller general's audit authority.

If one applied the traditional tests—private stock ownership, election of a majority of directors by private stockholders, and predominantly non-Treasury financing—a logical argument can be made that the Federal Reserve banks, Federal Land banks, and Federal Home Loan banks belong in a class apart from other government institutions. A logical rationale cannot be developed for the host of government-sponsored corporations, presumably created in the image of COMSAT, but without provision for private ownership. All they have in common with COMSAT is that they are declared by congressional fiat not to be agencies or instrumentalities of the United States government.

It is difficult to identify any unique attributes which are shared by such government-sponsored enterprises as the Corporation for Public Broadcasting, Federal National Mortgage

19. Joint Committee on Economic Report, Subcommittee on General Credit Control and Debt Management, hearings, March 11, 1952, p. 121.

Association, National Home Ownership Foundation, National Railroad Passenger Corporation, National Park Foundation, Securities Investor Protection Corporation, Student Loan Marketing Association, Legal Services Corporation, and U.S. Railway Association which warrant the nongovernment classification. Directors of the Corporation for Public Broadcasting, National Home Ownership Foundation, National Park Foundation, Securities Investor Protection Corporation, Legal Services Corporation, Student Loan Marketing Association and U.S. Railway Association are appointed by either the president or a Cabinet member, or are public officials designated to act *ex officio*. The National Home Ownership Foundation, for example, has an eighteen-member Board of Directors consistting of fifteen appointed by the president and the secretaries of housing and urban development and agriculture, and the director of the Office of Economic Opportunity. The board of the Securities Investor Protection Corporation is composed of five directors appointed by the president, and two named by the secretary of the treasury and the Federal Reserve Board. Except for the Federal National Mortgage Association, National Railroad Passenger Corporation, and Student Loan Marketing Association, there is no provision for private equity investment in the enterprises. None are financially self-sufficient, and all are supported directly or indirectly from the U.S. Treasury. Funds are obtained either by direct appropriations, as with the Corporation for Public Broadcasting, Legal Services Corporation, National Home Ownership Foundation, and U.S. Railway Association, or by grants and government guaranteed or Treasury-backed loans.[20]

Government-sponsored enterprises cannot be differentiated from their counterpart government agencies in terms of function, organization, and financing. The distinguishing charac-

20. For a discussion of government-sponsored enterprise, see Harold Seidman, "Government-sponsored Enterprise in the United States," in Bruce L. R. Smith, editor, *The New Political Economy*, Macmillan (London), 1975.

teristics of the enterprises are to be found exclusively in exemptions from the Government Corporation Control Act and laws applicable to federal personnel, funds, and contracts. Whatever the reasons advanced publicly, the objective has been to exclude expenditures from the budget and avoid controls.

According to the House Budget Committee, "the Congressional Budget Act has had the effect of significantly enhancing the value of off-budget status. Off-budget agencies are not covered by the new Congressional process and they are not included in the aggregate or functional amounts set forth in the Congressional budget resolutions."[21] Outlays of the so-called "Off-Budget" federal agencies and programs (Exchange Stabilization Fund, Federal Financing Bank, Pension Benefit Guaranty Corporation, Postal Service, Rural Electrification and Telephone Revolving Fund, Rural Telephone Bank, and U.S. Railway Association) and government-sponsored enterprises are estimated at $31.1 billion for 1980. The excluded outlays of government-sponsored enterprises have jumped from relatively small amounts in the 1960's to an average of $9.5 billion a year from 1973 to 1977.[22]

There are those who argue that exemptions from controls are necessary and desirable to safeguard corporate "independence" and avoid partisan political pressures.[23] But exemptions from the civil service laws are not designed to and have not prevented political appointments. Difficulties occur when an enterprise is controlled by directors and staff at odds with the incumbent administration. President Nixon vetoed the bill providing for two-year increased funding for the Corporation for Public Broadcasting because of "fundamental disagree-

21. House Committee on Budget, "Congressional Control of Expenditures," January 1977, p. 77.

22. The United States Budget for fiscal year 1979, pp. 248–49.

23. See testimony of Dr. James Killian on Corporation for Public Broadcasting in hearings before Senate Commerce Committee on S. 1160, 90th Congress, 1st sess., pp. 140–41.

ments concerning the direction which public broadcasting has taken and should pursue in the future."[24] The veto was followed by John W. Macy, Jr.'s, resignation as the corporation's president. Macy had been chairman of the Civil Service Commission under President Johnson.

The Carnegie Commission on the Future of Public Broadcasting confirmed that "appointments to the CPB board have become highly politicized." The Commission concluded that the Corporation had not succeeded in providing "insulation from federal pressure."[25]

Labeling as "private" what is in reality "public" for cosmetic reasons or to obtain fictitious budget reductions can contribute to loss of faith in our democratic institutions. Misbranding is no less heinous because it is practiced by the government. The most flagrant example is the Energy Security Corporation proposed by President Carter. Distinctions between what is public and what is private are becoming increasingly blurred, but we cannot abandon these distinctions altogether without fundamental alterations in our constitutional system. The maintenance of this distinction has been considered essential both to protect private rights from intrusion by the government and to prevent usurpation of government power.

If the Congress can turn public agencies into nongovernment institutions merely by waving its legislative wand, presumably there would be no legal bar to declaring that such agencies as the Tennessee Valley Authority and Federal Housing Administration are no longer agencies or instrumentalities of the United States. This device could be employed not only to exclude expenditures from the budget, but also to circumvent the civil service laws and regulations, conflict-of-interest statutes, and other laws which control the conduct and activities of officers and employees of the United States.

24. House Document 92–320.

25. Carnegie Commission on the Future of Public Broadcasting, *A Public Trust*, Bantam Books, 1979, pp. 70 and 75.

Intermingling of public and private duties places public officials in an ambiguous position. There are many unanswered questions. Do the secretaries of housing and urban development and agriculture serve as directors of the National Home Ownership Foundation in their official capacity, or as private citizens? To whom are federal officials accountable for their actions as directors? If the foundation is not an agency and instrumentality of the United States, what then are its responsibilities to the president, the Congress, and, ultimately, through them, to the people?

The ambiguous status of government-sponsored enterprises inevitably generates conflicts with the government sponsors. The Federal National Mortgage Association insisted that HUD Secretary Patricia Harris exceeded her authority in directing that 30 percent of FNMA's mortgage purchases be made in inner city areas.[26] The secretary is authorized by law to require that "a reasonable portion of the corporation's mortgage purchases be related to the national goal of providing adequate housing for low- and moderate-income families, but with reasonable economic return to the corporation."

The laws creating COMSAT, Corporation for Public Broadcasting, National Home Ownership Foundation, National Park Foundation, National Railroad Passenger Corporation, Securities Investor Protection Corporation, and U.S. Railway Association contain significant gaps. No express authority is conferred upon the president to remove directors whom he appoints. Is the power to remove implied in the power to appoint, or will the Supreme Court follow the doctrine laid down in the Humphrey and Wiener cases?

Other options are available to the Congress, which can minimize or eliminate these problems. Federally chartered or organized private corporations are by no means uncommon. These include national banks, federal savings and loan associations, small business investment companies, the Aerospace

26. *The New York Times,* February 22, 1978.

Corporation, and the Rand Corporation. But controls to protect the public interest have been provided by regulation, authority to give or withhold financial support, and contractual agreements without directly involving the government or government officials in the management of private organizations.

The New Federalism: Government by Contract. Why Congress favored the organizational approach typified by such government-sponsored enterprises as the Corporation for Public Broadcasting is a matter for speculation. It may reflect congressional disenchantment with the "think tanks" and other nonprofit corporations which have symbolized what Don K. Price calls "the new Federalism."[27] These institutions are creatures of the executive, not the Congress. Most of them were organized at the initiative of executive departments and financed under contracts which the Congress had no opportunity to review or approve. President Johnson launched the Urban Institute by press release. The pioneer nonprofit, the Rand Corporation, was sponsored by the Air Force in 1948, but it is doubtful that many members of the Congress were even aware of its existence until several years later.

The emergence of the nonprofit corporation is cited as "one of the most striking features of America's postwar organization."[28] As is characteristic of organization innovation in the United States, the nonprofit corporation evolved almost by accident and without conscious planning out of the need to devise institutional arrangements adapted to changing government requirements. Organization theories normally do not precede, but follow organizational innovation. By the time the theoretical justification is developed, an institution is likely to have achieved maturity and may be in its dotage.

27. Don K. Price, *Government and Science—Their Dynamic Relation in American Democracy,* New York University Press, 1954.

28. Bruce L. R. Smith. "The Future of the Not-for-profit Corporations," *The Public Interest,* No. 8, Summer 1967, a highly perceptive analysis of the growth, use, and potential of not-for-profit corporations.

Each major class of institutions is peculiarly a product of a particular epoch in United States history. Regulatory commissions were a response to problems growing out of the Industrial Revolution, notably the threat of monopolistic control of the nation's wealth and resources. Government corporations were born of war and depression. The dramatic developments resulting from the scientific and technological revolution commencing after World War II have had an enormous impact on the institutional structure and role of the federal government, business, and academic organizations.

Prior to World War II, the total federal research and development program is estimated to have cost annually about $100 million. In fiscal year 1950, total federal research and development expenditures were about $1.1 billion. In fiscal year 1980, the total is expected to reach $31.2 billion. The increase since 1950 demonstrates the extent to which major initiative and responsibility for promoting and financing research and development have shifted from private enterprise and universities to the federal government.

Given the magnitude of its new and rapidly expanding responsibilities, the government had no practical choice other than to enlist the support of outside organizations which had or could obtain the necessary manpower and institutional resources. The proportion of the research and development budget allocated to direct federal operations has steadily declined. In his report to President Kennedy on "Government Contracting for Research Development," Budget Director David E. Bell saw no alternative to continued government reliance on the private sector "for the major share of the scientific and technical work which it requires."[29]

Today more than 80 percent of federal expenditures for research and development are made through nonfederal in-

29. Bureau of the Budget, "Report to the President on Contracting for Research and Development," Senate Document No. 94, 87th Congress, 2nd Session, May 17, 1962, p. 2.

stitutions. Most of it goes to established business and academic institutions, either in the form of grants or under cost-plus fixed-fee contracts. Cost-plus fixed-fee contracts generally are negotiated on a noncompetitive basis and provide for government reimbursement of all allowable project costs. The formula for calculating the fee is negotiated by parties to a contract. Since the "fee" constitutes a contractor's profit, the Bell report expressed doubts about the appropriateness of paying fees to nonprofit organizations and recommended that "development" or "general support allowances" be substituted.

Employment of contractors to conduct or support operations on behalf of the government is by no means new. "Contracting-out" has an ancient lineage. So convinced an advocate of "laissez-faire" as Adam Smith drew the line at the prevalent eighteenth-century practice of contracting-out the collection of public revenues to tax farmers. Smith believed that "Government, by establishing an administration under their own immediate inspection of the same kind with that which the farmer establishes, might at least save the profit, which is almost always exorbitant."[30]

What is new are the so-called GOCO contracts providing for private industry or university management and operation of such government-owned facilities as the Oak Ridge and Argonne National Laboratories, and the nonprofit corporations, organized independently or under university sponsorship. The nonprofit corporations fall under four main categories: (1) university-affiliated research institutes or laboratories which perform some applied research or experimental tasks, such as the Applied Physics Laboratory of The Johns Hopkins University; (2) corporations like Aerospace and MITRE created to furnish systems engineering and technical management services; (3) "think tanks" established to provide operations research and analytical services; and (4) social research and demonstrations.

30. Adam Smith, *The Wealth of Nations,* The Modern Library, Random House, 1937, p. 384.

Many figures have been bandied about as to the number of nonprofit corporations which are for all practical purposes government "captives." Bruce L. R. Smith attributes claims about the proliferation of nonprofits to "idiosyncracies of definition." It is his view that there are about 20 organizations "that fit a reasonable definition of the [nonprofit] corporation as a nongovernmental entity with its own governing structure, dependent on government clients, but independent of the annual authorization and appropriation cycle of government agencies."[31]

All these corporations were organized by the government solely for the purpose of entering into contracts to furnish services to the government. In some instances, the government selected the "incorporators" of the nonuniversity-affiliated institutions. Charters were obtained under the laws of the state where the institution was incorporated. Individuals invited to serve as trustees were either picked by the contracting agency, or chosen with its approval. Except for grants made by the Ford Foundation to provide initial working capital to Rand and the Institute for Defense Analyses, financing came entirely from the federal government.

For anyone familiar with the Washington "establishment," the names of incorporators and trustees include few strangers. Roswell L. Gilpatric and Roger Lewis, who served respectively as deputy secretary of defense and assistant secretary of the Air Force, were incorporators of the Aerospace Corporation. At one time or another such well-known "in-and-outers" as Jerome Wiesner (director of OST), Harold Brown (secretary of the Air Force), General Lucius D. Clay, William C. Foster (director of Arms Control Agency), John Gardner (secretary of HEW), and James Killian (special assistant to President Eisenhower), to cite but a few, have served as "captive" corporation trustees. There is also considerable traffic back and forth at the executive and staff levels.

31. Smith, *op cit.*

In many respects the nonprofit corporations are indistinguishable from early government corporations chartered under state law. Seemingly, the Government Corporation Control Act provision that "no corporation shall be created, organized, or acquired by any officer or agency of the Federal Government . . . for the purpose of acting as an agency or instrumentality of the United States, except by or pursuant to an Act of Congress specifically authorizing such action" would apply to nonprofit corporations. Committee counsel raised this point during hearings on the Bell report but did not press his question.[32] The comptroller general has been discreetly silent on the subject.

General H. H. Arnold certainly did not intend to "create, organize, or acquire a corporation" when in 1945 he entered into a contract with the Douglas Aircraft Company for Project RAND. His objective was not to innovate, but to preserve the close association between the scientific community and the military which had been nurtured under Office of Scientific Research and Development auspices during World War II. The working partnership of the military and the scientists had produced significant advances in weaponry and in the deployment and use of weapons systems. This kind of capability could not be built into the formal Air Force organization structure without either bypassing the established chain of command or sacrificing direct access to the chief of staff. The first alternative was wholly unacceptable to the military, and the second to the scientists.

By 1948 RAND had proved itself and there was every indication that the program would be continued and expanded. But the association with the Douglas Aircraft Company was a source of increasing uneasiness because of the potential for conflicts of interest. University affiliation was considered and rejected. With the concurrence of the Air Force and the Doug-

32. House Committee on Government Operation, hearings on "Systems Development and Management," Part I, June 1962, pp. 57–58.

las Company, Rand was organized as an independent nonprofit corporation under the laws of the state of California.

Few realized at the time that Rand was to be the precursor of a new generation of federal instrumentalities. Rand itself fathered the System Development Corporation and Analytic Services, Inc. The Operations Research Organization established by the Army in 1947 as a Johns Hopkins University affiliate was converted in 1961 to the independent Research Analysis Corporation. In 1956 the Department of Defense asked a number of leading universities to sponsor the Institute for Defense Analyses. The Department of Defense organized the Logistics Management Institute in 1961. Use was confined to the military until 1968, when the Urban Institute was created.

Imposition of personnel "freezes" and inflexible personnel ceilings has spawned a new generation of nonprofit corporations to manage social demonstrations. Howard Rosen, director of Research and Development, Department of Labor, explained that the department had no choice but to organize the Manpower Demonstration Research Corporation, Corporation for Public/Private Ventures and Youthwork, to design and implement a complex $212.5 million youth employment and demonstration program. Speaking as one of the midwives of the Manpower Demonstration Research Corporation, Mr. Rosen stated: ". . . and you are told, don't hire anybody, but come in with these facts and information. Realistically, there is no alternative but a non-profit organization."[33]

Few of the copies captured fully the unique qualities which constituted the inner essence of Rand. The distinct characteristics which made Rand "different" were: (1) its extremely broad terms of reference; (2) a high degree of autonomy in the choice of research projects and in setting deadlines; (3) acceptance as part of the Air Force team; (4) independence of

33. National Academy of Public Administration, *Government-Sponsored Nonprofits,* November 1978, p. 15. See this report for a general discussion of nonprofits.

the established hierarchy and military chain of command; (5) access to top decision-makers; and (6) a research "atmosphere" conducive to original and nonconformist thinking.

Nonprofit "intermediaries" such as the Manpower Demonstration Research Corporation are performing tasks which government agencies would do themselves if they could hire the people. These are not advisory "think tanks," but program administrators. MDRC was designated to plan, design, and implement the Youth Incentive Entitlement project. It functions as a staff arm of the Labor Department, and its scope of operations is not left to the discretion of the corporation's directors.

Contract arrangements offer something far more tangible than an opportunity to create institutions with a suitable research environment. Nonprofit corporations, together with university-affiliated research centers and other types of contract organizations, provide a means for escaping irksome government controls and regulations. Salary limitations do not apply to contract personnel, nor do the ceilings on the number of civilian employees. The Armed Services find it easier to obtain money than to secure allocations of civilian "spaces," so there is a ready market for an organizational device which permits hiring outside the ceiling. Contract operations are funded under "contractual services" which ordinarily would receive far less intensive OMB and congressional scrutiny than the object classifications for personnel services. To some extent, the nonprofit corporation fills the void left by the taming and assimilation of the government corporation.

As an added fillip, contracting may broaden the base of public support by fostering alliances with politically influential organizations and groups in the private community. This was a major factor motivating the Agency for International Development to contract out its operations wherever possible. Links of gold can be stronger than links of steel. Don Price has observed that "this new system is breaking down the political opposition to federal programs even more effectively than did the system of grants to the states."[34] Debates about improper government competition with private enterprise generate considerably less heat when public programs are administered by private agencies.

This immunity from political opposition does not necessarily extend to independent nonprofit corporations. Institutions like Rand have no constituency other than their own employees and government sponsor. More and more they are being looked upon as the illegitimate offspring of the miscegenous mating of the public and private sectors. Profit-making companies resent the intrusion of nonprofit contractors into such fields as systems engineering and technical direction which traditionally have been reserved for competitive industry. Universities are also fearful about competition from the nonprofits. Viewed as a device for broadening the base of public support, independent nonprofit corporations are considerably less effective than other types of contractual arrangements.

Rather modest steps to develop a new set of ground rules were taken with the issuance of Bureau of the Budget Circular No. A-49 in February 1958. The circular directed agencies to develop criteria for the use of management and operating contracts. Several functions were ruled "off-limits" for contracting, including direction, supervision, and control of government personnel, and determination of basic government policies. Agencies were requested to consider other alternatives before contracting with an institution of higher learning to administer a large-scale applied research and development facility. The circular attracted little attention in the Department of Defense or the Congress and efforts to obtain compliance were minimal.

In the same year, the Bureau of the Budget raised with the secretary of defense the possibility of creating a new type of

34. Don K. Price, *The Scientific Estate,* Oxford University Press, 1968, p. 73.

organization to be called a Research Institute which would provide a means for reproducing within the government structure some of the more positive attributes of the nonprofit corporation. The suggestion was ignored at the time but revived in the Bell report, again with no results. The comptroller general in 1969 urged that the proposal be reconsidered.[35]

By 1961 contracting had grown to the point where, in the judgment of the House Appropriations Committee, "the Government is moving toward a chaotic condition in its personnel management because of this practice."[36] The committee stated in its report on the 1962 Defense Department appropriation bill:

> Some bold decisions must be made in regard to this mushrooming phenomenon before tremendous injury results to vital Defense programs and programs of other departments and agencies of the Federal Government.
>
> The employees of such organizations are paid indirectly by the taxpayer to the same extent as employees under civil service are paid directly by the taxpayer. The pertinent major difference is that their pay is higher. . . . To a considerable extent the use of contracts is merely a subterfuge to avoid the restrictions on civil service salary scales.

The committee recommended a $5 million reduction in the Aerospace Corporation budget because its salaries and overhead were too high.

Deep concerns were expressed also in the Bell report, although it concluded "many kinds of arrangements—both direct federal operations and various patterns of contracting now in use—can and should be used to mobilize the talent and facilities needed to carry out the Federal research and develop-

35. Comptroller General of the United States, report to the Congress on "Need for Improved Guidelines in Contracting for Research and Development with Government-sponsored Non-profit Contractors," February 10, 1969, p. 59.

36. House Committee on Appropriations, Department of Defense Appropriation Bill 1962, House Report No. 574, 87th Congress, 1st Session, June 23, 1961, pp. 53–54.

ment effort."[37] The need was emphasized for "discriminating" choices based on "getting the job done effectively and efficiently" and "avoiding assignments of work which would create inherent conflicts of interest."

The Bell report did recognize that affirmative measures were required both to arrest the progressive erosion of the government's in-house capability and to prevent nonprofit corporations from abusing their exemption from government controls and regulations. Salaries and related benefits and the use of fees to acquire capital facilities were singled out for special attention. Where the contracting system itself did not provide built-in controls, such as by competitive bidding, it was recommended that the basic standard for approving salaries and related benefits should be comparability with compensation paid to persons doing similar work in the private economy. It was proposed also that upon dissolution of a nonprofit corporation the government should have first claim on its assets. Contractors were successful in blunting the full force and effect of these recommendations, but they foreshadowed clearly the trend of government policies. The nonprofit corporation has ceased to be a sanctuary protected from government controls and congressional scrutiny.

Rather than be assimilated into the system, organizations such as Rand have sought to reduce their dependence on the federal government. Rand was aggressively seeking to develop outside business even before the involvement of two Rand employees in the disclosure of the "Pentagon Papers" threatened federal support.

The comptroller general views with considerable concern the efforts by Rand and other government-sponsored nonprofits to solicit outside business. He foresees that "there would be problems if these organizations that have operated on Government funds and acquired their capabilities with Government support were to be allowed to move freely into

37. Bureau of the Budget, *op. cit.* p. 8.

the private economy" where they would have an "unfair" competitive advantage.[38]

The Bell report saw in a variety of clients a means for enhancing the objectivity and independence of organizations engaged in operations and policy research. But these anticipated benefits, which may well be illusory, are more than offset by the loss of mutual confidence and trust. There is a great deal of difference between being *the* client and *a* client. Those advisers who are most influential share common goals and values and have no divided loyalties.

Herbert Roback, counsel to the Military Operations Subcommittee of the House Committee on Government Operations, graphically pictured a scene with an "Air Force general pacing up and down the room" and "a Rand fellow lying on the couch listening to him."[39] This kind of relationship was jeopardized seriously when Rand began serving the Office of the Secretary of Defense, and is bound to be eroded further as Rand becomes increasingly committed to clients other than the Air Force.

Government-sponsored nonprofit corporations are another manifestation of the prevailing anti-bureaucratic bias. The question is whether the nonprofits provide a cure or are merely symptomatic of basic but remediable deficiencies within the federal system.

The alternative of employing nonprofit intermediaries such as the Manpower Demonstration Research Corporation and "think tanks" on the Rand model should not be excluded when their superiority to government organizations can be demonstrated, but the decision should not be dictated by arbitrary and obsolete regulations. There is no bar to developing within the government institutions which can function with speed, flexibility, and independence. Organizational innovation should not be confined to the nongovernmental sector.

38. Comptroller General of the United States *op. cit.*, p. 50.
39. House Committee on Government Operations, *op. cit.*, p. 64.

The time has come to recognize the need for diversity in government institutions and in the application of government controls.

Proliferation of "twilight-zone" agencies is likely to continue as long as the president and the Congress insist on playing a political shell game with employment statistics and off-budget expenditures. Personnel ceilings control not the number of those working for the federal government, but the number of those reported as working for the federal government. The *Washington Post* estimates that the number of people paid by the federal government is well over double the number listed on the official civilian payroll.[40] Use of extra-governmental devices has enabled the president and the Congress to avoid facing up to the fact that they have created the conditions which now make it difficult for the bureaucracy to get things done.

40. *Washington Post,* July 10, 1978.

The time has come to recognize the need for diversity in government institutions and in the application of government controls.

The President and Congress [illegible] likely to continue to [illegible] the President and the Congress want to [illegible] a [illegible] such [illegible] employment statistics and [illegible] budget expenditures. [illegible] ceilings [illegible] on the number of those working for the federal government, but the number of those [illegible] working for the federal government [illegible] The [illegible] estimates that the number of people paid by the federal government [illegible] double the number listed on the official civilian payroll. [illegible] extra-governmental devices have pushed the president and the Congress [illegible] up to the [illegible] that they have created [illegible] which [illegible] make it [illegible] for the bureaucracy to get things done.

[illegible] Post, July [illegible]

III

Concluding Observations

11

Concluding Observations

If any thesis emerges from the previous chapters, it is that in the choice of institutional types and structural arrangements we are making decisions with significant political implications. In saying this, we do not imply that the administrative consequences of those decisions can be safely ignored. By allowing political expediency to dictate the design of administrative systems, a president can create major obstacles to the accomplishment of his basic political goals and the effective functioning of the democratic process. If present trends are not reversed, we run the risk that the federal structure will become not a reflection, but a caricature of our pluralistic society.

At the very time when the solution of urgent national problems demands diversity in government institutions, flexibility, and effective cooperation among executive agencies, the federal government is moving in the opposite direction. To the other powerful forces promoting fragmentation, compartmentalization, and rigidity, there must now be added the single-interest lobbies and the pressures arising from conflicts over civil service union jurisdictions.

An organization structure that provides access for particular groups within the community is not necessarily flawed, unless it prejudices policy outcomes, prevents team work, and permits private groups to exploit public institutions for their own benefit. The question is one of balance. One does not combat parochialism in the departments by bringing the interest-group brokers into the White House. In the design of any political structure, whether it be the Congress or the executive branch, it is important to build in arrangements that weigh the scale in favor of those advocating the national interest.

Structural arrangements and administrative systems can affect significantly the political balance and program results. But to prescribe reorganization as the cure-all for current frustrations reflects either a mistaken diagnosis or an inability to identify and come to grips with the real problems. Too often reorganization is employed to create the illusion of progress where none exists.

The federal government is well equipped to perform its traditional functions with reasonable effectiveness—to disburse money, to administer grants and contracts, to build dams, highways, and other public works, and to collect taxes. The government has not yet developed the capability to deal with the highly complex social and economic problems confronting the nation which, if they are to be resolved, demand radically new approaches. Alice Rivlin's suggestions for test and experimentation in her provocative book *Systematic Thinking for Social Action* are persuasive, but they require a fundamental change in political values and in the traditional "pork-barrel" approach to problem solving.[1]

Failure to devise new institutions and to modify control systems in the light of the varied needs of modern government is reflected in the increasing reliance on extra-governmental institutions "to get the job done." William J. Grinker, president, Manpower Research Development Corporation, and others accept it as "simply a fact of life that many restrictions

1. Alice M. Rivlin, *Systematic Thinking for Social Action,* The Brookings Institution, 1971.

under which bureaucracies work impede their ability to quickly hire or divert quality personnel to a new and complex undertaking." According to Grinker, there is no realistic alternative to the use of government-sponsored nonprofits and comparable twilight-zone agencies because "the government can, when necessary, spend money quickly, but it is less able to launch quickly a social program with a major, sophisticated research component."[2]

The nonprofits and government-sponsored enterprises are a means of avoiding, not solving, the critical problems confronting the government in the 1980's. It is more expedient to go outside the system altogether than to attempt the difficult and politically sensitive task of creating new institutional forms and reforming the central control systems. Often the central budget, personnel, procurement, and audit agencies would prefer to be bypassed than to alter their uniform rules to accommodate diversity or to depart from traditional ways of doing business.

Federal bureaucrats are today as much the victims as the cause of red tape. All too frequently the congressional and White House response to complex substantive issues is the imposition of additional procedural constraints. As a result, limited personnel resources must be diverted to activities which contribute little, if anything, to the delivery of services.

The Commission on Federal Paperwork decried the "heavy hidden 'taxes' of Federal paperwork and red tape which must be borne by the American people."[3] It estimated the cost at over $100 billion a year, but noted there were also psychological costs, namely the anxiety, frustration, and anger that people experience when dealing with excessive and seemingly purposeless paperwork. The commission limited its study to

2. National Academy of Public Administration, *Government-Sponsored Non-Profits,* November 1978, pp. 73 and 90.

3. Commission on Federal Paperwork, *Final Summary Report,* October 3, 1977, p. 2.

private citizens, recipients of federal assistance, businesses, governmental contractors, and state and local governments. If the commission had examined the federal government, it would have found that federal administrators are also frustrated by arbitrary controls and reporting requirements. The bureaucracy should not be criticized because it has lost or cannot develop the capability to perform effectively anything but traditional tasks when it is denied the discretion and managerial flexibility accorded to quasi-government institutions.

The blurring of the boundaries between public and private administration raises serious and unsolved problems of public accountability. David Lilienthal, former chairman of the Tennessee Valley Authority and Atomic Energy Commission, has posed the basic issue:

> I can think of few things that . . . can be more demoralizing to the dignity and strength of the Federal career service: the creation and proliferation of a body of super civil servants, men who perform governmental functions yet who are independent of government and its obligations as carried by Federal employees, men recruited and paid and supervised as if they were in private employment but who are in fact doing the public's work.[4]

Reorganizing the executive branch structure will not produce the necessary new approaches or responsible and accountable public institutions capable of performing *public* functions effectively. If competence in government and improved service delivery are the objectives, then the place to start is with a cost-benefit analysis of existing controls and regulations.

President Carter has advocated strongly the "deregulation" of private industry. In his 1978 State of the Union message he emphasized that the government was "vigorously pursuing the effort begun last year to reduce the burden of outdated, ineffective and nit-picking regulations." As persuasive a case can be made for "deregulating" the government.

4. David E. Lilienthal, "Skeptical Look at 'Scientific Experts' ", *New York Times Magazine,* September 29, 1963.

There are some hopeful signs. Alan K. Campbell, director, Office of Personnel Management, is committed to "general deregulation" of the personnel field. He recognizes that "the number, range and variety of Federal occupations and the diversity of Federal programs and conditions under which they operate require agencies to tailor personnel management programs to meet their own unique needs."[5] He warns that the gains from civil service reform will be lost if agencies "slide into a comfortable level of uniformity."[6] Personnel deregulation is a beginning, but comparable efforts to eliminate either purely symbolic or counterproductive regulations should be undertaken by the president, the Congress, and the central control agencies.

Deregulation cannot succeed without the support and cooperation of the Congress. Support will not be forthcoming as long as efforts to reorganize and improve executive branch management are viewed as potential threats to committee and subcommittee jurisdictions and congressional prerogatives. Proponents of the legislative veto, dual reporting requirements, and comparable arrangements which inject the Congress or its committees into the executive chain of command need to be persuaded that you do not strengthen the Congress as an institution by weakening the president and the department heads. These arrangements enable the bureaucracy to play off one branch of the government against another and make it more difficult to maintain accountability for executive actions. The Congress has found that it is incapable of satisfactorily controlling the U.S. Postal Service, regulatory commissions, and government-sponsored enterprises which it has exempted in whole or in part from presidential oversight and direction.

Atomization of political power will not make government more responsive. The notion that our governmental institu-

5. Statement of Alan K. Campbell before the House Committee on Post Office and Civil Service, March 20, 1979.

6. Office of Personnel Management, *Status Report on Federal Civil Service Reform,* March, 1979, p. 2.

tions can be reformed by emasculating them persists. When political power is fractionalized, the capability to obtain positive action is seriously impaired. All that is left is the power to veto—a situation conducive to stalemate.

Administration of federal services will not be brought closer to the consumers by so diffusing authority that effective delegation is impossible. Centralization of authority must precede decentralization. Whenever the exercise of executive authority is made contingent upon agreement by the Congress or others at the headquarters level, delegation outside of Washington presents difficult problems and is sometimes impossible. A department head can only delegate the powers vested in him.

Proposals to break up the present constituencies by moving from a functional to a regional or geographic executive branch structure merely would substitute one form of particularism for another. National purposes will not be strengthened by reorganizing to give primary emphasis to sectional interests. These are even more difficult to deal with than conflicts among program areas. A member of Congress can defend politically measures which favor one program area over another, but may feel constrained to demand "equal treatment" for the represented state or district. The pressure on the Congress to "logroll" and to spread the money around on a geographic basis without regard to peculiar local needs or national priorities would be increased rather than abated.

To revive the ancient debate about the relative merits of departmentalization according to major purpose, major process, clientele, materiel, or geography would be profitless and divert attention from the real issues. The doctrine of organization according major purposes advanced by the President's Committee on Administrative Management and the first Hoover Commission has brought about a more logical and consistent grouping of government activities within the executive departments and eliminated such organizational anomalies as the assignment of health functions to Treasury and education functions to Interior—anomalies by no means uncommon in the period prior to 1939. Changes in our national values, goals, and priorities may well argue for additional reforms in executive branch structure along the general lines considered by President Carter. None of these reorganizations could be expected by themselves to curb appreciably the power of the centrifugal forces within our governmental system or to get at the roots of our current difficulties.

The benefits that are supposed to flow from departmentalization are by no means automatic. All too often the general purposes which ostensibly are to be served by a department may be obscured or lost altogether by the way a department is structured internally. A department composed of a collection of small semi-autonomous units, each speaking for its own limited constituency, will not act as a cohesive whole and will be highly resistant to change. The walls between bureaus within a department may be as impenetrable as those between departments, sometimes more so. A joint Bureau of the Budget, Civil Service Commission, Labor Department survey team found that the Labor Department had become so "compartmentalized" that it was almost impossible to fit new programs into the existing structure.[7] As a result, the secretary was compelled to create a new bureau for each new program enacted by the Congress.

Reorganization studies have concentrated primarily on the organization of the executive branch with only relatively brief reference to internal departmental organization. Yet, as a determinant of organizational behavior, the latter is the most important. As a result of the recommendations of the first Hoover Commission, the Congress has removed some of the legal impediments to the exercise of secretarial authority. But it has shown no disposition to relax the extra-legal restraints against internal reorganizations which upset committee juris-

7. Joint Management Improvement and Manpower Review Team, "Review of Management Practices and Manpower Utilization in the Department of Labor," July 1963, pp. 2–2, 2–3.

dictions or threaten to alter the balance of power among constituencies or between the constituencies and the secretary.

Cabinet secretaries rarely bring to their jobs the unique combination of political insight, administrative skill, leadership, intelligence, and creativity required for the successful management of heterogeneous institutions with multiple and sometimes conflicting purposes. Most are content to be a "mediator-initiator" or a reactor to initiatives coming from the White House, the Congress, the bureaucracy, and the several constituencies represented by the department. Anything other than a passive approach is likely to encounter opposition from the Congress, which believes that major bureaus should be allowed to run themselves without undue secretarial interference. This is especially true of the so-called professional bureaus. We accept the principle of civilian control of the military profession, but not of the nonmilitary professions such as medicine, education, science, and engineering.

The Hoover Commission task force on departmental management recognized that "the external demands on a Secretary are such" that he cannot "give continuing attention to internal problems."[8] It assumed that the undersecretary, or, in the case of the Department of Defense, the deputy secretary, would become the "top internal point of departmental direction." Deputy secretaries of defense have been used in this way, as have such undersecretaries as Charles Murphy, who served under Secretary of Agriculture Orville Freeman, but these are the exceptions. An undersecretary suffers from much the same disabilities as the vice president and is subject to the same frustrations. Only under unusual circumstances is he able to establish the personal rapport and relationship of mutual trust with the secretary which are essential if he is to act as an "alter ego." He can exercise authority in his own right only when the secretary is absent or the secretarial post is vacant. Since

8. Commission on Organization of the Executive Branch of the Government, task force report on "Department Management," January 1949, p. 11.

anything he says is construed to represent departmental policy, he must be highly circumspect if he is to avoid the appearance of usurping secretarial prerogatives.

The failure of undersecretaries generally to evolve into general managers or executive vice presidents has left a vacuum within the departmental management systems which has never been satisfactorily filled. This vacuum cannot be filled merely by multiplying the number of staff advisers to the secretary. Attempts to use budget, planning, management, and analytical staffs to compensate for the deficiencies of line management are seldom successful and represent a misuse of staff talents. As one secretary expressed it, what he needed were "people to do the job," not more people to tell him how someone else should do the job.[9] Former HEW Secretary Folsom was making the same point when he said that we had made considerable progress in strengthening the staff resources available to a secretary and now his "chief concern was the need for more line officers."[10]

As departments are presently organized, a secretary is confronted with a dilemma. If he utilizes his assistant secretaries as line officers, then he has no one at the top political level with department-wide perspective whom he can use for assignments which cut across program jurisdictions. If he uses his assistant secretaries as staff, then he has no one between him and the bureau chiefs on whom he can rely to get jobs done. We find no consistent pattern within the executive departments, but the trend is toward using assistant secretaries in the line, with the notable exception of the Department of Transportation.

There is probably no pat solution to this dilemma. No two departments have identical managerial requirements. Each must have a system adapted to its own environment. It seems

9. Based on notes of personal conversation.

10. Senate Committee on Government Operations, Subcommittee on Executive Reorganization, hearings on "Modernizing the Federal Government," January–May 1968, p. 221.

clear, however, that present restrictions on establishing executive positions at the undersecretary and assistant secretary level, limiting the transfer or pooling of appropriations among organizational units to achieve common program objectives, and specifying the details of departmental organization and administrative procedures inhibit managerial innovation and experimentation. As James E. Webb points out, "if the organizational framework in which executives are fitted is rigid, the executive cannot be flexible."[11]

Departments are structured to administer national programs in accordance with uniform national standards. Solutions to many of our current problems require programs which are tailored to the special needs of a particular region or community. These types of programs by their very nature cut horizontally across established departmental jurisdictions at all levels of government. It is with respect to horizontal organization that the conventional wisdom of the orthodox doxology is least helpful. Hierarchical concepts of management cannot be applied to many of the new social programs which require the collaboration of a number of co-equal government organizations on a single project, without any one having final authority over the other.

The rigidities in our departmental systems are major deterrents to lateral communications and cooperative efforts. Agencies find it difficult to work together when they have incompatible administrative systems. It is as if we had designed one system to operate on 25-cycle current, and another on 60-cycle. Converters are expensive and inefficient.

Up to now, insufficient attention has been given either within the executive branch or within the Congress to the need for standardizing administrative provisions. Differences often reflect nothing more than historical accident or the predilections of a particular agency lawyer or congressional com-

11. James E. Webb, *Space-Age Management*, McGraw-Hill Book Co., 1969, p. 141.

mittee. Congress has no procedures for central review of proposed legislation to eliminate inconsistencies and conflicts in nonsubstantive administrative provisions. Administrative requirements in closely related programs may differ with respect to documentation to establish eligibility, control of property and funds, personnel standards, reporting procedures, geographic boundaries, auditing, planning, and definitions of common items such as "facilities."

For the horizontal programs, we need the "adaptive, rapidly changing temporary systems" advocated by Warren Bennis. Flexibility is essential so that the resources and people to solve specific problems can be drawn upon regardless of organizational boundaries. In designating project managers, there is a need for discretion to ignore traditional hierarchical distinctions among departments and agencies, secretaries, administrators, and directors.

In the final analysis, competent government, no matter how well organized, cannot be obtained without managerial skills. As James L. Sundquist notes in a highly perceptive article in the *Public Administration Review,* there is a tendency for politicians such as Jimmy Carter to confuse management with management improvement projects.[12] We must discard the notion that "anybody, chosen for whatever reason unrelated to management experience or talent, can run any government agency."[13] Whether the government succeeds or fails will depend on its ability to recruit and develop able career managers. We must get away from the idea that a neutral civil service capable of serving transient political executives has to be a sterile civil service isolated from the policy-makers.

The president's primary task is leadership: setting national goals and priorities and mobilizing public support for his pro-

12. James L. Sundquist, "Jimmy Carter as a Public Administrator: An Appraisal at Mid-Term," *Public Administration Review,* Vol. 39, No. 1, January–February 1979.

13. *Ibid.*

grams. Once he has established his goals, then he needs to consider carefully the means to be employed in reaching them. His decisions on program design, institutional type, organizational jurisdiction, and management system may well determine who will control and benefit from a program and, ultimately, whether national objectives are achieved. These decisions should not be governed solely by application of traditional organization doctrines. In evaluating the design and organization of new programs or proposed reorganizations of existing programs, the basic questions to be asked are:

1. What is the nature of the constituency that is being created, or acquired, and to what extent will it be able to influence policies and program administration?
2. Is the constituency broadly based or does it represent narrow interests antithetical to some of the public purposes to be accomplished by the program?
3. What committees of the Congress will exercise jurisdiction and to what extent do they reflect the interests of the constituencies to be served by the program, or those of groups hostile to program objectives?
4. What is the culture and tradition of the administering department or agency? Will it provide an environment favorable to program growth, stunt development, or produce a hybrid?
5. What are the constituencies to whom the administering agency responds? Would there be any obvious conflicts of interest?
6. Where are the loci of power with respect to program administration: the president, the agency head, the bureaus, congressional committees, professional guilds, interest groups, etc.? Are provisions made to assure an appropriate balance of power and to prevent domination by any single group? Are the ultimate powers of the president protected and supported?

7. To what extent and in what way is access to those with decision-making power limited?
8. Does the program design foster dominance by a particular professional perspective and will this result in distortion of program goals?
9. Is provision made for an "open" system engineered in such a way that there are no built-in obstacles to joint administration with related government programs and cooperative efforts?
10. What safeguards are provided to assure that no group or class of people is excluded from participation in the program and an equitable share in program benefits?
11. Do the type of institution and proposed organization provide the status, visibility, public support, and administrative system appropriate to the function to be performed?

Whether or not meaningful improvements in executive branch organization and in the management of the federal system can be obtained will depend in part on reorganization of the congressional committee structure. The particularistic elements in our society always will triumph over the general interest as long as they are nourished and supported by committees and subcommittees which share their limited concerns. At a minimum, committee and subcommittee jurisdictions should be compatible with current assignments of responsibilities within the executive branch and take into account interrelationships among programs so as to permit unified consideration of closely related and interdependent programs and evaluation of program objectives. Even modest reforms are unlikely, however, unless an informed and aroused electorate demands that the Congress modernize its organization and procedures. The assumption that only members of Congress are affected by congressional organization is no longer tenable.

The Hoover Commission doctrines were somewhat dated when they were first published. They have served their purpose, and most of the basic recommendations have been implemented. Our government has undergone revolutionary changes in the thirty years which have elapsed since the Hoover reports. The principles of organization advanced by the Hoover Commission have not lost their validity, but read by themselves they do not contribute materially to our understanding of current problems of government organization and management. It is fruitless to look to them for solutions.

We will compound the problems if we demand simple answers. The growing interdependence of the federal government, state and local governments, and many private institutions; increasing reliance on administration by grant and contract; and the greater utilization of multi-jurisdictional programs have added new dimensions to public administration. Whatever strategy is devised must be as sophisticated as the problems which it seeks to solve and retain sufficient flexibility to permit rapid adjustments to changing circumstances. It cannot deal with the executive branch as if it existed in isolation and must take into account the linkages between congressional and executive organization. If we persist in thinking of organization in terms of lines and boxes on an organization chart, our efforts to discover viable approaches to our current dilemma certainly will fail.

BOOKS

Adams, Sherman. *First Hand Report: The Story of The Eisenhower Administration,* Harper & Bros., 1961.

Alsop, Stewart. *The Center,* Popular Library, 1968.

Appleby, Paul H. *Big Democracy,* Alfred A. Knopf, 1945.

———. *Policy and Administration,* University of Alabama Press, 1949.

Bailey, Stephen K. "Managing the Federal Government" in *Agenda for the Nation,* The Brookings Institution, 1968.

Bailey, Stephen K., and Edith K. Mosher. *ESEA: The Office of Education Administers a Law,* Syracuse University Press, 1968.

Baldwin, Sidney. *Poverty and Politics,* University of North Carolina Press, 1968.

Baldwin, William L. *The Structure of the Defense Market, 1955–1964,* Duke University Press, 1967.

Barnard, Chester I. *The Functions of the Executive,* Harvard University Press, 1942.

Bennis, Warren G. *Changing Organizations: Essays on the Development and Evolution of Human Organization,* McGraw-Hill Book Co., 1966.

Bernstein, Marver H. *Regulating Business by Independent Commission,* Princeton University Press, 1955.

Biddle, Francis. *In Brief Authority,* Doubleday & Co., 1962.

Brownlow, Louis. *The President and the Presidency,* Public Administration Service, 1949.

———. *A Passion for Anonymity—The Autobiography of Louis Brownlow,* University of Chicago Press, 1958.

Bundy, McGeorge. *To Govern for Freedom,* Godkin Lectures, Harvard University, 1968.

Byrnes, James F. *All in One Lifetime,* Harper & Bros., 1958.

Carnegie Commission on the Future of Public Broadcasting. *A Public Trust,* Bantam Books, 1979.

Carter, Jimmy. *Why Not the Best?,* Bantam Books, 1976.

Cater, Douglass. *Power in Washington,* Vintage Books, 1964.

Crane, Katherine. *Mr. Carr of State—Forty-seven Years in the Department of State,* St. Martin's Press, 1960.

Cronin, Thomas E., and Sanford B. Greenberg, editors. *The Presidential Advisory System,* Harper & Row, 1969.

Crozier, Michel. *The Bureaucratic Phenomenon,* University of Chicago Press, 1963.

Cummings, Homer, and Carl McFarland. *Federal Justice,* The Macmillan Co., 1937.

Dahl, Robert A. *Pluralist Democracy in the United States: Conflict and Consent,* Rand McNally & Co., 1967.

Danhof, Clarence H. *Government Contracting and Technological Change,* The Brookings Institution, 1968.

Davidson, Roger H. and Walter J. Oleszek. *Congress Against Itself,* Indiana University Press, 1977.

Department of Labor. *The Anvil and the Plow,* 1963.

Derthick, Martha. *The Influence of Federal Grants,* Harvard University Press, 1970.

Derthick, Martha, and Gary Bombardier. *Between State and Nation: Regional Organizations of the United States,* The Brookings Institution, 1974.

Destler, I. M. *Presidents, Bureaucrats and Foreign Policy,* Princeton University Press, 1972.

Dickson, Paul. *Think Tanks,* Ballantine Books, 1972.

Downs, Anthony. *Inside Bureaucracy,* Little, Brown & Co., 1967.

Drucker, Peter F. *The Age of Discontinuity,* Harper & Row, 1969.

Emmerich, Herbert. *Essays on Federal Reorganization,* University of Alabama Press, 1950.

———. *Federal Organization and Administrative Management,* University of Alabama Press, 1971.

Evans, Rowland, Jr., and Robert D. Novak. *Nixon in the White House,* Random House, 1971.

Fenno, Richard F., Jr. *Congressmen in Committees,* Little, Brown and Co., 1973.

———. *The President's Cabinet: An Analysis in the Period from Wilson to Eisenhower,* Harvard University Press, 1959.

Fisher, Louis. *Presidential Spending Power,* Princeton University Press, 1975.

Fox, Harrison W., Jr., and Susan Webb Hammond. *Congressional Staffs: The Invisible Force in Lawmaking,* The Free Press, 1977.

Freeman, J. Leiper. *The Political Process: Executive Bureau–Legislative Committee Relations,* Random House, 1965.

Frieden, Bernard J., and Marshall Kaplan. *The Politics of Neglect,* The MIT Press, 1975.

Gardner, John W. *Excellence—Can We Be Equal and Excellent Too?,* Harper & Row, 1962.

———. *No Easy Victories,* edited by Helen Rowan, Harper & Row, 1968.

Gaus, John M. "The Citizen as Administrator" in *Public Administration and Democracy,* edited by Roscoe C. Martin, Syracuse University Press, 1965.

Gaus, John M., and Leon O. Wolcott. *Public Administration and the U.S. Department of Agriculture,* Public Administration Service, 1940.

Gilb, Corinne Lathrop. *Hidden Hierarchies,* Harper & Row, 1966.

Goldberg, Sidney D. and Harold Seidman, *The Government Corporation: Elements of a Model Charter,* Public Administration Service, 1953.

Greenberg, Daniel S. *The Politics of Pure Science,* The New American Library, 1967.

Greenfield, Meg. "Science Goes to Washington," reprinted in *The Politics of Science,* edited by William N. Nelson, Oxford University Press, 1968.

Grodzins, Morton. *The American System,* edited by Daniel J. Elazar, Rand McNally & Co., 1966.

Grosenick, Leigh E., editor. *The Administration of the New Federalism: Objectives and Issues,* American Society for Public Administration, 1973.

Gross, Bertram M. *The Managing of Organizations: The Administrative Struggle,* Vol. I, The Free Press of Glencoe, 1964.

Gulick, Luther, and L. Urwick, editors. *Papers on the Science of Administration,* Institute of Public Administration, Columbia University, 1937.

Haire, Mason. *Organization Theory in Industrial Practice: A Symposium of the Foundation for Research on Human Behavior,* John Wiley & Sons, 1962.

Halperin, Morton H. *Bureaucratic Politics and Foreign Policy,* The Brookings Institution, 1974.

Harris, Joseph P. *Congressional Control of Administration,* The Brookings Institution, 1964.

Heclo, Hugh A. *A Government of Strangers: Executive Politics in Washington,* The Brookings Institution, 1977.

Heren, Louis. *The New American Commonwealth,* Harper & Row, 1965.

Herring, E. Pendleton. *Public Administration and the Public Interest,* McGraw-Hill Book Co., 1936.

Hoover, Herbert C. *The Memoirs of Herbert Hoover: The Cabinet and the Presidency, 1920–1933,* The Macmillan Co., 1952.

Hughes, Emmet J. *The Living Presidency,* Coward, McCann, & Geoghegan, 1973.

Ickes, Harold L. *The Secret Diary of Harold L. Ickes: The Lowering Clouds, 1939–1945,* Vol. III, Simon and Schuster, 1954.

Janowitz, Morris. *The Professional Soldier—A Social and Political Portrait,* The Free Press of Glencoe, 1960.

Jones, H. G. *The Records of a Nation,* Atheneum, 1969.

Jones, Jesse H. *Fifty Billon Dollars: My Thirteen Years with the RFC (1932–1945),* The Macmillan Co., 1951.

Katz, Daniel, and Robert L. Kahn. *The Social Psychology of Organization,* John Wiley & Sons, 1966.

Kaufman, Herbert. *The Forest Ranger—A Study in Administrative Behavior,* published for Resources for the Future, Inc., by The Johns Hopkins Press, 1960.

———. "Reflections on Administrative Reorganization" in *Setting National Priorities: The 1978 Budget,* The Brookings Institution, 1977.

Keefe, William, J., and Morris S. Ogul. *The American Legislative Process—Congress and the States,* Prentice-Hall, 1964.

Kile, Orville Merton. *The Farm Bureau Through Three Decades,* The Waverly Press, 1948.

King, Ernest J., and Walter Muir Whitehill. *Fleet Admiral King—A Naval Record,* W. W. Norton & Co., 1952.

Kirkpatrick, Lyman B., Jr. *The Real CIA,* The Macmillan Co., 1968.

Kirst, Michael W. *Government Without Passing Laws,* University of North Carolina Press, 1969.

Koenig, Louis W. *The Chief Executive,* Harcourt, Brace & World, 1964.

———. *The Invisible Presidency,* Rinehart & Co., 1960.

Lambright, W. Henry. *Governing Science and Technology,* Oxford University Press, 1976.

Lawrence, Samuel A. *U.S. Merchant Shipping Policies and Politics,* The Brookings Institution, 1966.

Leiserson, Avery. *Administrative Regulation,* University of Chicago Press, 1942.

Levitan, Sar A. *Federal Aid to Depressed Areas: An Evaluation of the Area Redevelopment Administration,* The Johns Hopkins Press, 1964.

———. *The Great Society's Poor Law: A New Approach to Poverty,* The Johns Hopkins Press, 1969.

Library of Congress. *A Compilation of Basic Information on the Reorganization of the Executive Branch of the Government of the United States, 1912–1947,* Washington, September 1947.

Likert, Rensis. *New Patterns of Management,* McGraw-Hill Book Co., 1961.

Lilienthal, David E. *The Journals of David E. Lilienthal: The TVA Years, 1939–1945, The Atomic Energy Years, 1945–1950,* Vols. I and II, Harper & Row, 1964.

Maass, Arthur. *Muddy Waters—The Army Engineers and the Nation's Rivers,* Foreword by Harold L. Ickes, Harvard University Press, 1951.

MacMahon, Arthur W., and John D. Millett. *Federal Administrators—A Biographical Approach to the Problem of Departmental Management,* Columbia University Press, 1939.

MacNeil, Neil. *Forge of Democracy—The House of Representatives,* David McKay Co., 1963.

Mangum, Garth L. *MTDA: Foundation of Federal Manpower Policy,* The Johns Hopkins Press, 1968.

Mann, Dean E., and Jameson W. Doig. *The Assistant Secretaries,* The Brookings Institution, 1965.

Martin, Roscoe. *Grass Roots,* University of Alabama Press, 1957.

Marx, Fritz Morstein, editor. *Elements of Public Administration,* Prentice-Hall, 1950.

McConnell, Grant. *Private Power and American Democracy,* Alfred A. Knopf, 1967.

McGregor, Douglas. *The Human Side of Enterprise,* McGraw-Hill Book Co., 1960.

Meriam, Lewis, and Lawrence F. Schmeckebier. *Reorganization of the National Government: What Does It Involve?,* The Brookings Institution, 1939.

Millett, John D. *Organization for the Public Service,* D. Van Nostrand Co., 1966.

Moos, Malcolm, and Francis E. Rourke. *The Campus and the State,* The Johns Hopkins Press, 1959.

Morgan, Robert J. *Governing Soil Conservation: Thirty Years of the New Decentralization,* The Johns Hopkins Press, 1965.

Mosher, Frederick C. *Democracy and the Public Service,* Oxford University Press, 1968.

———, editor. *Government Reorganization: Cases and Commentary,* The Bobbs-Merrill Co., 1967.

———, and others. *Watergate: Implications for Responsible Government.* Basic Books, 1974.

Moynihan, Daniel P. *Maximum Feasible Misunderstanding,* The Free Press, 1969.

Musolf, Lloyd D., editor. *Communications Satellites in Political Orbit,* Chandler Publishing Co., 1968.

———. *Mixed Enterprise,* Lexington Books, 1972.

Navasky, Victor S. *Kennedy Justice,* Atheneum, 1971.

Nelson, William R. *The Politics of Science: Readings in Science, Technology and Government,* Oxford University Press, 1968.

Neustadt, Richard E. *Presidential Power—The Politics of Leadership,* John Wiley & Sons, 1960.

Noll, Roger G. *Reforming Regulation: An Evaluation of the Ash Council Proposals,* The Brookings Institution, 1971.

Nourse, Edwin G. *Economics in the Public Service,* Harcourt Brace & Co., 1952.

O'Leary, Michael Kent. *The Politics of American Foreign Aid,* Atherton Press, 1967.

Oleszek, Walter, *Congressional Procedures and Policy Process,* Congressional Quarterly Press, 1978.

Orlans, Harold. *Contracting for Atoms,* The Brookings Institution, 1967.

Perkins, Frances. *The Roosevelt I Knew,* The Viking Press, 1946.

Polenberg, Richard. *Reorganizing Roosevelt's Government: The Controversy over Executive Reorganization, 1936–1939,* Harvard University Press, 1996.

Pressman, Jeffrey L., and Aaron Wildavsky. *Implementation,* University of California Press, 1973.

Presthus, Robert. *The Organizational Society—An Analysis and a Theory,* Alfred A. Knopf, 1962.

Price, Don K. *Government and Science—Their Dynamic Relation in American Democracy,* New York University Press, 1954.

———. *The Scientific Estate,* Oxford University Press, 1968.

Reagan, Michael D. *The New Federalism,* Oxford University Press, 1972.

Reedy, George E. *The Twilight of the Presidency,* New American Library, 1970.

Ries, John C. *The Management of Defense-Organization and Control of the U.S. Armed Services,* The Johns Hopkins Press, 1964.

Rivlin, Alice. *Systematic Thinking for Social Action,* The Brookings Institution, 1971.

Rogow, Arnold A. *James Forrestal: A Study of Personality, Politics and Policy,* The Macmillan Co., 1963.

Rossiter, Clinton. *The American Presidency,* The New American Library, 1956.

Rourke, Francis E. *Bureaucracy, Politics and Public Policy,* Little, Brown and Co., 1969.

Ruttenberg, Stanley H., and Jocelyn Gutchess. *The Federal-State Employment Service: A Critique,* The Johns Hopkins Press, 1970.

Sanford, Terry. *Storm Over the States,* McGraw-Hill Book Co., 1967.

Schultze, Charles L. *The Politics and Economics of Public Spending,* The Brookings Institution, 1968.

Scott, William G. *Organization Theory: A Behavioral Analysis for Management,* Richard D. Irwin, Inc., 1967.

Seidman, Harold. "Government Sponsored Enterprise in the United States" in *The New Political Economy: Public Use of the Private Sector,* Macmillan, London, 1975.

Selznick, Philip. *TVA and the Grass Roots: A Study in the Sociology of Formal Organization,* University of California Press, 1949.

Sherman, Harvey. *It All Depends—A Pragmatic Approach to Organization,* University of Alabama Press, 1966.

Short, Lloyd Milton. *The Development of National Administrative Organization in the United States,* The Johns Hopkins Press, 1923.

Simon, Herbert A. *Administrative Behavior: A Study of Decision-Making Processes in Administrative Organization,* The Macmillan Co., 1957.

Simon, Herbert A., Donald W. Smithburg, and Victor A. Thompson. *Public Administration,* Alfred A. Knopf, 1950.

Simpson, Smith. *Anatomy of the State Department,* Beacon Press, 1967.

Smith, Bruce L. R., and D. C. Hague. *The Dilemma of Accountability in Modern Government,* St. Martin's Press, 1971.

Smith, Bruce L. R., editor. *The New Political Economy: The Public Use of the Private Sector,* Macmillan, London, 1975.

Smith, Frank E. *The Politics of Conservation,* Pantheon Books, 1966.

Sorensen, Theodore C. *Decision-Making in the White House: The Olive Branch and the Arrows,* Foreword by President John F. Kennedy, Columbia University Press, 1963.

Stanley, David T. *The Higher Civil Service,* The Brookings Institution, 1964.

Stanley, David T., Dean E. Mann, and Jameson W. Doig. *Men Who Govern,* The Brookings Institution, 1967.

Stewart, Irwin. *Organizing Scientific Research for War,* Atlantic Monthly Press Book, Little, Brown and Co., 1948.

Stimson, Henry L., and McGeorge Bundy. *On Active Service in Peace and War,* Harper & Bros., 1947.

Sundquist, James L. *Politics and Policy: The Eisenhower, Kennedy and Johnson Years,* The Brookings Institution, 1968.

Sundquist, James L., and David W. Davis. *Making Federalism Work,* The Brookings Institution, 1969.

Tacheron, Donald G., and Morris K. Udall. *The Job of the Congressman,* The Bobbs-Merrill Co., 1966.

Talbot, Ross B., and Don F. Hadwiger. *The Policy Process in American Agriculture,* Chandler Publishing Co., 1968.

Thomas, Morgan, and Robert M. Northrop. *Atomic Energy and Congress,* University of Michigan Press, 1956.

Truman, David B. *The Governmental Process,* Alfred A. Knopf, 1964.

Truman, Harry S. *Memoirs of Harry S Truman: Years of Decisions, Years of Trial and Hope,* Vols. I and II, Doubleday & Co., 1955–1956.

Waldo, Dwight. "Public Administration and Culture" in *Public Administration and Democracy,* edited by Roscoe C. Martin, Syracuse University Press, 1965.

———. *The Administrative State: A Study of the Political Theory of American Public Administration,* The Ronald Press Co., 1948.

Wallace, Schuyler C. *Federal Departmentalization: A Critique of Theories of Organization,* Columbia University Press, 1941.

Wann, A. J. *The President as Chief Administrator—A Study of Franklin D. Roosevelt,* Public Affairs Press, 1968.

Warner, W. Lloyd, Paul P. VanRiper, Norman H. Martin, and Orvis F. Collins. *The American Federal Executive,* Yale University Press, 1963.

Warren, Sidney, editor. *The American President,* Prentice-Hall, 1967.

Wayne, Stephen J., *The Legislative Presidency,* Harper & Row, 1978.

Webb, James E. *Space-Age Management,* McGraw-Hill Book Co., 1969.

White, Leonard D. *The Federalists,* The Macmillan Co., 1948.

Wildavsky, Aaron. *The Politics of the Budgetary Process,* Little, Brown and Co., 1964.

Wilson, Woodrow. *Congressional Government,* Meridian Books, 1956.

Zeigler, Harmon. *Interest Groups in American Society,* Prentice-Hall, 1964.

PERIODICALS, PAMPHLETS, AND REPORTS

Acheson, Dean. "Thoughts about Thoughts in High Places," *The New York Times Magazine,* October 11, 1959.

Advisory Commission on Intergovernmental Relations. *Multistate Regionalism,* April 1972.

———. *Statutory and Administrative Controls Associated with Federal Grants for Public Assistance,* May 1964.

———. *Categorical Grants: Their Role and Design,* 1977.

———. *The Intergovernmental Grant System as Seen by Local, State, and Federal Officials,* 1977.

———. *Improving Federal Grants Management,* 1977.

———. *Summary and Concluding Observations,* 1978.

Allison, Donal V. "The Development and Use of Political Power by Federal Agencies: A Case Study of the U.S. Forest Service," May 1965 (unpublished thesis, University of Virginia).

Anderson, Patrick. "Deputy President for Domestic Affairs," *The New York Times Magazine,* March 3, 1968.

Argyris, Chris. "Some Consequences of Separating Thought from Action," *Ventures,* Graduate School, Yale University, Spring 1968.

Arnold, Peri E. "The First Hoover Commission and the Managerial Presidency," *Journal of Politics,* Vol. 38, 1976.

Bartlett, Joseph W., and Douglas N. Jones. "Managing a Cabinet Agency: Problems of Performance at Commerce," *Public Administration Review,* Vol. 34, No. 1, January-February 1974.

Beam, David R. "Public Administration is Alive and Well and Living in the White House," *Public Administration Review,* Vol. 38, No. 1, January-February 1978.

Bell, Daniel. "Toward a Communal Society," *Life,* May 12, 1967.

Berman, Larry. "OMB and the Hazards of Presidential Staff Work," *Public Administration Review,* Vol. 38, No. 6, November-December 1978.

Bolton, John R. *The Legislative Veto: Unseparating The Powers,* American Enterprise Institute for Public Policy Research, 1977.

Bombardier, Gary. "The Managerial Function of OMB: Intergovernmental Relations as a Test Case," *Public Policy,* Vol. 23, No. 3, Summer 1975.

Brademas, John. "Federal Reorganization and its Likely Impact on State and Local Government," *Publius,* Vol. 8, No. 2, Spring 1978.

Bruff, Harold, and Ernest Gellhorn. "Congress and Control of Administrative Regulations: A Study of Legislative Vetoes," *Harvard Law Review,* Vol. 90, 1977.

Caldwell, Lynton K. "Restructuring for Coordinative Policy and Action," *Public Administration Review,* Vol. 28, No. 4, 1968.

Carey, William D. "On Being Fed Up with Government," *The Bureaucrat,* Spring, 1972.

———. "Presidential Staffing in the Sixties and Seventies," *Public Administration Review,* Vol. 29, No. 5, 1969.

———. "Reorganization Plan No. 2," *Public Administration Review,* Vol. 30, No. 6, November-December 1970.

Citizen's Board of Inquiry into Hunger and Malnutrition in the United States. *Hunger, U.S.A.,* New Community Press, 1968.

Colm, Gerhard, and Luther Gulick. *Program Planning for National Goals,* National Planning Association, November 1968.

Commission on Intergovernmental Relations. *The Administrative and Fiscal Impact on Federal Grants-in-Aid,* June 1955.

Commission on Organization of the Executive Branch of the Government. *Budget and Accounting,* June 1955; *Departmental Management,* task force report, January 1949; *Federal Business Enterprises,* March 1949; *General Management of the Executive Branch,* February 1949; *Legal Services and Procedures,* March 1955; *Public Welfare,* task force report, June 1949.

Committee for Economic Development. *Modernizing Local Government,* July 1966.

———. *Modernizing State Government,* July 1967.

Council of State Governments. *Federal Grant-in-Aid Requirements Impeding State Administration,* November 1966.

———. *Integration and Coordination of State Environmental Programs,* 1975.

Cronin, Thomas E. "The Swelling of the Presidency," *Saturday Review,* February 1973.

David, Paul T. "The Vice-Presidency: Its Institutional Evolution and Contemporary Status," *The Journal of Politics,* November, 1967.

Davidson, Roger H. "Our Changing Congress," Paper delivered at Conference on Congress and Presidency, Lyndon B. Johnson Library, November 1977.

Dean, Alan L. "The Goals of Departmental Reorganization," *The Bureaucrat,* Spring 1972.

Dempsey, John R. "Carter Reorganization: A Midterm Appraisal," *Public Administration Review,* Vol. 39, No. 1, January-February 1979.

Derthick, Martha. "On Commissionship: Presidential Variety," *Public Policy,* Vol. 19, No. 4, Fall 1971.

Devine, William R. "The Second Hoover Commission Reports: An Analysis," *Public Administration Review,* Vol. 15, No. 4, 1955.

Drew, Elizabeth B. "How to Govern (or Avoid It) by Commission," *Atlantic Monthly,* May 1968.

Drummond, Roscoe. "Is the Government Ready for the Future?", *Saturday Review,* August 29, 1964.

Emmerich, Herbert. "Administrative Problems of Multipurpose Diplomacy," *Public Administration Review,* Vol. 29, No. 6, 1969.

———. "Complexities of Administered Diplomacy," *Public Administration Review,* Vol. 29, No. 6, 1969.

Etzoni, Amitai. "The Third Sector and Domestic Missions," *Public Administration Review,* Vol. 33, No. 4, July-August 1973.

Fairlie, Henry. "Thoughts on the Presidency," *The Public Interest,* Fall 1967.

Fesler, James W. "Administrative Literature and the Second Hoover Commission Reports," *American Political Science Review,* March 1967.

Fielder, Frances, and Godfrey Harris. *The Quest for Foreign Affairs Officers—Their Recruitment and Selection,* Carnegie Endowment for International Peace, 1966.

Fox, Douglas M. "The President's Proposals for Executive Reorganization: A Critique," *Public Administration Review,* Vol. 33, No. 5, September-October 1973.

Frankel, Charles. " 'Culture,' 'Information,' 'Foreign Policy,' " *Public Administration Review,* Vol. 29, No. 6, 1969.

Furnas, Howard. "The President: A Changing Role?", *The Annals of the American Academy of Political and Social Science,* November 1968.

Gardner, John W. "How to Prevent Organizational Dry Rot," *Harpers,* October 1965.

Gordon, Kermit. *Reflections on Spending,* The Brookings Institution, 1967.

Green, Harold P. *Nuclear Technology and the Fabric of Government* (Paper No. 7, Program of Policy Studies in Science and Technology), The George Washington University, January 1965.

Hardin, Charles M. *Food and Fiber in the Nation's Politics,* National Commission of Food and Fiber, August 1967, U.S. Government Printing Office, 1967.

Harr, John Ensor. "The Managerial Crisis," *The Annals of the American Academy of Political and Social Science,* November 1968.

Halperin, Morton H. "Why Bureaucrats Play Games," *Foreign Policy,* No. 2, Spring 1971.

Heclo, Hugh. "Political Executives and the Washington Bureaucracy," *Political Science Quarterly,* Vol. 92, Fall 1977.

———. "OMB and the Presidency—the Problem of 'Neutral Competence,' " *The Public Interest,* No. 38, Winter 1975.

Henry, Laurin L. "Presidential Transitions: The 1968–69 Experience in Perspective," *Public Administration Review,* Vol. 29, No. 5, 1969.

Heyman, Victor K. "Government by Contract: Boon or Boner?", *Public Administration Review,* Vol. 21, No. 2, 1961.

Hickman, Martin B., and Neil Hollander. "Undergraduate Origin as a Factor in Elite Recruitment and Mobility: The Foreign Service—A Case Study," *The Western Political Quarterly,* Vol. 19, No. 2, June 1966.

Hoover, Dale M., and James G. Maddox. *Food for the Hungry,* A Statement by the NPA Agriculture Committee, National Planning Association, February 1969.

Hornig, Donald F. "United States Science Policy: It's Health and Future Direction," *Science,* February 7, 1969.

House Committee on Post Office and Civil Service. "A Report on the Growth of the Executive Office of the President 1955–1973," Committee Print No. 19, 92nd Congress, 2nd Sess.

Ink, Dwight. "A Management Crisis for the New President: People Programs," *Public Administration Review,* Vol. 28, No. 6, 1969.

Jessup, Paul F. "The Theory and Practice of Nonpar Banking," unpublished dissertation, Northwestern University, 1964.

Kaufman, Herbert. "Administrative Decentralization and Political Power," *Public Administration Review,* Vol. 29, No. 1, 1969.

Klima, Otto, Jr., and Gibson M. Wolfe. "The Oceans: Organizing for Action," *Harvard Business Review,* May-June 1968.

Kolodziej, Edward J. "The National Security Council: Innovations and Implications," *Public Administration Review,* Vol. 29, No. 6, 1969.

Kraines, Oscar. "The President Versus Congress: Keep Commission, 1905–1909," *The Western Political Quarterly,* Vol. 23, No. 1, March 1970.

Kristol, Irving. "Decentralization for What?" *The Public Interest,* No. 11, Spring 1968.

Lacy, Alex B., Jr. "The White House Staff Bureaucracy," *Transaction,* January 1969.

Landau, Martin. "Redundancy, Rationality, and the Problem of Duplication and Overlap," *Public Administration Review,* Vol. 29, No. 4, 1969.

Long, Norton E. "Power and Administration," *Public Administration Review,* Vol. 9, No. 4, 1949.

———. "Reflections on Presidential Power," *Public Administration Review,* Vol. 29, No. 5, 1969.

Mansfield, Harvey C. "Federal Executive Reorganization: Thirty Years of Experience," *Public Administration Review,* Vol. 29, No. 4, 1969.

———. "Reorganizing the Federal Executive Branch. The Limits of Institutionalization," *Law and Contemporary Problems,* Vol. 35, Summer 1970.

Masters, Nicholas A. "House Committee Assignments," *American Political Science Review,* June 1961.

McKinley, Charles. "Federal Administrative Pathology and Separation of Powers," *Public Administration Review,* Vol. 11, No. 1, 1951.

Meyers, Will S., Jr. "Fiscal Balance in the American Federal System," *State Government,* Winter 1968.

Miles, Rufus E., Jr. "The Case for a Federal Department of Education,'" *Public Administration Review,* Vol. 27, No. 2, 1967.

———. *A Cabinet Department of Education,* American Council on Education, Washington, D.C., 1976.

———. "Considerations for a President Bent on Reorganization," *Public Administration Review,* Vol. 37, No. 2, March-April 1977.

Miller, S. M., and Martin Rein. "Participation, Poverty and Administration," *Public Administration Review,* Vol. 29, No. 1, 1969.

Moe, Ronald C. *Executive Branch Reorganization: An Overview,* Senate Committee on Governmental Affairs, Committee Print, March 1978.

Mosher, Frederick C. "Some Observations about Foreign Service Reform: Famous First Words," *Public Administration Review,* Vol. 29, No. 6, 1969.

Mosher, Frederick C., and Richard Stillman, II. "Symposium on Professions in Government," *Public Administration Review,* Vol. 38, No. 2, March-April 1978.

National Academy of Public Administration, *Government-Sponsored NonProfits,* November 1978.

———. *Reorganization in Florida,* September 1977.

Neustadt, Richard E. "On Constraining the President," *New York Times Magazine,* October 14, 1973.

Orlans, Harold. "The Political Uses of Social Research," *Annals of the American Academy of Political and Social Sciences,* Vol. 384, March 1971.

Parris, Judith H. "The Office of Management and Budget: Background Responsibilities, Recent Issues," Congressional Research Service, July 27, 1978.

Patterson, Samuel C. "The Professional Staffs of Congressional Committees," *Administrative Science Quarterly,* Vol. 15 (1970).

President's Committee on Administrative Management. *Administrative Management in the Government of the United States,* January 1937.

President's Commission on Postal Organization. *Towards Postal Excellence,* June 1968.

Price, Don K. "Reflections and Comments," *Public Administration Review,* Vol. 29, No. 6, 1969.

Raymond, Jack. "Growing Threat of Our Military-Industrial Complex," *Harvard Business Review,* May-June 1968.

Redford, Emmette S. "The President and the Regulatory Commissions," report prepared for the President's Advisory Committee on Government Organization, November 17, 1960.

Roback, Herbert. "Congress and the Science Budget," *Science,* May 31, 1968.

———. "Do We Need a Department of Science and Technology?", *Science,* Vol. 165, July 4, 1969.

———. "The Congress and Super Departments," *The Bureaucrat,* Spring 1972.

———. "Problems and Prospects in Government Reorganization," Selected Papers of the National Academy of Public Administration, No. 1, January 1973.

Rourke, Francis E. "The Politics of Administrative Organization: A Case History," *The Journal of Politics,* Vol. 19, August 1957.

Rowe, James, Jr. "Cooperation or Conflict? The President's Relationships with an Opposition Congress," *Georgetown Law Journal,* Vol. 36, 1947.

Russell, Gary. "The Bureaucratic Culture and Personality of the U.S. Coast Guard," unpublished master's thesis, University of Connecticut, 1974.

Sayre, Wallace S. "Premises of Public Administration: Past and Emerging," *Public Administration Review,* Vol. 18, No. 2, 1958.

Schick, Allen. "The Budget Bureau That Was: Thoughts on the Rise, Decline and Future of a Presidential Agency," *Law and Contemporary Problems,* Vol. 35, Summer 1970.

Seidman, Harold. "Crisis of Confidence in Government," *Political Quarterly* (*London*), January-March 1972.

———. "The Government Corporation: Organization and Controls," *Public Administration Review,* Vol. 14, No. 3, 1954.

———. "The Government Corporation in the United States," *Public Administration* (Great Britain), Summer 1959.

———. "The Theory of the Autonomous Government Corporation: A Critical Appraisal," *Public Administration Review,* Vol. 12, No. 2, 1952.

Seidman, Harold, Dominic Del Guidice, and Charles Warren. *Reorganization by Presidential Plan: Three Case Studies,* National Academy of Public Administration, 1971 (mimeographed).

Segal, David R., and Daniel H. Willick. "The Reinforcement of Traditional Career Patterns in Agencies Under Stress," *Public Administration Review,* Vol. 28, No. 1, 1968.

Senate Committee on Government Operations, Subcommittee on Intergovernmental Relations. *The Federal System as Seen by Federal Aid Officials,* 1965.

———. *The Federal System as Seen by Local Officials,* 1963.

Smith, Bruce L. R. "The Future of the Not-for-Profit Corporations," *The Public Interest,* No. 8, Summer 1967.

Solomon, Anthony M. "Administration of a Multipurpose Economic Diplomacy," *Public Administration Review,* Vol. 29, No. 6, 1969.

Souers, Sidney W., "Policy Foundation for National Security," *American Political Science Review,* June 1949.

Steiner, Gilbert Y. "How to Win the Coordination Sweepstakes," *Public Management,* February 1968.

Sundquist, James L. "Jimmy Carter as a Public Administrator," *Public Administration Review,* Vol. 39, No. 1, January-February 1979.

Thomas, Norman C., and Harold L. Wolman. "The Presidency and Policy Formulation: The Task Force Device," *Public Administration Review,* Vol. 29, No. 5, 1969.

Waldo, Dwight. "Organization Theory: An Elephantine Problem," *Public Administration Review,* Vol. 21, No. 4, 1961.

Walker, David B. "Curbing the New Feudalists," *The Bureaucrat,* Spring 1972.

———. "The State of American Federalism 1977," *Publius,* Vol. 8, No. 1, Winter 1978.

———. "Federal Aid Administrators and the Federal System," *Intergovernmental Perspective,* Vol. 3, No. 4, Fall 1977.

Walker, Lannon. "Our Foreign Affairs Machinery: Time for an Overhaul," *Foreign Affairs,* January 1969.

Wann, A. J. "Franklin D. Roosevelt and the Bureau of the Budget," *Business and Government Review,* University of Missouri, March-April 1968.

Wildavsky, Aaron. "Government and the People," *Commentary,* August 1973.

Wood, Robert C. "Federal Role in the Urban Environment," *Public Administration Review,* Vol. 28, No. 4, 1968.

Index